OXFORD ENGLISH MONOGRAPHS

General Editors
PAULINA KEWES LAURA MARCUS PETER McCULLCUGH
SEAMUS PERRY LLOYD PRATT FIONA STAFFORD
DANIEL WAKELIN

Conspicuous Silences

Implicature and Fictionality in the Victorian Novel

RUTH ROSALER

OXFORD
UNIVERSITY PRESS

OXFORD
UNIVERSITY PRESS

Great Clarendon Street, Oxford, OX2 6DP,
United Kingdom

Oxford University Press is a department of the University of Oxford.
It furthers the University's objective of excellence in research, scholarship,
and education by publishing worldwide. Oxford is a registered trade mark of
Oxford University Press in the UK and in certain other countries

© Ruth Rosaler 2016

The moral rights of the author have been asserted

First Edition published in 2016

Impression: 1

All rights reserved. No part of this publication may be reproduced, stored in
a retrieval system, or transmitted, in any form or by any means, without the
prior permission in writing of Oxford University Press, or as expressly permitted
by law, by licence or under terms agreed with the appropriate reprographics
rights organization. Enquiries concerning reproduction outside the scope of the
above should be sent to the Rights Department, Oxford University Press, at the
address above

You must not circulate this work in any other form
and you must impose this same condition on any acquirer

Published in the United States of America by Oxford University Press
198 Madison Avenue, New York, NY 10016, United States of America

British Library Cataloguing in Publication Data

Data available

Library of Congress Control Number: 2016934697

ISBN 978–0–19–876974–3

Printed in Great Britain by
Clays Ltd, St Ives plc

For Michael and Lea Schuldiner

Preface and Acknowledgements

I began researching this work a decade ago, when I first read *Lady Audley's Secret* for an undergraduate course on Victorian literature. The narration of the novel immediately interested me, but it was only in the encouraging atmosphere of my MA course that I felt confident enough to attempt articulating what exactly about the narration was interesting. This proved nearly impossible with the terminology and information then at my disposal, and it took three years of fumbling inquiry before I learned that linguistics had formulated terminology that allowed me to express what I'd encountered. Finding pre-existing terminology for the phenomenon I was discussing—even if I was asserting original ideas about the phenomenon—was necessary; as a graduate student, I didn't feel that I yet had the credibility to coin my own terminology about a seemingly unknown phenomenon and still be taken seriously, let alone obtain a doctorate. More than anything else, this work is motivated by what I felt at that point: we literary theorists rightly pride ourselves on our ability to articulate unquantifiable, slippery phenomena, and we should know the words with which to discuss the effects of a slippery yet pervasive aspect of communication.

Implicature can be found in all texts, of course, but (as I hope to show here) it dominates the narration of some literary texts and strongly impacts the way in which the reader thinks about the occurrences that are narrated. Exploring these uses of implicature informs not only historically oriented literary criticism (such as that regarding the Victorian era) but also the more theoretical criticism that, even when attentive to the demands of postmodernism, strives to encompass as much of the general literature-reading experience as possible (such as that discussing narrative omniscience and fictionality). This work might be of most interest to scholars of Victorian literature, in that roughly three-quarters of it discusses the use of central, sustained implicatures within Victorian novels, and how they were shaped by and understood within their historical contexts. It is my hope, however, that the work may be understood as commenting on more basic and widespread literary phenomena as well—specifically, the impact that a reader's categorization of a text as 'fictional' has on his or her interpretation of the text, and the use of implicatures that are sustained rather than fleeting. I feel that this work may be of interest to scholars studying the nature of narrative in general as well as the linguists whose work allowed its articulation.

I am heavily indebted to Helen Small and Deborah Cameron for their dedicated support throughout my DPhil. My research has benefited greatly from their knowledge and their tireless attention, and I am very grateful for the opportunity to have studied with them. I would also like to thank Billy Clark for his invaluable advice and our many discussions on pragmatic stylistics. Billy generously donated his time to help me better understand the field, and our discussions changed the way I perceived the discipline and the place of my own research within it. I am additionally grateful for the advice of Richard Walsh, Matthew Reynolds, Helen Barr, and the anonymous reviewers contacted by Oxford University Press, who all provided insightful feedback that shaped this text in important ways. Many thanks to Andrew McCann (who introduced me to *Lady Audley's Secret* and then proceeded, as my honours thesis supervisor, to provide excellent advice on the skills and practices necessary in tackling extended writing projects) and to Gretchen Gerzina (who, among other things, singlehandedly gave me the confidence to apply to graduate school). A big thank you to Stella Pratt-Smith, Jessica Hancock, and Juliann Schamel for carefully reading early versions of the manuscript and for the humour-filled commiserations that eased the stress of the DPhil process; equal thanks to Jessie Bray for lending her eyes and brain to later versions of the manuscript and for the humour-filled commiserations that eased the stress of our first postdoctoral teaching jobs. Sowmya Kypa and Toby Schuldiner kept this project afloat with their many well wishes and phone calls, and my sanity thanks them for it. My husband, Joshua Rosaler, has the ability to make me laugh in any situation, and he kindly exercised this talent in the late nights before deadlines, tense moments before examinations, and despairing, apocalyptic-seeming hours after setbacks. Here's to eighty years more of the same!

My biggest thanks, of course, go to Michael and Lea Schuldiner, who have always been ready with good advice but have never pressed me into accepting it. This work could not possibly have been written without their measureless and loving support, which came in every form imaginable. I am very, very lucky.

I am grateful to Palgrave for allowing my chapter in *Pragmatic Literary Stylistics* (eds. extraordinaire Siobhan Chapman and Billy Clark) to be integrated into this work.

Contents

Introduction: Pragmatics and Fictional Narrative	1
Narratological Discussions of Gaps	4
Pragmatic Stylistics	10
Implicature and Fictionality in Post-Gricean Pragmatic Stylistics	21
Aims and Methods of This Work	29
1. The Unarticulated Antinarratable: Illegitimate Pregnancy and the Pragmatics of Politeness	35
Introduction	35
Historical Context	38
The Pragmatics of Politeness	43
Jessie Phillips: Trollope's Call for Change	50
Ruth: Gaskell's Careful Protest	60
Adam Bede: Eliot's Appeal for Sympathy	74
2. Unspoken Desires: Representations of Semiconsciousness and Control	86
Introduction	86
Victorian Discourses on the Unconscious	87
Narratological Discussions of Represented Intersubjectivity and Consciousness	94
The Mill on the Floss: Eliot's Narration of Resisted Attraction	100
Orley Farm: Interpretations, Infatuations, and Crime	112
3. The Narrative Tease: Open Secrets in Sensation Fiction	123
Introduction	123
Sensation Fiction and Literary Realism	128
Reading for Subversive Messages: Tonal Ambiguity in *Lady Audley's Secret*	138
Hidden Identities and Sly Communications: Narrative Games in *Our Mutual Friend*	148
Representing Fate in Fiction: Artificial Plotting in *Armadale*	157
Conclusion	169
Reference List	175
Index	183

Introduction

Pragmatics and Fictional Narrative

In chapter fourteen of *Vanity Fair*, William Thackeray incorporates a conspicuous silence into the narration of the chapter's central events. Despite this silence, however, the narrative clearly communicates the information which, on an explicit level, the narrator appears to withhold. The chapter begins with the aged Miss Crawley returning home with a mystery guest. The guest is first referred to as 'a young lady', and emphasis is placed on this 'young companion' by detailing her actions instead of Miss Crawley's (1968, 167). The reader learns that Miss Briggs, Miss Crawley's devoted companion of decades, is upset that a 'stranger was administering [Miss Crawley's] medicines—a stranger from the country—an odious Miss...' (1968, 168, ellipsis in original). Although it neglects to name her, this passage continues to portray the actions of the unidentified 'new companion' as central to the chapter, following her as she greets Rawdon Crawley (Miss Crawley's nephew) and leads him downstairs for a private conversation (1968, 168). For two pages more this mystery character is conspicuously referred to as 'the new nurse', the 'young person', and 'the person' repeatedly (1968, 168–9), with the narrator asking, 'Who could this young woman be, I wonder?' (1968, 168).

The emphasis placed on this mystery guest's unknown identity is salient, transgressing many of the narrative rules the text has previously established. It is not only that this lack of central narrative information (the main actor's identity) is repeatedly noted, or that the omission of the information obtrusively breaks away from the focalization code of the passage (all other characters, even those not previously known to the reader, are named by the narrator). The lack of narrative information is particularly conspicuous because it is out of keeping with the focalization code of the entire narrative. The preceding chapters have established a context in which the (often intrusive) narrator is omniscient, cattily ridiculing the innermost secrets and tendencies of a large roster of characters. It is, then, especially noticeable that the narrator appears not to know the most basic elements of a character's identity, let alone those of a character who is central to the passage.

Soon after, the identity of the 'young lady' is explicitly given as 'Miss Rebecca Sharp (for such, astonishing to state, is the name of her who has been described ingeniously as "the person" hitherto)' (1968, 170). However, the narrator's revelation is not a true revelation at all, in that the reader is likely to have been certain of 'the person['s]' identity for the duration of the narrator's evasiveness. Becky Sharp has been the narrative's protagonist for thirteen chapters, and unmistakeable clues suggest Becky's identity even as the narrator explicitly withholds it. Becky's perfect execution of tasks and trademark sarcasm are present in the actions attributed to 'the person', and she is, at that point in the narrative, the character most likely to be holding private conversations with Rawdon Crawley. The context of the omniscient narrator's 'gaps' of information communicates what is explicitly withheld, ironizing the 'astonish[ment]' over Becky's identity and rendering plainly disingenuous narratorial inquiries such as 'Who could this young woman be, I wonder?' The narrator's blatant obfuscation provides an implicit commentary on the obvious whereabouts of his protagonist, suggesting that Becky's presence at those whereabouts is accompanied by transparently dubious intentions (just as the reader can detect Becky's presence, he or she can detect the audacious motivations which spur it). This obfuscation also poses Becky's identity as a puzzle, albeit only facetiously: it allows the reader to 'guess' correctly and creates an in-joke between narrator and reader.

The above reading highlights a deliberate refusal of explicitness that can be found in many descriptions in fiction. This work discusses the way in which Thackeray and other Victorian authors communicate narrative propositions without explicitly stating them. This practice is most precisely denoted by the term 'implicature'. Broadly speaking, an implicature is the aspect of an utterance that relies on the utterance's relationship to its context, rather than on its semantic import, to communicate meaning. While all utterances contain implicatures (in that all utterances' meanings are impacted by their context), some rely more heavily on those implicatures than others. Sometimes what is implicated by an utterance (or, in other words, discernible only through hearer inference) far outweighs what is explicitly expressed through its semantic import. In the passage discussed above, for instance, Thackeray provides an abundance of narrative details that, when read together, communicate Becky's presence; while his facetious tone in introducing 'Miss Rebecca Sharp' indicates that he expects the reader to have ascertained Becky's identity from the accumulation of the narrative details provided, he does not explicitly communicate her presence before that point. When read in the context

Introduction 3

of the other narrative details, each one 'implicates' Becky's presence in the passage.

Laurence R. Horn and Gregory Ward characterize implicature as

> a component of speaker meaning that constitutes an aspect of what is **meant** in a speaker's utterance without being part of what is **said**. What a speaker intends to communicate is characteristically far richer than what she directly expresses; linguistic meaning radically underdetermines the message conveyed and understood. (2006, 3, emphasis in original)

As Horn and Ward note, much of the responsibility for communication usually falls onto non-coded (that is, not figurative or explicit) methods of communication: even when listening to an explicit utterance, the listener infers as well as decodes information. There is no communicative method in which context does not impact what is expressed, and, even with the most explicit communications, this impact is inferred by the listener. Methods of communication rely on the listener's inferences to a greater or lesser extent, and 'implicature' is the term for communications which place more emphasis on the listener's powers of inference than on his or her ability to decipher the information linguistically encoded in the utterance. It involves, as Roger Fowler characterizes it, 'what is said "between the lines"'; it is communication that relies heavily on the interaction between text and context to generate meaning (1996, 135). Implicature is a central topic of study within the linguistic field of pragmatics, which concentrates on the effect that context has on the interpretation of utterances.

To date, literary criticism has paid a great deal of attention to the use of implicature in character dialogue but has largely neglected this aspect of communication in the narration of fictional plot. Linguistic criticism (pragmatic stylistics included) has explored this technique extensively but, as I will show, has tended to neglect larger, more central instances of implicature and authors' exploitations of contexts of fictionality to generate implicatures. This is partly because most literary criticism (including linguistic criticism of fiction) has failed to look beyond explicit and figurative modes of communication in its analysis of fiction, and partly because pragmatic stylistics has largely failed to consider fictionality itself as a context, indicative of certain background assumptions that fiction writers can exploit to generate implicatures. A schema that refers to implicature and contexts of fictionality can more clearly explain how Thackeray communicates Becky's presence than most schemas currently available within literary and linguistic criticism. After all, it is only within fiction that a narrator can assume a truly omniscient perspective; Thackeray's narrator regularly knows the impossible, detailing characters' secret thoughts and feelings for us. This context highlights the narrator's sudden reticence, causing the reader to pay closer attention to the surrounding narrative details than they otherwise might, and indicating the narrator's potentially facetious tone. In this way, the perceived fictionality of the text impacts the reader's interpretation of the text's implicatures.

This work discusses the previously underexamined role that implicatures can play in fictional narrative and, conversely, the role that a fictional context can play in generating implicatures. I aim to do far more than justify an acknowledgement of pragmatic stylistics—and specifically the idea of implicature—in mainstream literary criticism; although discussion of implicature is almost completely circumscribed within the domain of stylistics, stylisticians have been convincingly justifying this acknowledgement for decades. That said, my critical aims are based on the idea that pragmatic stylistics has much to offer mainstream literary criticism, and it is a secondary aim of mine to echo previous stylisticians who have sought to enrich diverse strands of literary criticism with concepts taken from linguistics. Primarily, however, I hope to illustrate how authors use sustained implicatures to communicate central elements of plot without stating them, and how narrative techniques using implicature often rely on a narrative's fictionality (that is, on the recognizable liberties and constraints associated with its being invented) for their effect. I also hope to show that, in addition to being motivated by such intuitive considerations as politeness and efficient characterization, implicature may be used for its own sake because it is a source of reading pleasure.

The remaining sections of this introduction trace the history of concepts that are central to my argument through the evolving fields of narrative theory, pragmatics, and pragmatic stylistics. This overview will highlight some critical gaps that persist in many narratological and pragmatic stylistics studies, and will suggest that the relevance theoretical approach which follows offers the most revealing way of addressing these neglected areas. This introduction's emphasis on narrative theory and pragmatic stylistics is balanced by an emphasis on historicist criticism in the chapters that follow; the narratological and pragmatic stylistic concepts introduced here can explain how societal and historical forces impacted the formulation, expected interpretation, and actual interpretation of (specifically) fictional utterances.

NARRATOLOGICAL DISCUSSIONS OF GAPS

While to date there has not been much literary criticism concerned with why authors use implicature to communicate plot, there has been a great deal written on 'gaps' in the explicit narration of plot. Pierre Macherey writes that what 'is important in [a literary] work is what it does not say', but he clarifies that 'this is not the same as the careless notation "what it refuses to say"' and that '.... what the work *cannot say* is important' (1986, 87). Geoffrey Wall explains that Macherey is interested in the 'repressed presence of those ideological materials which are transformed in the labour of literary production' (1986, viii). Toni Morrison's concept of 'unspeakable things unspoken' is similar, though as much psychological as political in emphasis: it refers to the narration of traumatic experiences, or, as Abdellatif Khayati writes, it resonates 'with the silence surrounding many things repressed in the African American unconsciousness, or distorted beyond recognition in the American Africanist discourse' (1999, 318). Perhaps the best-known discussions of gaps within literary theory occur within its psychoanalytic branch, in which Sigmund Freud's concept of 'repression' is applied to notable absences within narratives. Freud once defined repression as 'turning something away, and keeping it at a distance, from the conscious' (1995, 569–70). In applying the concept of psychoanalytic repression to narratives, explicit language would roughly correlate with 'the conscious'. While Macherey, Morrison, and Freud discuss narrative silences, then, their work focuses more on the political, ideological, and psychological forces producing inevitable literary silences than on the technical manipulation of strictly unnecessary silences within literary texts.

Robyn Warhol's recent, groundbreaking scholarship has led narrative theorists to consider other types of gap in their analyses of fictional texts.[1] In her 2006 discussion of Gerald Prince's work, Warhol posited various categories into which Prince's concept of the 'unnarratable' could be divided. Warhol discusses the unnarratable as

> 'that which is unworthy of being told,' 'that which is not susceptible to narration,' and 'that which does not call for narration' or perhaps 'those circumstances under which narration is uncalled for.' Prince [defines] the 'unnarratable' as 'that which, *according to a given narrative*, cannot be narrated or is not worth narrating either because it transgresses a law (social, authorial, generic, formal) or because it defies the powers of the particular narrator (or those of any narrator) or because it falls below the so-called threshold of narratability (it is not sufficiently unusual or problematic)'.
>
> (Prince 1988, 1 cited in Warhol, 2006, 222, emphasis in original)

---

[1] While narratological discussions of gaps do predate Warhol's scholarship, none of these discussions are extensive. Mieke Bal, for instance, provides a smart but cursory discussion of narrative gaps in *Narratology: Introduction to the Theory of Narrative* (1997, 103–4).

Warhol expands on Prince's statements, using his definition as a starting point for discussion of different types of 'unnarratable' information. Warhol does not mean to provide 'an exhaustive list of all possible forms of the unnarratable' (2006, 222) but instead focuses on the four categories of the unnarratable that are most closely indicated by Prince's definition. These categories are the 'subnarratable', the 'supranarratable', the 'antinarratable', and the 'paranarratable'.

The subnarratable is material that is inevitably omitted in consideration of the finite space available to any narrative. It is 'what needn't be told because it's "normal"', or, in context, generically or otherwise conventionally predictable (Warhol 2006, 222). The absence of much that is subnarratable from narrative is standard, and it is its inclusion that is unusual and that calls into question the reliability of the narration, alerting the reader that there is more to the story than what is being explicitly narrated.

Unlike the subnarratable, which 'is not worth narrating', the supranarratable 'can't be told' (Warhol 2006, 222). Warhol defines the supranarratable as 'what can't be told because it's "ineffable"', clarifying that it comprises 'those events that defy narrative, foregrounding the inadequacy of language or of visual image to achieve full representation, even of fictitious events' (2006, 223). The supranarratable is never present in fiction because it is impossible to represent. Warhol points out that it is, however, possible to indicate the presence of the supranarratable by asserting the impossibility of narrating it. George Eliot uses this technique when communicating Hetty Sorrel's extraordinary beauty in *Adam Bede*:

> It is of little use for me to tell you that Hetty's cheek was like a rose-petal, that dimples played about her pouting lips, that her large dark eyes hid a soft roguishness under their long lashes, and that her curly hair, though all pushed back under her round cap while she was at work, stole back in dark delicate rings on her forehead, and about her white shell-like ears... of little use, unless you have seen a woman who affected you as Hetty affected her beholders, for otherwise, though you might conjure up the image of a lovely woman, she would not in the least resemble that distracting kitten-like maiden. (2005, 146)

While this passage presents lush and evocative detail of Hetty's physicality, Eliot's professed inability fully to communicate Hetty's attraction ('It is of little use for me to tell you') invalidates the description, displacing the burden of it from the text to the reader's imagination. The details given are characterized as insufficient, marking the extent of Hetty's beauty as both emphasized and withheld.

Introduction

The 'antinarratable' is both worthy of being narrated and capable of being represented. Its unnarratability results from its 'transgress[ion] of social laws or taboos': it is 'what shouldn't be told because of social convention' (Warhol 2006, 224). Warhol points out that

> Sex in realist Victorian novels, for instance, is always antinarratable, and can only be known by its results as they play themselves out in the plot (for instance in the presence of new babies, disillusioned hearts, or ruined reputations). As I have written elsewhere, Victorian narrative uses euphemism, allusion, metaphor, and especially metonymy to signify sexual connection between characters, but never narration. (2006, 224)

Warhol's claim that sex 'can only be known by its results as they play themselves out in the plot' suggests that the audience's knowledge of the characters' sexual activities in these novels is necessary to the coherence of the narratives. However, many of the culture-specific, once-pervasive codes used to effect the mentioned tropes are now antiquated; current readers, for instance, may be unfamiliar with Victorian-era euphemisms. The continuing popularity of these novels demonstrates the presence of some subtle means of communication that demarcate the figurative language employed *as* figurative (that is, which alert current readers that the euphemism must be interpreted as a euphemism). Implicature is this 'subtle means'.[2]

Warhol is particularly interested in the 'paranarratable', or 'what wouldn't be told because of formal convention' (2006, 226). 'Formal conventions' are, briefly, those conventions that are associated with the genre or medium in which the narrative is told (as opposed to 'social conventions', which are associated with their social context). Surprisingly, she depicts the paranarratable as more rigidly unnarratable than the antinarratable. Warhol writes that

> Laws of literary generic convention are more inflexible, I believe, than laws of social convention, and have led throughout literary history to more instances of unnarratability than even taboo has led. My students always look puzzled when I tell them that there were many more possibilities for the life-stories of real Victorian women than there were for Victorian heroines: it's counterintuitive, because fiction would seemingly be limited only by imagination, while 'real life,' as the students call it, is bound to follow the dictates of what undergraduates like to call 'society.' (2006, 226)

While Warhol's description of the paranarratable rings true, the introduction of the concept problematizes her other categories of the unnarratable.

---

[2] The Victorian fiction author's use of implicature to convey sexual acts will be discussed in Chapter One.

For instance, Warhol characterizes 'the visual revelation' of the protagonist's penis in the film *Boogie Nights* (1997) as the introduction of antinarratable material, but then notes that that 'moment in *Boogie Nights* functions as neonarrative [a generic innovation] for Hollywood film, but it would be unremarkable in, for example, a porn film, as it would in a photograph by Robert Mapplethorpe' (2006, 228). With the existence of porn films and sexually explicit art in mind, the protagonist's penis becomes visually paranarratable rather than antinarratable. The same logic can be discovered in the representation of Victorian sexuality: as Warhol observes in her discussion of the antinarratable, it is in 'realist' Victorian novels that the representation of sex is omitted from the text. This statement is not at odds with the existence or the content of Victorian pornography. While Warhol does discuss the possibility of manipulating the unnarratable into instances of neonarrative, she does not address the implied tendency of the subnarratable and antinarratable to collapse into the paranarratable. In other words, the subnarratable and the antinarratable are only unnarratable within certain texts; within other texts, subnarratable and antinarratable material may be admissible information. In effect, her conclusions indicate that, apart from the supranarratable, all unnarratable information is a product of its generic context; of the subnarratable, antinarratable, and paranarratable, only the paranarratable is a verifiable concept. While Warhol's categories are critical to discussions of underlying authorial motivations for gaps, their collapsibility illustrates the necessity of acknowledging all gaps' contexts when analysing their narrative significance.

Warhol's taxonomy of the unnarratable uses authorial motivation to distinguish between different types of gap that appear in texts. While she focuses primarily on gaps that are irrelevant to my critical aim (in that they represent the complete absence, rather than inexplicit presence, of information in texts), Warhol's emphasis on authorial motivation is relevant because an author's motives for omitting information from a text are likely to be similar to his or her motives for employing implicature instead of explicit narration. The antinarratable, for instance, is often a source of implicature, in that it is both 'worthy' and capable of being told but is often not explicitly mentioned. The author's ability to communicate occurrences that were at once integral to his or her plot and unmentionable in polite society evidences implicature's strong presence in Victorian fiction and highlights the need for identification and analysis of implicature in literary criticism. Warhol's categories of the unnarratable are integral to the scholarship presented here: Chapters One and Three, for instance, could be said to centre on authors' uses of implicature to either downplay or emphasize the antinarratable content found in their narratives.

Victorian uses of implicature highlight another way in which 'gaps' in narratives have not been adequately differentiated in critical literature. In her 2007 article 'Narrative Refusals and Generic Transformation in Austen and James: What Doesn't Happen in *Northanger Abbey* and *The Spoils of Poynton*', Warhol asserts that the 'narrative refusal', or the explicit discussion of unnarrated events, can be 'a strategy for addressing the unnarratable in fiction, rather than simply keeping quiet about it' (259). She further defines 'narrative refusal' in terms of 'disnarration' and 'unnarration', the two particular strategies in question. 'Disnarration', as defined by Gerald Prince, is made up of the 'terms, phrases, and passages that consider what did not or does not take place' (1988, 3). 'Unnarration' is Warhol's own term and refers to 'asserting that what did happen cannot be retold in words, or explicitly indicating that what happened will not be narrated because narrating it would be impossible' (2006, 222).[3] When discussing the nonfactual, and consequently ambiguous, portrayal of the beloved's affection for the heroine in *The Spoils of Poynton*, Warhol notes that 'narrative refusal does not block narrative transmission' (2007, 259). However, she also claims that 'disnarration [is] responsible for readers' puzzlement over [*The Spoils of Poynton*'s] action' (2007, 263) and at other points characterizes the novel as 'obscured by James's disnarration' (2007, 262). Warhol seems to claim that narrative refusals both communicate and obscure diegetic information simultaneously; however, she never explicitly comments on this dual (and sometimes simultaneous) application of narrative refusals.

A similar ambiguity is found in many narratological discussions of gaps. In *The Cambridge Introduction to Narrative*, H. Porter Abbott identifies a crux as a 'critical point, often a gap, in a fictional narrative where there is an insufficiency of cues, or where cues are sufficiently ambiguous, to create a major disagreement in the intentional interpretation of the narrative' (2008, 231). Abbott does not differentiate between genuine omissions (those we cannot fill in) and the 'false omissions' that implicatures fill, and consequently leaves unacknowledged 'gaps' in which explicit narration is not used but narrative information is still unambiguously communicated to the reader. This is not to say that a discussion of narrative ambiguity is not informative and necessary in its own right; as Abbott points out, there are conspicuous narrative gaps that function to communicate ambiguity rather than unambiguous narrative information. However, there are also gaps in explicit narration in which unambiguous, central narrative information is nonetheless communicated; despite its pervasiveness this second possibility has been neglected by narrative theory. A discussion of

---

[3] In the above example of supranarratability in *Adam Bede*, George Eliot uses unnarration to communicate Hetty's beauty.

implicature would clarify this ambiguity by showing how the language used to construct some omissions functions simultaneously to communicate information inexplicitly, and by differentiating omissions of this kind ('false' omissions) from those omissions which are 'true'.

Warhol's discussion does not take into account the exploitation of narrative gaps for psychological mimesis, nor does it address narrative gaps' potential uses in the creation of narrative games or the communication of inexplicit plot lines. The narrative omission of Becky's identity in chapter fourteen of *Vanity Fair* pertains to no content that could be classed as subnarratable, supranarratable, antinarratable, or paranarratable, but it does further an inexplicit plot line in which Becky continues to milk everyone she meets for as much money as possible (her kindness to Miss Crawley is due to the latter's large fortune, old age, and liking for Becky's secret fiancé, Rawdon). While Warhol states that her four categories were 'not meant to be an exhaustive list of all possible forms of the unnarratable', the instances of omission (and accompanying implicature) in *Vanity Fair* are not even unnarratable: if we review Warhol's carefully detailed definition of the unnarratable, we see that the motivation behind Thackeray's omissions is incongruent with the types of motivation that Warhol discusses. While Warhol details motivations that pertain to the author's interaction with real-life readers via the text, the motivation behind the omissions in *Vanity Fair* involves rather the author's desire to fashion a certain narrative tone and to communicate Becky's motives (and a derisive judgment on those motives) by way of something other than explicit description.

Warhol does not discuss the potential exploitation of the concept of the unnarratable to effect implicature, such as the author's use of narrative refusals to claim a supranarratability or antinarratability that is ironic. This manipulation of narrative refusals (and other similar techniques) to communicate inexplicit propositions is little recognized in narrative theory, although it can be central in portraying the psychology of characters, and the narrative games it can create may greatly affect the tone of a text. Chapters Two and Three will discuss the exploitation of unnarratable categories to generate implicatures that impact both character portrayal and narrative tone. These illustrations of the central role implicature sometimes plays in fiction will both disambiguate and inform narratological conceptualizations of gaps.

PRAGMATIC STYLISTICS

Pragmatics acts as a counterweight in linguistics, providing a venue in which to discuss meaning that is not directly reliant on semantics. Originating in the 1960s with Searle's speech act theory and H. P. Grice's theories about implicature, pragmatics is now a prominent field within linguistics. It is internationally studied, with watershed theories continuing to appear today.

While pragmatic stylistics is not a large field, it is an established discipline within stylistics, is recognized by pragmaticists, and is on the cusp of narrative studies.[4] To date, pragmatic stylistics has remained primarily the province of specialists, so it is necessary to provide a short introduction to the field before addressing its contribution to discussions of narrative gaps and implicature. In the process of covering this fairly general ground I will introduce concepts and terminology that are relevant to my argument, and will provide a foundation on which to characterize the contribution of this work to discussions in pragmatic stylistics, narrative theory, and the Victorian novel.

The main strands of pragmatic stylistics can be quite disparate in their approaches. All critics agree, however, in situating pragmatic stylistics clearly within the larger literary subfield of stylistics. Varying characterizations of the field can at times be found within the work of a single critic: one leading practitioner, Jacob L. Mey, has characterized pragmatic stylistics as the study of the 'user's role in the societal production and consumption of texts' (2006, 256) and alternatively as the 'science of the unsaid' (2001, 194). While these two definitions emphasize different aspects of the same field, they also represent an undecided primary aim within it. Roger D. Sell writes that

> Basically the aim [of pragmatic stylistics] is to relate the writing and reading of literary texts to the linguistic and sociocultural contexts in which those processes have taken place. This means that literary pragmatics is at one and the same time linguistic and literary, and its unifying emphasis on contextualization also gives it a strongly historical slant. (1994, 232)

Sell's definition of pragmatic stylistics does justice to how comprehensive the field is, describing pragmatics as concerned with both the sociocultural and the textual contexts in which texts are manufactured and interpreted. In reality, the wider scope of the field is usually neglected in favour of a more linguistic or sociological orientation. Pragmatic stylistics is unified,

---

[4] I have adopted what I gather to be the most common appellations of stylistics-related concepts. I use 'stylistics' to denote the linguistic study of literature and 'pragmatic stylistics' to denote the subfield of stylistics in which the pragmatics of literature is discussed. Until around the mid-1990s, 'literary pragmatics' was the term most commonly used to denote this subfield. Since the late 1990s, however, 'pragmatic stylistics' has become the favoured term in the United Kingdom ('literary pragmatics' continues to be the popular name for the field throughout continental Europe).

however, by its emphasis on explaining existing interpretations of texts rather than generating new readings (Furlong 2007, 3; Pilkington et al. 1997, 141).

The three main strands of pragmatic stylistics are those based on speech act theory, those focused on fictional worlds theory, and those that concentrate on individual pragmatic phenomena within texts and usually decline to comment on the ontological status of fictional entities. All three strands tend to deemphasize the distinction between fiction and nonfiction. Despite this deemphasis, these strands include important arguments on which the discussions here build.

Mary Louise Pratt's *Toward a Speech Act Theory of Literary Discourse* (1977) is still considered the seminal text on the incorporation of speech act theory into pragmatic stylistics, and is one of the most frequently discussed texts in the field.[5] Pratt concentrates on the idea of 'appropriateness conditions' (otherwise known as 'felicity conditions'): the extralinguistic conditions which must be met in order for the speech act (the utterance) to be correctly or felicitously performed (1977, 81). Pratt believes that 'literature itself is a speech context' that must be assumed in order for the reader to experience literature *as* literature: the assumption of literariness is the appropriateness condition that must be met in order to experience the literariness of a text (1977, 86).

This thesis has interesting implications. Importantly, it disassociates 'literariness' from the text itself and instead identifies 'literariness' versus 'nonliterariness' as a schema which the reader imposes upon the text (Pratt 1977, 87); Pratt writes that 'with a context-dependent linguistics, the essence of literariness or poeticality can be said to reside not in the message but in a particular disposition of speaker and audience with regard to the message' (1977, 87). Pratt's thesis also indicates that authors can manipulate the assumed literariness of their texts to generate implicatures, purposefully violating conventions of discourse to communicate unwritten information. When discussing passages from Laurence Sterne's *Tristram Shandy* and Jane Austen's *Pride and Prejudice*, Pratt writes:

> we know the violations in the Sterne and Austen passages are intentional because of what we know about the circumstances under which literary works are composed, edited, selected, published, and distributed. The literary

---

[5] Speech act theory was developed by J. L. Austin and John Searle in the 1960s. It famously includes the assertion that, when speaking, a person performs a 'locutionary act' ('producing a recognisable grammatical utterance in the given language'), an 'illocutionary act' (the act that is intended by the utterance, such as 'promising', 'commanding', or 'greeting'), and a 'perlocutionary act' ('achieving certain intended effects in his hearer in addition to those achieved by the illocutionary act') (Pratt 1977, 80–1).

pre-paration [sic] and preselection processes are designed to eliminate failures which result from carelessness or lack of skill. . . . The preparation and selection processes are designed to reduce the likelihood of there being any 'other way' in works of literature. Textual criticism is built on this assumption. This is not to say, of course, that we do or should assume all literary works to be somehow perfect. It means only that in literary works, the range of deviations which will be construed as unintentional is smaller than in many other speech contexts. Put the other way around, in literary works the range of deviations which will be construed as intentional is much larger.
(1977, 170).

Pratt's conclusions are aligned with the primary theses proposed here; however, her terminology is not. Pratt adamantly advocates that the 'fiction/nonfiction distinction is neither as clear-cut nor as important as we might think' (1977, 143), and she uses the term 'literature' to indicate both fictional and nonfictional texts.[6] Pratt's inclusion of nonfiction in her definition of 'literature' does not make the conclusions glossed above any less valid; it does, however, render her conclusions no more than a starting point for my discussion. While Pratt successfully argues that 'literariness' is most usefully envisioned as a reader assumption rather than as a quality inherent to the text, and that readers' assumptions of literariness do equate an assumption of 'pre-paration and preselection', she does not comment on the effect that an assumed context of fictionality has on reader interpretation.

Pratt's demotion of the distinction between fiction and nonfiction is difficult to maintain. Many of the implicatures which she analyses rely on the fiction reader's assumption of the narrative's fictionality and on his or her familiarity with certain conventions specific to fiction. Pratt repeatedly, for instance, returns to the narrative meanderings and half-propositions of *Tristram Shandy*'s narrator (1977, 163–6, 169, 170, 174, 175, etc.). While she initially explains the reader's tolerance for (and active endeavour to interpret meaning from) superficially inept narration as a result of the text's having been 'composed, edited, selected, published, and distributed', she later acknowledges that the reader is able to make sense of (and not be annoyed by) this faulty narration because of the assumed fictionality of the narrator; Tristram Shandy may be a terrible narrator, but Sterne is not (1977, 174). The seemingly inept narration of the novel functions to display Tristram's 'naiveté or ignorance' without explicitly describing it;

---

[6] See also pages 91, 96, and 199–200 of *Toward a Speech Act Theory of Literary Discourse* for Pratt's arguments against the importance of the distinction between fiction and nonfiction in critical theory.

Tristram shows his ignorance and confusion in spite of himself, adding a level of dramatic irony to Sterne's writing (Pratt 1977, 174).

Pratt explains the role that fictionality plays in the creation of such implicatures by characterizing all fiction as 'imitation speech acts' (1977, 173). In these imitation speech acts the real-life author mimetically portrays a fictional speaker, and it is the duality between the two 'sources' of text that makes many implicatures possible (Pratt 1977, 173–4). Pratt resolves these implicatures' reliance on fictionality by reminding her readers that 'fictive or "imitation" speech acts are readily found in almost any realm of discourse, and our ability to produce and interpret them must be viewed as part of our normal linguistic and cognitive competence, and not some special by-product of it' (1977, 200). While Pratt's reasoning is sound, it is still the fictionality of these texts (or mimetic quality of the utterances) that allows these implicatures to occur. It is Tristram's status as 'invented' that triggers readers' background assumptions about fiction and causes them to interpret the text differently from how they would interpret nonfiction texts. In this way, reading *Tristram Shandy* differs greatly from interpreting speech acts that are found in nonfiction 'realm[s] of discourse'; the reader's literary competence allows him or her to have complete faith in the earnestness of the narrator (Tristram) while attributing irony to the author (Sterne). Such a complete schism is impossible in nonfiction texts, and shows that there are greater differences in how fiction and nonfiction are interpreted than Pratt suggests. As illustrated above, these differences extend to the potential implicatures generated by and deduced from the text.

The second major strand of pragmatic stylistics is based on fictional worlds theory, popularized by Marie-Laure Ryan. My own proposals are compatible with much of what this strand of pragmatic stylistics asserts, but they resist some of its larger implications about the experience of reading fiction. Fictional worlds theory is based on the philosophical concept of possible worlds theory, which discusses probability as a series of hypothetical alternate worlds. In possible worlds theory our objective reality is discussed as the 'Actual World' (AW). Surrounding our AW is a 'universe of possibilities', which is constituted of all conceivable situations not found in our AW (Ryan 1991, 18). These unactualized conceivable situations are 'Alternative Possible Worlds' (APWs) and are made up of hypotheticals, counterfactuals, and 'unactualized possible worlds and... unactualized possibilities' (Ryan 1991, 18). An APW is itself surrounded by its own specific 'universe of possibilities', and those in an APW conceive of their world as an AW and can only conceive of our AW as an APW of their own.

In her text *Possible Worlds, Artificial Intelligence, and Narrative Theory*, Marie-Laure Ryan discusses the ontological status of fictional objects; as she writes, the 'main legacy of possible-world theory to textual semiotics is an interest in the problem of truth in fiction and in the relations between semantic domains and reality—two questions considered heretic by orthodox structuralism' (1991, 3). Like Pratt, she distinguishes between literature and fiction (1991, 1); unlike Pratt, she makes defining 'fictionality' one of her primary aims (1991, 3). As follows from the basic tenets of fictional worlds theory, the 'problematic status of fiction as a nonexistent object is tackled by possible world theories by defining fictional worlds as possible states of affairs' (Downing 2000, 11). Ryan assigns the status of APW to all fictions, but it is not the APW status of a narrative that defines it as fiction; rather, it is the 'recentering' of our experience around the APW. Ryan explains that

> For the duration of our immersion in a work of fiction, the realm of possibilities is thus recentered around the sphere which the narrator presents as the actual world. This recentering pushes the reader into a new system of actuality and possibility. As a traveler to this system, the reader of fiction discovers not only a new actual world, but a variety of APWs revolving around it. (1991, 22)

'Recentering' is intuitively appreciated as central to the activity of reading fiction; it is how readers identify with and are able to cognitively process a narrative, and how some readers even temporarily lose track of their AW in the fiction-reading process. Ryan insists that 'recentering' is at the core of experiencing fictionality. She writes:

> Because of the common modal structure of most textual universes, both fictional and nonfictional discourse may contain factual statements, referring to the actual world of the system, and nonfactual ones, representing its alternatives. In a nonfactual statement, the speaker describes an APW from an external point of view, while in fiction, the writer relocates to what is for us a mere possible world, and makes it the center of an alternative system of reality. If this recentering is indeed the gesture constitutive of fiction... nonfictional texts describe a system of reality whose center is occupied by the actually actual world; fictional ones refer to a system whose actual world is from an absolute point of view an APW. (1991, 24)

The prominence of 'recentering' in Ryan's account of experiencing fictionality is much of what makes her theory a pragmatic one: while she devotes much of her book to streamlining Searle's and Pratt's earlier claims, she also differentiates fictional worlds theory from previous pragmatic stylistic theories based on speech act theory. For instance, she disagrees with Pratt about what can constitute a fiction: while Pratt believes that 'hyperbole, teasing, "kidding around," imitations, verbal play' and more qualify as fiction (1977, 63), Ryan points out that, 'while the pretense of fiction lures the hearer into an alternative system of reality in order to contemplate it for its own sake, verbal play remains much more firmly rooted in the AW. The point of the devil's advocate who argues for a cause he or she does not believe in is to address real issues', not those of a fictional world (1991, 63).[7]

Ryan's and Pratt's theories are similar in that they both advocate an assumed duality of sources in fictional texts: the implied author and narrator. Ryan writes that the 'referential divorce between the I of the actual world and the relocated I of the textual universe in fictional communication invites us to reconsider the problem of fictionality in terms of the relation between the two subjects and their respective discourse' (1991, 61). Although Ryan and Pratt arrive at this conclusion of communicator duality through two different approaches to pragmatic stylistics, they agree that it is intrinsic to fictionality; it is one way in which 'the problem of fictionality' may be considered and articulated. Ryan builds on this proposition, claiming that one of the fundamental differences between fictional and nonfictional literature is that, in fiction, it is possible for the narrative voice to be overridden by perceived authorial intention. In nonfiction, where the narrator and the author are assumed to be the same person, such an override (with its accompanying irony-laden implicatures) is not possible (Ryan 1991, 113). Both Pratt's and Ryan's theories, then, evidence the difference that the assumption of a fictional (as opposed to a nonfictional) context will make in text interpretation, but Ryan's writing addresses the fiction–nonfiction divide explicitly.

While Ryan's text is largely about readers' interpretations of fiction, her distinction between the author and narrator of fictional narratives is one of the few concrete discussions she provides of how a context of fictionality affects reader interpretation. In her schema, the AW reader is temporarily transported to the APW of the fiction—negating in many ways the APW *as* an APW and correspondingly emphasizing the aspects of a fiction reader's experience which allow him or her to interpret the fiction as a nonfiction. While fictional worlds theory posits a convincing argument about how readers rationalize the ontological status of fictional narratives, it deemphasizes the reader's understanding of the text as a fiction and in consequence pays little attention to how the fictionality of the text affects the reader's interpretation of it.

---

[7] While Ryan's assertions about 'recentering' do not pertain only to realistic fiction, she does claim that the types of mental shifts that a reader performs when 'recentering' are reflective of the mode of fiction that is being read (1991, 43–4).

The third strand of pragmatic stylistic enquiry—which provides pragmatic analyses of various literary conventions—is predictably fragmented but is also unified to an extent by its post-Gricean approach. H. P. Grice's 1967 lectures on the Cooperative Principle are generally considered as the 'landmark event in the development of a systematic framework for pragmatics' (Horn and Ward 2006, xi). Grice claimed that this Cooperative Principle regulates all conversations: 'Make your conversational contribution such as is required, at the stage at which it occurs, by the accepted purpose of direction of the talk exchange in which you are engaged' (1975, 45). He divided the Principle into the maxims of Quantity, Quality, Relation, and Manner, all of which express conversational 'rules' that people unconsciously acknowledge when conversing (1975, 45–6).

Grice's most prominent legacy to the field of pragmatics is his coinage of the term 'implicature', which he introduced in his discussion of the Cooperative Principle. In Grice's schema, implicature occurs when a speaker 'flouts' a maxim by 'BLATANTLY fail[ing] to fulfill it' (1975, 49, emphasis in original). He famously provides the following example of implicature:

> A is writing a testimonial about a pupil who is a candidate for a philosophy job, and his letter reads as follows: 'Dear Sir, Mr. X's command of English is excellent, and his attendance at tutorials has been regular. Yours, etc.' (Gloss: A cannot be opting out, since if he wished to be uncooperative, why write at all? He cannot be unable, through ignorance, to say more, since the man is his pupil; moreover, he knows that more information than this was wanted. He must, therefore, be wishing to impart information that he is reluctant to write down. This supposition is tenable only on the assumption that he thinks Mr. X is no good at philosophy. This, then, is what he is implicating.)
>
> (1975, 52)

This passage discusses the thought process by which hearers, according to Grice's model, discern implicatures. As the example illustrates, the blatancy involved in 'flouting' maxims negates the seeming insincerity of it: as Grice explains, the blatancy involved in flouting a maxim itself often signals an (unarticulated) meaning that is not truly in violation of the Cooperative Principle. Moreover, the indirect quality of the speaker's utterance takes on a meaning in itself and indicates the speaker's attitudes concerning the communicative act.[8]

---

[8] It is important to note that implicatures are defeasible. In other words, because implicatures only partially stem from the semantic meaning of utterances, they are capable of being negated (someone may state, for instance, that they do not possess peanut butter, after having implicated that they do). Conversely, communications that are primarily reliant on the semantic meaning of utterances are rarely capable of being negated (after a person

Since Grice's introduction of the concept, several theorists have attempted to refine the idea of implicature and to articulate more fully the aspects of language that allow speaker meaning to diverge from the semantic meaning of an utterance. One of the most influential post-Gricean approaches, and the one that is adopted here, is relevance theory.[9] Developed by Dan Sperber and Deirdre Wilson in their 1986 book *Relevance: Communication and Cognition*, the theory attempts to explain how humans communicate and the cognitive processes behind communication. Relevance theory does away with almost all of the maxims Grice postulates within his Cooperative Principle, claiming that the only true arbiter of communication is relevance. Sperber and Wilson posit two central principles to explain successful human communication: the 'Cognitive Principle', which claims that 'human cognition tends to be geared to the maximisation of relevance', and the 'Communicative Principle', or 'Principle of Relevance', which claims that 'every act of ostensive communication communicates a presumption of its own optimal relevance' (1999, 260–1). 'Ostensive communication', or 'ostension', is shorthand for 'ostensive-inferential communication', with which the communicator indicates that he or she intends to communicate information (although that information may be as vague as expressing an attitude through a slight change in body language or as specific as choosing a flavour by pointing to it at an ice cream parlour). The terms 'ostensive' and 'inferential' refer to the actions of the speaker and audience, respectively: the audience 'infers' what the speaker has made 'ostensive'. While Sperber and Wilson agree with previous theorists that there are two fundamental 'modes of communication: coded communication and ostensive-inferential communication', they argue that there is a degree of ostension and inference involved in all types of communication, primarily coded or not (1999, 63). 'Whereas ostensive-inferential communication can be used on its own', they write, 'coded communication is only used as a means of strengthening

explicitly states that they possess peanut butter, it is usually absurd for them to then claim that they do not possess it).

Although implicatures are often perceived as certain information, their logically defeasible quality adds an ambiguous element to them; implicatures *are* capable of being contradicted, whereas explicit language is not. As previously stated, however, this work focuses on those instances of implicature that unambiguously communicate central narrative information. Such is the case with implicatures that are referred to throughout the remainder of a narrative, and on which the coherence of a plot relies. In an attempt to isolate implicatures that communicate information as a certainty, I have chosen to concentrate only on implicatures that are central to fictional plots.

[9] The capitalization of these terms varies from text to text. I have followed the advice of Billy Clark (2011), who suggests that 'relevance theory' need not be capitalized but that associated principles should be (personal interview).

ostensive-inferential communication. This is how language is used in verbal communication' (1999, 63).

Ostension plays such a large role in all communication because it focuses the hearer's attention on the most relevant aspects of the communication. In a schema in which meaning is synonymous with the speaker's intention in communicating, ostension is necessary because it 'makes manifest an intention to make something manifest' (Sperber and Wilson 1999, 49). Because 'to communicate is to imply that the information communicated is relevant' (vii), ostension also 'comes with a tacit guarantee of relevance' to the audience (49).

According to relevance theory, then, ostension and inference (and the speaker's associated action, implicature) are necessary parts of all communication, and communication is only divisible into 'coded' (explicit or figurative) and 'non-coded' (implicature-heavy) language to the extent that it relies on ostension to a greater or lesser degree. That being said, Sperber and Wilson do provide an (avowedly problematic) differentiation between 'explicit' and 'implicit' language. They write that

> On the analogy of 'implicature' we will call an explicitly communicated assumption an *explicature*.... An explicature is a combination of linguistically encoded and contextually inferred conceptual features. The smaller the relative contribution of the contextual features, the more explicit the explicature will be, and inversely. Explicitness, so understood, is both classificatory and comparative: a communicated assumption is either an explicature or an implicature, but an explicature is explicit to a greater or lesser degree.
>
> This is an unconventional way of drawing the distinction between the explicit and the implicit 'content' of an utterance. On a more traditional view, the explicit content of an utterance is a set of decoded assumptions, and the implicit content a set of inferred assumptions. Since we are claiming that no assumption is simply decoded, and that the recovery of any assumption requires an element of inference, we deny that the distinction between the explicit and the implicit can be drawn in this way.   (1999, 182, emphasis in original)

While such definitions of explicit and implicit language might be more difficult to apply than definitions that characterize them as simple antonyms, Sperber and Wilson's characterizations of explicitness and implicitness are more valuable than less nuanced definitions that ignore the inherent greyness of the explicit–implicit distinction. Moreover, Sperber and Wilson do provide criteria by which the explicit versus the implicit nature of language can be measured: as they write, the 'smaller the relative contribution of the contextual features, the more explicit the explicature will be, and inversely'. This criterion acknowledges that there are such things as 'more explicit' and 'less explicit' language: that, although the dividing line between the two categories may be unclear and even moveable, divisions can be argued for persuasively. A sentence, then, of which the primary meaning is evident when the sentence is removed from its immediate context is explicit compared to a sentence for which it is necessary to know the context in order to comprehend its primary, intended meaning. Although this distinction may not always be so clearly made, it does indicate that implicature is a detectable and definable occurrence and that it is useful in the analysis of specific implicatures.

Sperber and Wilson also discuss how the indirectness of an utterance communicates meaning in itself. Why would a speaker make his or her hearers work harder by having them infer an implicit meaning rather than explicitly tell it to them? Sperber and Wilson conclude that 'it follows from the principle of relevance that the surplus of information given in an indirect answer must achieve some relevance in its own right' (1999, 197). In the famous example of implicature provided by Grice above, the perceived indirectness of A's testimonial alerts the reader that Mr X must be 'no good at philosophy' by suggesting that it would be impolite to explicitly communicate the blatantly missing information. When the reader considers the testimonial's purpose, the perceived impoliteness of the withheld information is attributed to A's low estimation of Mr X's worth as a philosopher. There are many different intentions a speaker might have when causing information to be inferred rather than more explicitly communicating it; relevance theory is one approach towards discussing how the hearer correctly infers the information as well as the intention that motivates the indirect mode of the communication.

Sperber and Wilson also comment on implicature's ability to communicate a more nuanced representation of a person's psychology through mimicry. When analysing the implicatures that sometimes communicate the missing information in gaps, Sperber and Wilson write that these 'utterances as it were exhibit rather than merely describe the speaker's mental or emotional state: they give rise to non-propositional effects which would be lost under paraphrase' (1999, 220). One form of mimetic representation that relies on these implicatures is free indirect discourse, the use of a character's representative vocabulary and style in third-person, past-tense narration. Free indirect discourse is entertaining largely because of its heavy reliance on irony. Sperber and Wilson assert that ironic utterances are 'echoic': a 'speaker has in mind what so-and-so said, and has a certain attitude to it: the speaker's interpretation of so-and-so's thought is relevant in itself' (1999, 238). They go on to reject the

> classical account of irony as saying one thing and meaning, or implicating, the opposite. The most obvious problem with the classical account—and

with its modern variant, the Gricean account—is that it does not explain why a speaker who could, by hypothesis, have expressed her intended message directly should decide instead to say the opposite of what she meant. It cannot be too strongly emphasised what a bizarre practice this would be.... Genuine irony is echoic, and is primarily designed to ridicule the opinion echoed. (1999, 240–1)

Sperber and Wilson contend that, while an ironic utterance might express the opposite of what it explicitly states, the true intention (and, correspondingly, the meaning) of ironic utterances is to express the speaker's attitude towards the material rather than to mimic or provide an antithesis to that material (1999, 241). Relevance theory's contribution to our understanding of irony has significant implications for pragmatic stylistics: it allows for a more nuanced discussion of how and why authors use ironic utterances when straightforward ones are available and, more broadly, might reflect on how and why authors construct implicatures of all kinds when the explicit discussion of material is possible. Relevance theory is also particularly appropriate for analysing the structure and motivations behind the use of free indirect discourse; it provides a conduit by which one may explore the cognitive effects of exposing character psychologies, with an emphasis on uncovering why mimetic character portrayal is generally considered more successful than descriptive character portrayal.

IMPLICATURE AND FICTIONALITY IN POST-GRICEAN PRAGMATIC STYLISTICS

Pragmatic stylisticians have written much about narrative gaps but often concentrate on gaps that are inherent to all textual communication and the techniques writers employ to bridge them. In *Discourse Analysis* (1983), Gillian Brown and George Yule discuss the gaps that result from writing sentences, in that one sentence necessarily presents a separate piece of information from another. They conclude (and others have built on their proposal) that 'human beings do not require formal textual markers before they are prepared to interpret a text. They naturally assume coherence, and interpret the text in the light of that assumption' (1983, 66). This concept is often termed the 'assumption of coherence' (Brown and Yule 1983, 67). Brown and Yule conclude further that a 'sequence of events in time, told as a narrative in English, will often be presented in the order in which they happened and often, with an unstated implication of a relationship in which the second event in some sense follows from the first (e.g. *was caused by*)' (1983, 144, emphasis in original). These conclusions have important ramifications for the study of literature: if Brown and Yule are right, authors do not have to spell out characters' actions in order for them to be implied but can instead posit a minimal amount of information to convey much more. It is pragmatic phenomena such as these that provide building blocks for the inexplicit communication of concrete plots in fictional texts. However, Brown and Yule's conclusions do not help us to understand how authors lead readers to infer character actions that are less visibly represented: how, for instance, a reader may infer the connection between a first and second event without the second event itself being narrated.

Jacob L. Mey has written much on the inevitable role that textual gaps play in the reading of narrative. Following Brown and Yule, Mey acknowledges that readers automatically fill in narrative gaps; however, this also means that 'people always hear what they expect to hear; in other words, in the presence of any noise, they preferably hear old, familiar input rather than new, unfamiliar one [sic]; many popular stories and jokes capitalize on this' (1999, 303). In *Pragmatics: An Introduction* (2001), Mey stresses the author–reader cooperation necessary for the 'construction' of literary texts, which stems partly from the author's awareness and manipulation of inevitable gaps:

> The pragmatic act of reading implies an open-ended invitation to the reader to join the author in the co-creation of the story, by filling in the holes that the text leaves open. Just as the 'said', the speaker's explicit verbal act, in many cases is dispensable, given a sufficient backdrop and the listener's pragmatic act of understanding the 'unsaid', so the reader's act of understanding is not dependent on what is found in the actual text (or co-text) in so many words, but on the total context in which those words are found— and are found to make sense, through an active, pragmatic collaboration between author and reader. It is this spontaneous, mostly unconscious 'plugging' of the textual gaps that characterizes us as competent and 'versatile' readers ... ; conversely, this characteristic carries with it an obligation on the part of the author to offer us a readable, 'pluggable' text.   (2001, 255)

In Mey's characterization of reading, the reader's inferences 'create' the plot alongside the author's explicit guidance. In this schema, it is expected that readers 'read between the lines', allowing for the creation of unarticulated plot to be the norm rather than the exception. However, Mey does not discuss the extent to which this practice can be extended, focusing on the setting of fictional scenes rather than on the reader's ability to correctly infer significant blocks of information that have not been articulated: no pragmatic stylistician has yet discussed the reader's ability to make sense of fictional narratives which, if posed in a nonfictional context, would be far more ambiguous (and might be dismissed as unintelligible). While Mey rightly notes some of the heightened, publication-related constraints fiction authors must work with (2006, 257), he does not comment on how a reader's assumption of a text's fictionality may transform his or her perception of that text from an otherwise incoherent narrative into a display of ostensive-inferential communication. The passage from *Vanity Fair*, for instance, does not immediately make explicit Becky's identity. However, in the context of Thackeray's otherwise omniscient narration, the phrase 'the person' is so evasive that it is out of place, causing it to be interpreted as ostensive. This ostension highlights the clues to Becky's identity, allowing the reader to infer her presence in the passage. The same passage would be interpreted differently if approached in a nonfiction context, in which the narrator truly might or might not know the identity of 'the person' described, causing the phrase 'the person' to be ambiguous.

As the preceding glosses have indicated, pragmatic stylisticians rarely distinguish between fiction and nonfiction, possibly acknowledging a few distinctions between the two categories but denying that there is any difference in the way proposed principles apply to fiction and nonfiction. This tendency has a history as old as pragmatic stylistics: in 1975 Wolfgang Iser argued against the previous antonymic characterization of fiction and nonfiction, emphasizing that 'fiction is a means of telling us something about reality' (7). In 2000, Laura Hidalgo Downing used 'possible world theory as text theory' to address the 'problems' associated with the non-real status of fiction (11). Downing uses fictional worlds theory to represent the fictional world as a potential reality. As with Iser's more functional, speech-act-based approach, Downing's theory deemphasizes the distinction between fiction and nonfiction, neglecting the ways in which fiction is read differently from nonfiction. Pragmatic stylisticians who are less aligned with speech act theory or fictional worlds theory have tended to follow suit. In 'A Historical but Non-determinist Pragmatics of Literary Communication', Roger D. Sell historicizes the synonymity between 'literature' and 'fiction', differentiating between the two and adopting a view of 'literature' in his article that includes both fiction and nonfiction (2001, 6).[10]

---

[10] It would be wrong to neglect the work of Catherine Emmott, whose book *Narrative Comprehension: A Discourse Perspective* is a notable exception to the trend described above. Emmott asserts that fictionality provides a 'lack' of real-life context, which must be rectified in the text itself. She writes that in 'real life we are always rooted in a specific physical context', saying that her '.... book looks primarily at how the illusion of situatedness and embodiment in specific contexts within a fictional world is achieved' (1997, 58). While Emmott, then, distinguishes between fiction and nonfiction, her characterization of fiction is rooted less in the special conventions that fiction brings to the context in which it is read and more in those that it lacks.

In *The Rhetoric of Fictionality: Narrative Theory and the Idea of Fiction*, Richard Walsh argues strongly for the impact fictionality has on the interpretation of fictional texts. His theoretical orientation comes closest to the one adopted in this work. In an argument directed against the ontological descriptions of fiction by speech act theory and fictional worlds theory, Walsh proposes that

> fictionality is best understood as a communicative resource, rather than as an ontological category. Fictionality is neither a boundary between worlds, nor a frame dissociating the author from the discourse, but a contextual assumption by the reader, prompted by the manifest information that the authorial discourse is offered as fiction. (2007, 36)

Walsh also believes that fictionality is the dominant 'contextual assumption by the reader', claiming that 'the generic marker of all fictional narrative, literary or cinematic, is that the rhetoric of fictionality is the dominant framework for the communicative gesture being made, and therefore defines the terms in which it solicits interpretation' (2007, 7). Walsh sees the tendency within pragmatic stylistics (and narrative theory as well) to conflate fiction and nonfiction as detrimental to the articulation of a pragmatics of fiction. He discounts some of the approaches to describing fictionality that I responded to earlier; he also confronts theorists' 'disavowal' of the concept of fictionality, tying this disavowal to a failure to isolate fictionality's substance and articulate the distinction between fiction and nonfiction (2007, 14–15). Uniquely, among the critics treated here, he recognizes a place for genre and convention (as aspects of a 'recognizably distinct rhetorical set') in helping to form the meaning of a text, but he characterizes them as things to be 'invoked' rather than only displayed; they are reader assumptions which may be reinforced by the text, not reinforced by the text, or otherwise manipulated (2007, 15).

I am concerned with the distinction between fiction and nonfiction as it influences the way in which readers interpret fictional texts and consequently influences how readers interpret implicatures in fictional texts. I define 'fictionality' in opposition to 'nonfictionality', using the term to concentrate on the text's assumed lack of literal truthfulness. Although narratorial omniscience will be discussed extensively, I have opted to use the term 'fictionality' instead of the phrase 'conventions of fiction' because my ultimate intention is to illustrate authorial manipulation of these texts' assumed fictionality, and not manipulation of the various conventions according to which fiction is traditionally constructed. By this definition nonnarrative, nonliterary texts such as sarcastic comments also qualify as fictional (Pratt 1977, 91), but this work is concerned solely with the fictionality of literary prose. Like Walsh, I discuss fictionality as 'a contextual assumption: that is to say in the comprehension of a fictive utterance, the assumption that it is fictive is itself manifest' (2007, 30).[11] However, my primary thesis differs from Walsh's; moreover, I discuss aspects of fictionality on which Walsh has not commented and which are fundamental to the way in which some implicatures are interpreted in fictional texts. Here, again, my point of departure may also be found in Walsh's work: while Walsh believes (as do I) that the 'rhetoric of fictionality is brought into play whenever a narrative is offered or taken as fiction, regardless of issues of form, style, or reference', he also suggests that 'it is the case that most fictions do in fact exhibit characteristics indicative of their fictional status, in the form of transgressive narratorial situations such as omniscient narration or internal focalization, but these are neither necessary nor sufficient conditions of fictionality' (2007, 44). I disagree with Walsh in that I consider omniscient narration to be potentially a sufficient (although not a necessary) condition of fictionality: I argue not only that omniscient narration indicates fictionality but also that (if not negated by other contextual factors) narratorial omniscience may create the context in which a narrative is interpreted as a fiction.[12] This assertion is evidenced by the ways in which omniscient narration is often manipulated by authors to create implicatures: these implicatures rely heavily on the fictionality of the text in order to be effective (they would fail if interpreted in a nonfictional context, where omniscient narration is unlikely to be assumed by the reader).

Clearly this assertion depends on how one defines 'omniscience'. The *Oxford English Dictionary*'s second definition applies specifically to fiction:

[11] The distinction between fiction and nonfiction is sometimes characterized as problematic, largely because overlapping genres such as 'creative nonfiction' exist. There are scholars who argue that this 'in-betweenness' is not possible: Dorrit Cohn argues that the 'oxymoronic subtitles featured on the title pages of these newer crossbreeds... [make] it clear that they were largely written and read for their transgressive shock value.... Biographies that act like novels, far from erasing the borderline between the two genres, actually bring the lines that separates them more clearly into view' (1999, 29). The clarity with which fiction can be distinguished from nonfiction, then, is debatable. Regardless of the validity of these genres, however, there are narratives that are unreservedly assumed to be fictional, and it is this reader assumption of fictionality, nonfictionality, or an in-betweenness that affects the reader's interpretation of the text and consequently must be considered in an analysis of that interpretation. It is the assumed *context* of fictionality that I am interested in, rather than whether or not a narrative can be unarguably categorized as a fiction.
[12] I concede that omniscience is rarely the defining characteristic of fiction; in this I agree with Walsh when he claims that omniscience is not 'necessary' to fictional texts. It is also the case that omniscience is largely limited to third-person narratives, and a definition of fictionality that would be characterized solely by omniscience would exclude all first- and second-person narratives.

omniscience is 'an attribute of the author or a third-person narrator: a full and complete knowledge concerning all the events of a narrative, and the private motives, thoughts, etc., of all the characters'. It is this definition of omniscience that I intend to adopt here. Omniscient narration can, for instance, imply that a narrator is impartial or has a very large, if not infinite, knowledge of his subject matter. In fiction, there are gradations of impartiality and distance that are evoked by third-person, otherwise omniscient narrators; however, this distance is very often fluid and fluctuates throughout a novel, resulting in narratives where a hardly perceptible, objective narrative voice will suddenly break into individuated, opinionated narration. I have chosen to focus primarily on the epistemic connotations of 'omniscience', although I will at times comment on the narrative voice's distance from the characters it discusses. I am also not concerned with instances in which a narrator's knowledge is large but limited: while there are nonfiction narrators who tell readers more than they can be expected to have known previously (such as a specialized scientist detailing his or her research to laypeople), these narrators are not truly 'omniscient', in that they do not and cannot know everything. Conversely, a fictional narrator potentially is omniscient, and third-person omniscient narrators regularly do know the impossible (such as their characters' thoughts) and are perceived by readers as capable of communicating anything (unlike nonfiction narrators, who, as Pratt and Ryan assert, are identified with the only-human implied author). Revered texts (such as the Bible and the Koran) might appear to be the one exception to this rule. However, they are revered precisely because they are considered to be omnisciently narrated. People who do not revere these texts usually consider them as fictions, disagreeing that the omniscient viewpoint is truly omniscient (that it is 'mistaken' (not of their personal religious or nonreligious beliefs) or impossible (because omniscience is impossible)). Nonfiction texts that attempt omniscience often lay themselves open to criticism for assuming fuller knowledge than their authors can possess.

I am not the first scholar to associate narratorial omniscience with fictionality. In her 1999 book *The Distinction of Fiction*, Dorrit Cohn defines fiction partly by its potential display of omniscient narration:

> In fiction cast in the third person, this presentation involves a distinctive epistemology that allows a narrator to know what cannot be known in the real world and in narratives that target representations of the real world: the inner life of his figures.... this fictional stamp, as one theorist proposes, makes such a text 'epistemologically illegitimate' to the point where its speaker must appear as 'insane' to someone who mistook it for a historical text. (1999, 16)

Cohn (1999, 23) is careful to point out that this aspect of her work follows propositions supplied earlier by Kate Hamburger. Cohn's own work has been carried forward in other narratological texts: both Alan Palmer (2004, 5) and Monika Fludernik (2009, 6) have echoed her close alignment of fictionality with a potential narratorial omniscience in their respective writings. Cohn's use of the term 'fictional stamp' is telling, in that she (and the other narrative theorists named) tend to view omniscience as a convention potentially exhibited by fictional texts, rather than as a convention potentially assumed by readers of fictional texts. This second (and, as far as I know, original) formulation of how assumed narratorial omniscience impacts the interpretation of fictional texts allows us to explore how authors are able to manipulate this reader assumption, exploiting the reader's expectations in order to effect implicatures. While previous associations of fictionality with narratorial omniscience have been groundbreaking and insightful in their own right, they have only addressed the fiction author's ability to exploit readers' expectations of narratorial omniscience in a limited way.

While the figure of the narrator is potentially useful in articulating the implicatures that arise out of omniscient narration, the concept is not endorsed by all literary scholars. Narration is, many times, carried out by no more than a narrative voice; because the narrative voice conveys minimal personal characteristics, it is not always appropriate to assign an owner to it. Pratt's and Ryan's reliance on the narrator as the performer of the fictional act is controversial and forms part of a larger debate about how literary theory should view the concept of the narrator. Shlomith Rimmon-Kenan, for instance, argues against Seymour Chatman's claim that 'every text has an implied author and implied reader, but a narrator and a narratee are optional' (Rimmon-Kenan 2006, 89). Instead, Rimmon-Kenan 'calls for the inclusion of the narrator and the narratee as constitutive, not just optional, factors in narrative communication.... In [her] view there is always a teller in the tale, at least in the sense that any utterance or record of an utterance presupposes someone who has uttered it' (2006, 89). The issue of the necessity (or redundancy) of the narrator takes on special significance in pragmatic stylistic debates on fictionality. Walsh has argued that, in speech act theories that emphasize the role of a fictional narrator, 'the problem of fictionality is not accounted for, but merely displaced onto the (non-speech) act of pretending or imitating' (2007, 75). Walsh believes, essentially, that a critical emphasis on narratorial discourse detracts from the fictional discourse being offered by the author and effectively allows scholars to ignore the narrative's fictional status in their analysis of a text (2007, 84–5). Literary criticism too often adopts this fallacy, and it often describes fictional discourse as a report rather than as a creation (some of my responses to other theorists are loosely based on this assertion). However, I believe that a scholarly emphasis on the inherent tension between authors and their fictional narrators (like that adopted by Pratt and by Ryan) is worthwhile. While it is true that 'the reader is not obliged to hypothesize a narrator who really is omniscient in order to naturalize the authorial imaginative act' (Walsh 2007, 73), the reader's experience of the narrative as fictional motivates him or her to dissociate the narrative discourse from the author's other (fictional and nonfictional) discourses, keeping in mind that the narrative voice is definitively not representative of the author's. However, although this debate is relevant to my argument, it is not my primary goal to weigh in on the scholarly disagreement over the necessity or redundancy of the narrator figure. As a compromise, I will use the term 'narrative voice' for more distant, less conspicuous narrative voices and will use the term 'narrator' only when the narrative voice becomes unambiguously individuated.

While critics are far from being in agreement on what constitutes fiction, few will dispute that omniscient narration is only present in fictional discourse. Readers rarely read—nor are they expected to read—nonfictional discourse as if it were narrated omnisciently; the possibility of knowing everything as a certainty is a known fiction. The fictionality of omniscient narration translates into an overarching fictionality of discourse, making omniscient narration (as some narrative theorists would argue) perhaps the sole sufficient (but not necessary) marker of fictionality. By recognizing the inherent fictionality of narratorial omniscience I aim to sidestep the controversy surrounding definitions of fictionality and to concentrate instead on the effect that assumed fictionality has on the fashioning and interpretation of texts.

When the author of an omniscient narrative chooses to communicate information through implicature rather than primarily through standard, coded language, the reader is faced with the puzzle of why an omniscient persona (the narrator) would opt to communicate material that is integral to the rest of the narrative in an inexplicit or ambiguous way. It is this implicitly posed question that often motivates readers to attempt to decipher the vagueness surrounding implicatures; it also emphasizes the relevance of the implicatures to their surrounding contexts. Because intentional vagueness or ellipsis is especially suspect in a context of omniscient narration, and because omniscient narration is only possible in a fictional context, the effect of many implicatures found in omniscient narration relies on that context. This aspect of implicature and omniscient narration has been neglected, resulting in pragmatic stylisticians' questionable views on how readers interpret fictional statements (with most of them asserting that there is little difference between the interpretation of fictional and nonfictional texts) and both pragmatic stylisticians' and narrative theorists' inattentiveness to the significance granted to ellipses and implicature in omnisciently narrated texts.

AIMS AND METHODS OF THIS WORK

My discussion of these topics is deliberately situated within pragmatic stylistics, narrative theory, and historicist scholarship on the Victorian novel; it is necessary to engage all three schools of criticism to articulate the effects this work examines. I hope to contribute to pragmatic stylistics in two ways. My primary aim is to analyse the use of salient implicatures: those that communicate central elements of plot. These implicatures are often notably sustained, forcing the reader to rely on them for hundreds of pages at a time. While the discussion of implicature is fundamental to the entire field of pragmatics, pragmaticists (pragmatic stylisticians included) usually concentrate on smaller, pervasive implicatures in which the evasion or circumlocution of the speaker or author is less conspicuous. I am concerned with instances in which such less explicit narration takes on a central role in communication, and specifically in the communication of fictional narratives: when it is necessary to communicate central antinarratable actions of a novel, when it is used to imitate the undefined intentions of the characters, or when the entertainment provided by inexplicitness itself is the overt effect intended by the author. In this last case (when the circumlocution itself is the effect intended by the author), implicature is granted an additional layer of salience that is not visible in implicatures employed for other purposes. I am especially interested in the use of strictly unnecessary narrative implicatures to communicate actions central to fictional narratives (which is the topic of Chapter Three). I hope that this discussion will be doubly original: as far as I have been able to discover, pragmatic stylisticians have not discussed narrative indirectness as a technique used for its own sake, and they have shied away from discussing how a narrative is affected by having its central action narrated through implicature.[13]

---

[13] A notable exception is Billy Clark's article 'Salient Inferences: Pragmatics and *The Inheritors*' (2009). Clark reconsiders previous interpretations of *The Inheritors* in light of the central, salient implicatures in the narrative. His aims are different from my own: his emphasis is on the inferences that the reader makes, rather than on the construction of the implicatures which spur those inferences. He is also largely uninterested in the range of authorial motivations behind constructing implicatures: those he discusses are all motivated by the author's desire to communicate the psychology of characters.

My secondary goal is to convince pragmatic stylisticians to consider fictionality as a context that should be acknowledged in analyses of how readers interpret fictional texts. My discussion of central, salient implicatures in fiction involves an examination of conspicuous narrative gaps in a third-person-omniscient narration (and therefore a fictional) context. Fictionality affects the way readers interpret prominent gaps of explicit communication in narratives: while readers are likely to be confused or angered by inexplicitness found in many kinds of nonfictional narrative, they are often amused when they encounter it in a fiction, even if it is centrally located. Omniscient narration, specifically, creates a context which causes a narrator's apparent obtuseness to be interpreted as facetious; this dynamic is possible in texts which are not omnisciently narrated, but with two important caveats: either the implicature created is not as certain ('strong', in pragmatics terminology) or another context must be created which renders the narrative statements clearly facetious. This phenomenon alone evidences the need to differentiate between fictional and nonfictional contexts when analysing how readers interpret implicatures.

Both of these discussions will contribute to the ongoing concerns of pragmatic stylistics and stylistics. I also believe that they will contribute significantly to narratological discussions of gaps and omniscient narration in fictional novels. As this introduction has illustrated, pragmatic stylistics and narrative theory often overlap in the issues that they discuss; a pragmatic stylistic analysis of implicatures within fiction will inform many ongoing narratological debates. Importantly, it will also provide a vocabulary for and means of analysing phenomena that, as far as I can tell, narrative theory is currently unable to articulate. This is especially true of my characterization of narratorial omniscience as a reader's assumed context rather than only as a convention overtly exhibited by the text. As noted in the previous section, omniscience has only been discussed as a potential marker of fiction, rather than as a potential reader assumption that authors of fiction can exploit. Discussing omniscience as an assumed context will allow me to articulate authorial exploitations of readers' expectations (stemming from the perceived fictionality of the text) that are currently neglected by narratological criticism.

I also hope that my discussion of Victorian fiction in its Victorian context will provide greater insight into the pragmatics of fiction from that period: this undertaking is intended to develop new perspectives for Victorian literary studies and to contribute to the burgeoning field of historically oriented pragmatic stylistics. As mentioned previously, pragmatic studies definitively concentrate on both the linguistic and social contexts of a text's production, but in practice these studies often examine one context more intently than the other. I have attempted to incorporate discussions of historical and generic contexts, focusing both on ideological trends of specific eras and the reader's assumption of a text's fictionality. Discussing fiction *as* fiction from another era highlights its particular historical contexts, providing a more unified pragmatic reading of it than would be possible by concentrating on its generic characteristics alone. By examining the manipulation of contemporary readers' background assumptions, I add to the body of scholarship that focuses specifically on the creation and reception of Victorian fiction in the Victorian era.

Lastly, I consider realist novels alongside works that more obviously draw on melodrama or were identified with the specific genre of 'sensation fiction'. As discussed in Chapter Three, many of the works conventionally identified as realist themselves use implicature to put realism under strain at certain points. Pragmatic stylistic readings of these novels need to consider ways in which conventions and expectations of genre and literary modes may affect the working of implicature. In turn, it is my hope that pragmatic stylistics has a contribution to make to a longstanding critical interest in refining how we describe the characteristic features of realism, and how we draw its limits.

The organization of this work reflects a goal of illustrating how the study of pragmatic stylistics, narrative theory, and Victorian novels can inform each other. Each chapter is centred on authorial motivations that underlie prominent uses of implicature in Victorian novels. It is hoped that the following case studies will further the claim that the pragmatics of fictional texts differs from that of nonfictional ones, in that fictionality presents a specific context which (alongside the other contexts in which a book is read) influences the reader's interpretation of the text.

While my discussion benefits from concentrating on novels from a specific period (mid-Victorian), the novels discussed here were chosen primarily because they make exceptionally central use of implicature rather than because of the historical moment at which they were written. Nevertheless, my choice of primary texts has some historical logic. My first chapter attempts to chart the evolving representation of a sensitive topic in early- to mid-Victorian England, discussing, in chronological order, three novels that span sixteen years (1843–59). The texts considered in my second and third chapters were published within nine years of each other (1857–66). The short span of years within which these novels were published allows for a better understanding of the cultural context in which they were written and originally interpreted. This understanding allows me to comment on how contemporary readers might have been expected to interpret the implicatures with which I am concerned and why some types of implicature were commonly used.

Chapter One discusses pragmatic theories of politeness and the representation of illegitimate pregnancy in early- to mid-Victorian fiction. As a variable concept that is both defined and largely affected by its context, politeness is a central concern in pragmatic theory. While many pragmaticists have discussed politeness, however, few have attempted to relate politeness theories to written discourse. In the small amount of literature available on politeness within written discourse, there is a tendency to conflate fictional with nonfictional writing. This conflation obscures key differences in how the pragmatics of politeness functions in fictional and nonfictional texts. The chapter uses relevance theoretical analyses to illustrate how existing politeness theoretical models may be expanded to apply to fictional texts.

This chapter relies heavily on historical pragmatics to account for how authors of polite fiction represented illegitimate pregnancy in the 1840s and 1850s. The New Poor Laws of 1834 introduced legislation that left unwed mothers with drastically less support than they had hitherto received. The legislation was perceived as the cause of a widespread increase in infanticide that was not to abate for several decades. Illegitimate pregnancy (how it would be best treated by the law and society) became a major topic of debate and, with Frances Trollope's 1843 novel *Jessie Phillips: A Tale of the Present Day*, was introduced into polite fiction. Before the novel's publication, many thought discussion of illegitimate pregnancy inappropriate for mainstream fiction. Trollope explicitly challenged this assumption, and, when further (if ineffective) reforms were passed the year after her novel was published, other novelists followed suit. However, some succeeding novelists felt it best to represent illegitimate pregnancy in less direct ways, using more implicature as their works dealt more heavily with the most negative consequence of illegitimate pregnancy: infanticide. Close readings of *Jessie Phillips* (1843), Elizabeth Gaskell's *Ruth* (1853), and George Eliot's *Adam Bede* (1859) highlight how the perceived 'impoliteness' of the fictional representation of illegitimate pregnancy constrained authors in their writing and show how implicature was used to circumvent mid-Victorian politeness standards for fiction.

Chapter Two is concerned with authors' uses of implicature as a means of representing characters' internal mental states and processes, both conscious and unconscious. Because psychological representation is an inherent aspect of most fiction writing, this chapter is more psychological than historicist in its focus; however, it still attempts to address some of these novels' cultural contexts, and specifically the psychological debates and concepts of the era. Authors often employ actions to delineate character psychologies, and the metonymic function of these narrated actions often qualifies as implicature. However, there are yet other instances of representation that more concretely shun explicit description in an effort to communicate character psychology indirectly. These instances usually revolve around a character's semiconsciousness of or denial of information. The lack of explicit reference to this information in the description of a character's thoughts may mimetically illustrate the character's lack of consciousness while also explicitly delineating other, competing aspects of it. These uses of implicature are resonant of (and often are) free indirect discourse. However, the use of implicature in these instances may not always be unproblematically categorized as free indirect discourse: sometimes only a striking lack of information is present in a narrative, rather than the particular nuances of a given character's language that definitively make up free indirect discourse.

As in Chapter One, a short introduction of applicable theoretical and historical context is provided before a discussion of the novels' implicatures. After a preliminary discussion of 'the unconscious' in mid-Victorian psychological debates, Chapter Two takes the representation of courtship in mid-Victorian novels as a case study through which to discuss authors' employment of implicature in portraying certain characters' lack of self-awareness. 'Falling in love' is often represented as a gradual and unconscious process in the Victorian novel, and one which reticent characters are likely to deny, even to themselves. In Eliot's *The Mill on the Floss* (1860), Maggie Tulliver dabbles in what she knows to be an illicit and hurtful courtship; her denial of the seriousness of her flirtation with Stephen eventually leads to the social crisis of the novel. In *Orley Farm* (1862), Mr Furnival does not admit to himself that he is in love with his client, Lady Mason, and his feelings disproportionately influence his perceptions of and actions regarding her case.

Chapter Three turns to humorous 'meta-' narrative instances of salient implicature in sensation fiction. These uses of implicature encourage the reader not only to grasp unarticulated information but also to appreciate the opaque, sometimes teasing or riddle-like quality of the narrative language. The chapter focuses on the conspicuous omissions surrounded by implicatures in M. E. Braddon's *Lady Audley's Secret* (1862), Charles Dickens's *Our Mutual Friend* (1865), and Wilkie Collins's *Armadale* (1866). These uses of implicature satirize the realist tendency towards limited omniscience and create an enjoyable reader experience that results from the narrative's assumption of the reader's knowledge, rather than an assumption of the lack thereof. These novels depend on dramatic irony to maintain the reader's interest: in *Lady Audley's Secret* the author's use of implicatures creates a satirically 'polite' distance from Lady Audley's commission of murder, and in *Our Mutual Friend* and *Armadale* the reader is pulled into collaboration with characters whose true identities are secrets assumed to be shared with the reader for significant portions of the texts. In these novels, indirection is not a means towards acknowledging social convention, nor is it an aid to characterization; it is rather an end in itself. Scholars have identified the usefulness of implicature in communicating otherwise inexpressible subject matter, but few have commented on the enjoyment readers derive from narrative indirection and the stylistic performativity it makes available to the author. While pragmaticists have successfully articulated implicature's centrality in the creation of irony, they have rarely discussed the enjoyment to be derived from the use of implicature itself. This last chapter attempts to show that the above texts rely, at times, on implicature for their effect, rather than solely on the commentary the implicature provides on 'hidden' diegetic facts. In doing so it aims to uncover a facet of reader entertainment that has not previously been articulated.

1

The Unarticulated Antinarratable

*Illegitimate Pregnancy and the
Pragmatics of Politeness*

INTRODUCTION

Authors' writings are likely to be affected by their perceptions of what they think their audience will approve: if nothing else, the market in which the book trade is rooted demands this of them. Those who do not take into account the constraints of public taste or audience appropriateness, or are not capable of accommodating readers' expectations, suffer loss of sales or worse. This was equally true in the Victorian era, with the advent of large circulating libraries that sought to regulate the fiction that reached the public. William St Clair explains that

> The owner of Mudie's, the largest and dominant circulating library, which operated nation-wide in a highly monopolised market, read some novels personally before deciding whether to make a bulk purchase, and if his decision, or that of his managers, was negative, an author could find that his book remained uncirculated, little read, and unlikely to be reprinted at a less expensive price for a wider readership, and that his authorial career and future commercial prospects were severely set back. (2009, 725)

Mudie's impact on the publishing industry was enormous: in his history of the 'House of Blackwood', David Finkelstein describes Charles Mudie as the 'Chief among trade buyers': his circulating library, 'started in the 1840s, was by the early 1860s one of the biggest purchasers and distributors of texts, accounting for up to 60 percent of sales of a print run' (2002, 43–4). Moreover, Mudie notoriously 'insisted that his stock exclude trash and anything that would upset family values': this commercial institution consciously imposed and responded to perceived public taste, limiting the publication of what Mudie thought the public would dislike (Law and Patten 2009, 152).

Lending libraries, however, were not the only institutions to constrain authors. Finkelstein notes that 'publishers act[ed] as filters' in 'attempts to impose an overarching identity on [their] products' (2002, 19). The leading Edinburgh publishers of fiction—Blackwood's, for example—'took steps to mould, manipulate, and control work produced under the firm's imprint in order to conform to particular cultural values and perceived tastes', a practice which, according to Finkelstein, should 'remind us that texts are inevitably products of a social transaction between producers and readers' (2002, 152). As products of a social transaction, Victorian fictional texts were obviously subject to and indicative of the social constraints placed upon them by various (and differing) classes of Victorian readers.

This chapter will discuss narratives in which implicature is used to represent subject matter to which these constraints applied: specifically, illegitimate pregnancy. This subject matter is, due to social convention, usually incommunicable in mainstream Victorian narratives, or 'antinarratable'; social convention, or regard for politeness, may force writers to use implicature in their writing. While previous pragmatic stylisticians have noted that considerations of politeness do play a role in the creation of literary texts, they have not registered the impact that fictionality can have on the way politeness is represented and incorporated into fictional texts. The relevance theoretical analyses in this chapter will attempt to address this critical gap.

This chapter, then, will draw on examples from early- and mid-Victorian fiction to illustrate politeness-related implicature. As is indicated by the above discussion of unofficial censors of Victorian texts, the Victorian era, as varied as it was, is particularly suitable for the study of how politeness considerations are incorporated into fictional texts. The early- and mid-Victorian eras are known for the strict sexual code by which they were ruled; regardless of this generalization's disputable truth, it is popularly held and has formed a prominent aspect of Victorian studies. The analysis of politeness strategies in mid-Victorian texts enriches pragmatic theories of politeness by using an established context of politeness-related contemporary thought to test its relevance to fiction, and it enriches Victorian studies by providing further nuance to the much-debated issue of mid-Victorian sexual morality and its representation in the mid-Victorian novel. Through a pragmatic analysis of key scenes in the novels *Jessie Phillips*, *Ruth*, and *Adam Bede*, I will demonstrate how Frances Trollope, Elizabeth Gaskell, and George Eliot respectively communicate their characters' seductions and illegitimate pregnancies through implicature. Implicature largely appeased the 'unofficial censors' (such as Mudie's) who disapproved of the explicit representation of pregnancy, much less illegitimate pregnancy, in 'polite' fiction.

The Unarticulated Antinarratable

These novels react to and exploit audience expectations of politeness in different ways. While both *Jessie Phillips* and *Ruth* are usually categorized as social problem novels in today's criticism, *Ruth* is often regarded as the more polished novel, and *Adam Bede* is usually discussed as an example of classical realism.[1] Trollope, Gaskell, and Eliot had similar (but not identical) goals in writing *Jessie Phillips*, *Ruth*, and *Adam Bede*, but their specific aims, methods, and subcultures were somewhat different. While Eliot wrote *Adam Bede*, as well as her other novels, with the overarching aim of broadening individual readers' sympathies, Gaskell wrote *Ruth* in reaction to her encounters with unwed mothers, and hoped her novel would spur societal reform. Trollope's aim was much the same as Gaskell's, but her comparatively blunt appeals may have resulted partly from her desire to motivate concrete legal reformation. In greater consideration of fictional boundaries, Eliot and Gaskell use more implicature than Trollope to ease the presence of antinarratable content in their 'polite' literature.

Early- and mid-Victorian attitudes towards illegitimate pregnancy will be discussed before an examination of how those attitudes are represented through implicature in the above three novels. The discussion of these attitudes will necessarily be only introductory; my emphasis is on the use of implicature in response to these cultural attitudes, rather than on the attitudes themselves. The examination of these novels' historical contexts confirms illegitimate pregnancy's antinarratability and illustrates the correlation between the degree of readerly offence and the degree of explicitness in illegitimate pregnancy's representation. That these pregnancies are truly 'communicated' before their explicatures is evident from these novels' coherence. Traditional close readings cannot adequately explain how it is that, for instance, for the first four hundred pages of *Adam Bede* the reader is not confused by the superficially unexplained, irrelevant phenomena that Eliot interjects. Rather, our understanding of what is inexplicit but nevertheless plain is best explained by relevance theory. In the resulting readings of these novels I hope to say as much about how we 'read between the lines' as about the historical context of these novels' creation.

---

[1] It is worth noting that the concept of the 'social problem novel' would not materialize until the next century; Trollope and Gaskell would not have considered themselves as part of a tradition of social problem novelists (Guy 1996, 3, 41). However, this does not mean that Trollope and Gaskell did not hope to effect some level of reform while writing their novels; as the following discussions will show, historical documents suggest that this was the case. It is this perceived intention—both in their respective writings and in historical documents about them—that led to Trollope and Gaskell being labelled as social problem novelists in the twentieth century.

HISTORICAL CONTEXT

While illegitimate pregnancy was necessarily openly discussed by medical and social reformers, a Victorian novelist hoping to establish a very public (because marketed) but unnecessary (because fictional) literary discourse on the subject would do well to minimize explicit discussion of it. In some newspapers, by contrast, factual reporting granted potentially lewd material a moralistic, purposeful cover that fiction could not as easily assume. In his survey of mid-nineteenth-century newspaper articles, Thomas F. Boyle writes that 'police reports of mid-nineteenth-century newspapers consistently offer graphically detailed accounts of the sexual misbehaviour of all classes of the citizens of the "Age of Improvement"' (1984, 212). Eric Trudgill observes that the 'novelist's freedom... was very restricted, but most of the respectable newspapers throughout the century carried accounts of salacious sex crimes and crim. con. or divorce actions' (1976, 137). The restrictions on fiction writers applied more to certain types of novels than to others: Matthew Rubery reports, for instance, that the 'deprecating label "Newspaper Novel" soon became synonymous with a subgenre of fiction derived from actual criminal reports or, as the derogatory term would come to be used by critics, with all varieties of sensation narrative' (2009, 48). The respectability of these novels was compromised by this association with newspapers. The double standard concerning the subject matter allowed in newspapers and 'polite' fiction could be frustrating to those serious fiction writers who hoped to represent British society as realistically as possible and to effect social change through their novels.

In his work Boyle attempts to explain the prudery that middle-class Victorians are still (too generalizingly) known for. After glossing the story of a little girl who was stabbed while urinating over a grate (later realized to be an opening into a lower-class home) and a quack doctor who impregnated and then gave abortion pills to his patient, Boyle writes that 'one can only understand the deep-seated and evangelical nature of the Victorian ideology of respectability if one understands the gross reality which it set itself in opposition to. Indeed one can see the "official consciousness" in this light as a justifiable act of defensive self-preservation' (1984, 221–3). Boyle equates public (indiscreet) displays of sexuality with the disempowered status of the lower classes, whose children and women were perceived as being (and often were) susceptible to seduction, rape, and abuse. The description of the Victorian middle classes as prudish, exaggerated as it may be in many subsequent historical accounts, allowed those classes' members to identify themselves as unlike the disempowered lower classes and proudly to proclaim their bodies as private and safe.

Boyle's explication of this middle-class mentality (which had its many contradictions and exceptions) allows us to understand taboos that were, if not strictly followed in private life, part of polite 'official consciousness', forming easily accessible background assumptions on which fiction readers could draw. In a society where the body was carefully guarded from actual, physical intrusion, childbirth became indicative of sexuality and pregnancy a display of indecorous carnality (MacPike 1984, 56–7). Leigh Summers explains:

> Pregnancy was, of course, the most obvious demonstration of women's carnal animality, as well as a reminder of the female body's predilection for unseemly, squeamish and occasionally painful bodily functions. Consequently, Victorian standards of decency demanded the concealment of the pregnant body and denied any public discussion of either the experience of pregnancy or its *accoutrements*.... Pregnancy taboos were implemented and obeyed for several reasons. They operated primarily to ensure that an image of womanly innocence was maintained despite evidence of sexual experience. They were essential too in perpetuating the illusion (and male fantasy) of the continued 'virginality' and 'innocence' of married women despite the somatic betrayal that revealed they had indulged in, and possibly enjoyed, sexual intercourse. (2001, 39, emphasis in original)

John Hawkins Miller also speculates as to why the 'Victorians were often excessively prudish about public discussion of the physiology of pregnancy and birth' (1978, 23). His reasoning echoes that of Summers; he notes that 'the process of birth—with its attendant pain and potential for death—was an unwanted reminder of the physical, barnyard facts of life from which many middle-class Victorians preferred to look away as if they were not there' (1978, 40). Miller claims that

> The reluctance to discuss the indelicate subject of pregnancy and labour stems not only from ancient taboos about the ritual uncleanliness of women, but also from the transference to the woman of the dark and 'dirty' sexual drives of the male.... Perversely, however, women became tainted by the male sexual drive, and the only road to redemption was through the uncleanliness of childbirth to the temple of pure and undefiled motherhood. (1978, 41)

The pregnant body, here, is the sexual equivalent of used goods: a body that has been violated and is no longer wholly its own. With illegitimate pregnancy, however, this seemingly unconscious attitude is forced to the surface.

The situations of unwed mothers and unwed expectant mothers were considered among the worst in Victorian society. Unwed mothers faced a loss of respectability that was thought to dictate the rest of their lives: Ann Higginbotham writes that the unmarried mother 'was commonly assumed to have little future beyond prison, the streets, or the river. Her fall condemned her to a life of degradation and crime' (1992, 281). Josephine McDonagh notes that 'extra-marital pregnancies often led a woman to the loss of regular employment, homelessness, being disowned by family and friends, and being cast out of parishes that were unwilling to pay poor relief for illegitimate children' (2003, 2). It is no wonder, then, that the 'unmarried mother, it was assumed, would seek above all to conceal her fall from virtue by destroying the evidence of her sin, the illegitimate infant' (Higginbotham 1992, 260). Contemporary Victorian discussions often conflated the issues of illegitimate pregnancy and infanticide, positing ways in which 'fewer girls would be seduced; fewer children murdered' (*Infanticide* 1862, 2) in the hope of diminishing 'Bastardy, and its attendant Infanticide' (Brownlow 1864, 59).

This conflation had a long history, and was first legally represented by the 1624 Act to Prevent the Destroying and Murthering of Bastard Children. McDonagh writes that the act 'reflected the common supposition that the shame of the illegitimacy was motive enough to provoke a woman to commit the deed.... Towards the end of the eighteenth century... the concealment of a pregnancy had come to be taken as evidence of an intention to murder the child' (2003, 3). While the act was officially repealed in 1803, concealment continued to be a chargeable offence throughout the nineteenth century, with amendments concerning the application of the law being made as late as 1861 (McDonagh 2003, 4). The lesser charge of concealment was often invoked when a woman's infanticidal intentions were unproven or when a jury was sympathetic with an obviously infanticidal mother (Krueger 1997, 274).

In 1834 the New Poor Laws were introduced, and with them the unpopular Bastardy Clause. The new laws placed the responsibility (and, correspondingly, the blame) for an illegitimate birth solely on the unmarried mother and made it harder for her to access aid. It was not long before the press noticed that the 'entire exemption of the reputed father, not only from the costs of midwifery and maintenance (of the mother), but also from the costs of an application to the justices for the maintenance of the child, operates as a premium upon seduction, and inflicts a grievous burden upon the parish to which the woman belongs' ('Hints' 1841, 4). Other newspapers directly blamed the perceived spike in infanticide on the 'bastardy law, which has given such encouragement to profligacy and illegitimacy' ('Died' 1843).

There is limited truth in these representations of Victorian illegitimate pregnancy and infanticide. Officially, illegitimate pregnancy was stigmatized but in reality premarital sex was not uncommon. Michael Mason reports that, until 1860, between a third and a half of all brides were pregnant (at least in many parts of England)... courtship, or relations between the sexes—readily including full intercourse... were expected to lead to marriage [and] illegitimate birth was usually the result of a disruption of marriage intentions, when a courtship involving intercourse and pregnancy issued in an unmarried mother rather than in a pregnant bride.   (1994, 67–8)

Lionel Rose quotes an 1866 article from the *Saturday Review* which 'reminded its readers that among the working classes sexual intercourse "is regarded as an incident of honourable courtship and is—or at least used to be—followed by the solemnisation of marriage"' (1986, 20). Carolyn A. Conley traces the stigma associated with premarital sex back to the Marriage Act of 1753, which first added the legal component to the distinction between married and unmarried couples. In agreement with Mason and Rose, however, Conley notes that, although 'such a distinction would make bearing an illegitimate child considerably more shameful... the stigma would be traumatic only for those who were concerned about respectability' (1991, 112). While illegitimate birth was stigmatized, then, premarital sex was a pervasive and an understood (if hushed) part of courtship culture. However, illegitimate childbirths comprised only about 7 per cent of mid-century births, and these births were 'quite strongly associated with low social rank' (Mason 1994, 70–1). Although these births' association with low social rank might indicate that some higher-class men (in accordance with press assertions) took advantage of lower-class women, it is noteworthy that, in practice, premarital sex wholly unassociated with future marriage seems to have been relatively infrequent.

Neither pregnancy nor abortion was considered as unambiguous as it is today. Summers explains the mentality surrounding early- and mid-Victorian pregnancy:

'denial' was a particularly useful strategy in family limitation... at least until 1860 (and as late as 1880), women, rather than the medical profession, determined whether or not they were pregnant.

Pregnancy was determined by women upon the experience of 'quickening'. Quickening was the common nineteenth-century term to describe foetal movement. Until the foetus quickened (approximately four months after insemination), the woman's cessation of menstrual periods could be construed either as an 'unnatural obstruction' or a pregnancy, depending entirely on the woman's interpretation of the biological changes experienced by her own body. The removal of an 'unnatural blockage' was not a criminal offence. Until the woman herself declared she had experienced quickening, the foetus was not accorded legal or medical human status, and both the woman and her physician felt justified in using drugs or mechanical devices to remove the 'obstruction' and bring order to her menses. Recipes for the removal of obstructions were, at least until the 1880s, found in women's household advice manuals.[2]   (2001, 50–1)

Summers is describing abortion rather than infanticide, but her description nonetheless complicates a schema (accepted both in Victorian times and now) in which pregnancy is deemed a categorical 'she is or is not' matter. Victorian ideas of infanticidal intention were also complicated by a woman's perceived ability to influence her pregnancy (that is, to keep or 'unblock' a potential pregnancy): concealment is thus no longer a 'she did or did not' issue but rather an ambiguous state in which a woman might truly have thought her pregnancy was something else.

As indicated above, illegitimate pregnancy and infanticide were often conflated in the Victorian press. That the 'first born of unmarried parents [should be] the class of infants most exposed to violent deaths' was common knowledge, and much commented on (qtd. in Higginbotham 1992, 257). The debate over how best to stop infanticide was present in public literature from the passing of the 1834 Poor Laws through to the 1860s. While pamphlets often provided a preemptive apology for 'details, that may, even by well meaning persons be considered indelicate' (Osborne 1835, 3), both pamphlets and newspapers usually provided direct, unambiguous discussions of 'pregnancy', 'illegitimate offspring', and the 'Bastardy Clauses' ('Hints' 1841, 4). Not only was infanticide explicitly named but also headlines such as 'Infanticide in the Metropolis', 'Infanticide and Its Cause', and 'Thoughts and Suggestions Having Reference to Infanticide' (Brownlow 1864) were common. There was also explicit discussion of seduction as a pervasive practice largely responsible for both illegitimate childbirth and infanticide (Brownlow 1864, 47–8; 'Church' 1854, 4; *Infanticide* 1862, 5; Osborne 1835, 11).

It is important to recognize the close connection these concepts had. Today they are often discussed as wholly separate occurrences whereas in Victorian Britain infanticide was considered primarily as a consequence of illegitimate pregnancy. Similarly, illegitimate pregnancy could be said to represent the pregnancy that the middle classes hoped to keep invisible: illegitimate pregnancy was public evidence that a woman had been violated or had allowed herself to fall. Infanticide hardened her image as solely

---

[2] Jennifer Thorn echoes Summers's historical gloss, claiming that 'though abortion after quickening (usually understood as the fifth month of pregnancy) remained officially a capital crime through the period, a wide variety of sources indicate that abortion at many stages of unwanted pregnancy was regularly practiced and that the killing of newborn bastards was understood as a kind of belated birth control, regrettable but nonetheless understandable' (2003, 25).

sexual by repudiating the motherhood that was considered woman's 'natural' role and an unwed mother's only chance of partial redemption. Infanticidal mothers were the ultimate fallen women: having transgressed sexual (and, by association, class) boundaries, these infanticidal women murdered in an attempt to reclaim their station instead of publicly atoning by raising the illegitimate child.

While typically only hinted at or cursorily mentioned in the world of polite fiction, illegitimate pregnancy was actually 'paranarratable' rather than 'antinarratable' in the early- to mid-Victorian period: as mentioned previously, there was an explicit and vocal debate concerning illegitimate pregnancy in nonfictional literature. Although understood as a serious topic of reform debate, the sexual activity it represented made illegitimate pregnancy an inappropriate subject for polite entertainment. In understandable attempts to incorporate an intense national debate into their literature, later 'polite' fiction authors devised techniques by which to communicate the fact of illegitimate pregnancy and to reflect upon its causes and consequences while minimizing the risk of offending their readers.

These techniques can be articulated using relevance theory, and their explication can show how current pragmatic theories of politeness may helpfully inform the analysis of the inexplicit in Victorian fiction.

THE PRAGMATICS OF POLITENESS

As the introductory chapter showed, aspects of pragmatic theory, and especially relevance theory, may be readily adapted to inform literary criticism. While most pragmaticists aim their theories at real-life conversation, pragmatic stylisticians have adopted these theories as the basic tenets by which they analyse certain aspects of written discourse. Jacob L. Mey writes that 'Grice's notion of "implicature," as it is called, is of the utmost importance with regard to explaining how authors and readers go about "cocreating" the literary work ... a text is not the exclusive work of the individual author but always presupposes the active collaboration of an audience, the readers' (2006, 256–7). It is this necessary collaboration between author and readers that makes pragmatics applicable to fiction. Mey notes that 'this is, eventually, why books are bought and sold: not because they are indispensable for our material existence, but because they represent a personal communication from an author to a potential readership—a communication that, in order to be successful, will have to follow certain rules'—that is, implicit rules (2006, 257). It is this same dynamic that necessitates an author's observance of the antinarratable: it is important that an author acknowledge social constraints because the unfolding of the narrative involves an intimate collaboration of the reader with the author. The reader's outlook need not be the same as that of the author, but it must be sufficiently similar: the potential reader must, to at least a certain extent, be able to identify with the implied reader. Nonobservance of the conventional designation of certain topics as antinarratable would alienate 'decent' potential readers. This does not mean that the author may not create an ironic narrator who jocosely assigns ridiculous opinions to his or her narratees (as Thackeray, Dickens, and Eliot often do). It does, however, mean that the author's irony must be sufficiently clear and his or her good opinion of the implied reader evident (and, as in Thackeray, Dickens, and Eliot, narrators' obviously ironic assignations of narratee opinion create a fictional, stigmatized third party in reaction to which the author and the readers may bond).

There is a long history within pragmatics of theorizing politeness, and a few pragmatic stylisticians have used these theories to articulate the heightened cooperation that literary discourse necessitates. The remainder of this section will provide brief discussions of pertinent theories of politeness and how they have been applied to pragmatic stylistics. Penelope Brown and Stephen Levinson's *Politeness: Some Universals in Language Usage*, originally published in 1978, revolutionized linguistic conceptions of the phenomenon, and, although Peter Grundy's (2000) discussion of politeness does not concentrate on written discourse, his definition of the concept can easily be applied to analyses of texts. Roger D. Sell (1991) and Elizabeth Black (2006) are two pragmatic stylisticians who have applied politeness theories to literary discourse. I mean to supplement these politeness theoretical accounts of the literature-reading experience with relevance theoretical analyses that illustrate how the politeness theories may be modified to better describe both nonfiction-reading and fiction-reading experiences.[3]

Brown and Levinson famously applied the sociological concept of 'face' to the politeness of linguistic interactions. 'Face' has two aspects: 'negative face' and 'positive face'. 'Negative face' denotes the 'want of every "competent adult member" that his actions be unimpeded by others' (1999, 62). Brown and Levinson define 'positive face' as referring to the 'want of

---

[3] Much of what has been written about relevance theory and the way we think about politeness is exploratory, discussing the ways in which existing politeness theories may be supplemented by relevance theory (Christie 2007; Jary 1998). Not much has been written that discusses how relevance theory and politeness theory, combined, may describe unique characteristics of written discourse; in fact, Christie notes that 'the processes of communication through speech and writing are seen by relevance theory to be analogous' and refers to hearers and readers (and speakers and writers) interchangeably throughout her article (Christie 2007, 293).

every member that his wants be desirable to at least some others' and explain that this 'want' 'includes the desire to be ratified, understood, approved of, liked or admired' (1999, 62). 'Face' affects what speakers say when they perpetrate a 'face-threatening act'—that is, when they are forced to communicate material that might be threatening to a listener's independence or self-esteem. The linguistic markers that speakers use to ameliorate face-threatening acts are treated by Brown and Levinson as markers of politeness. Speakers may opt, for instance, to perform the act either 'on record' (unambiguously) or 'off record'; if they perform the act 'on record', they may choose to perform it either with or without redressive action, and that redressive action can seek to emphasize the hearer's positive or negative face (Brown and Levinson 1999, 68–71). These strategies involve various effects such as humour, heightened formality, apologies, ambiguous hints, and flattery. Employing implicatures while performing a face-threatening act would be considered as executing it off record.

According to Peter Grundy, politeness is the 'exercise of language choice to create a context intended to match the addressee's notion of how he or she should be addressed' (2000, 145). Although he does not discuss politeness in literary discourse, Grundy's pragmatic definition of 'politeness' highlights its relevance to the analysis of literature: no literature, fiction or nonfiction, is capable of success (financial, persuasive, or even comprehension-wise) if it does not 'create a context [that matches] the addressee's notion of how he or she should be addressed'. This definition indicates why it is that we so often associate politeness with 'decorum' and 'etiquette', and in fact Grundy does characterize 'politeness phenomena [as] one manifestation of the wider concept of etiquette, or appropriate behaviour' (2000, 146). This characterization does not sit well with previous pragmatic theories of politeness, all of which attempt to distance politeness from its 'proper' connotations and emphasize its pivotal role in cooperative interaction.[4] Grundy himself problematizes the distinction, writing that the

> folk view of politeness as the speech style of the over-classes is strongly indicative of value for the speaker. Thus the value-neutral way in which 'politeness' is used as a term of pragmatic description applicable to all communicative instances of language use is easily confused with the quite different, but widely held, ideological attitude to politeness in society at large. (2000, 164)

---

[4] Geoffrey Leech notes that there 'is an unfortunate association of the term with superficially "nice", but ultimately insincere, forms of human behaviour, and it is therefore tempting to write off politeness... as being a trivial and dispensable factor which is no more than a "garnish" on the serious use of language' (1990, 83).

Such a claim is complicated by the fact that politeness is implicated in different ways in different cultures (including different class cultures). While the 'folk view of politeness as the speech style of the over-classes' (Grundy 2000, 164) is not the only type of politeness, it is certainly a specimen of the 'exercise of language choice to create a context intended to match the addressee's notion of how he or she should be addressed' (Grundy 2000, 145). Moreover, it is one that would have been dominant and—if we can trust literary representations of Victorian culture— influential for the Victorian middle classes. While it would be wrong to conclude that the pragmatic definitions of politeness and 'decorum' are collapsible, they are certainly more compatible (at least in the domain of Victorian studies) than is assumed in current pragmaticist scholarship.

Roger D. Sell's discussion of politeness in literary discourse is marked by an ambiguity similar to Grundy's in regard to the possible distinction between politeness and decorum. Sell opens his discussion with an Augustan definition of politeness, associating it with 'mental cultivation and polished manner, elegant refinement and neo-classical good taste. Such qualities... were epitomized in a polite conversation that was well-informed and pleasurable—easy, free, natural, pliant, humorous' (1991, 208). Sell does, however, treat his readers to a short history of 'politeness', noting the suspicion with which the concept came to be regarded throughout the eighteenth and nineteenth centuries (1991, 210). Like Grundy, Sell mentions the shift in the primary meaning of the term (from 'decorum' to the value-neutral politeness discussed by Brown and Levinson) but, also like Grundy, he does not explain the shift or how the two concepts are related.

Sell explicitly points out the dearth of scholarship on politeness within literary discourse, writing that 'there is a major vacuum here in literary research' (1991, 222). Moreover, he notes that critics concerned with politeness in literary discourse 'discuss, not the politeness *of* literary texts, which would have something to do with the relationship between the writer and the readers, but the politeness *in* literary texts, which is a question of relationships between personae and characters dramatized within the world of mimesis' (1991, 217, emphasis in original). In attempting to partially fill the critical gap he has just identified, Sell helpfully differentiates between 'selectional' and 'presentational' politeness, identifying them as the two types of politeness applicable to literary discourse. Selectional politeness entails the observance of 'taboos and conventions of social and moral decorum operative within [an author's] culture, never saying anything, and never using any words, which would be in the least way threatening the readers' positive or negative face' (1991, 221). Sell's concept of presentational politeness entails the closest observance of Grice's Cooperative Principle possible (1991, 221–2). However, while all of his examples are fictional, Sell is concerned with both fictional and nonfictional texts (that is, all literary discourse). Sell's lack of distinction between two different types of text conflates their respective qualities and for that reason lessens the degree of insight offered into the study of politeness in fiction. Fiction and nonfiction differ in many aspects, two of which are the certainty with which they may communicate information (an omniscient narrator, for instance, may be more certain of facts than a nonfictional narrator) and the planes in which the information they communicate will be significant (information in nonfiction texts relates to the reader's real-life world, while information in fictional texts does not). In light of these differences, it is notable that Sell does not, for instance, articulate how fictional content is capable of threatening real-life readers' faces.

In her book *Pragmatic Stylistics*, Elizabeth Black notes that the applicability of politeness theories to character dialogue is obvious but that their relevance to the 'communicative flow between the narrator and reader is less clear' (2006, 72). Black believes that there 'is an inherent impoliteness in being invited to read a book. It is an imposition, which threatens our negative face. It makes demands on our time, and... it may seek to overturn our schemata, to change our minds about things we may hold dear.' (2006, 74). This assertion seems to be in contradiction with a general characterization of fiction as entertainment: readers, for the most part, control what fiction they choose to read, and they read it because it is enjoyable, not because they feel obliged to. As noted in the initial segment of this chapter, the very concept of marketing a book is based on the book's attractiveness, and arguably it would be a face-threatening act to prohibit people from reading books. While a novel does make demands on a reader's time, so does any activity, and (because fiction is often marketed as entertainment) it is generally time that a reader willingly opts to spend reading. While a novel must be interesting in order for this preference to occur, 'politeness', as defined above, seems less relevant to a person's general desire to read fiction. Similarly, while Black's assertion that novels 'may seek to overturn our schemata' is undoubtedly true, this is not an assumption with which most readers begin reading novels.

Black also claims that 'a very serious type of FTA [face-threatening act] that occurs on the authorial or narratorial level lies in the choice of topic' (2006, 75). However, Black does not suggest a possible explanation regarding why choice of topic can be inflammatory (like Sell, she does not articulate why fictional content is capable of offending readers personally). The applicability of the 'face' concept to the analysis of fictional (specifically narratorial, not character) discourse appears to not yet have been questioned in pragmatic stylistics scholarship. The concepts of face and face-threatening acts clearly can apply, in that it is necessary that an author not offend his actual readers in order to be read (and earn a paycheck). But the relationship between author and reader is more indirect and more complex than that in face-to-face dialogue: while a narrator (such as those of Thackeray, Fielding, or Sterne) may explicitly insult his narratee, such blatant face-threatening acts often have the counterintuitive effect of flattering the actual reader by implicitly contrasting the reader's behaviour with that of the narratee. Moreover, the tactic appeals to the reader's intelligent discrimination between author and narrator: the narrator has committed the face-threatening act rather than the (actual or implied) author.[5] This suggests that it would be much harder for an author to offend his readers than for a speaker to offend his hearers. The reader's awareness of his or her own anonymity is also suggestive of this conclusion: in most cases the reader is aware that the author cannot personally attack his or her face and that, even if the author were to do so, the offence would be registered privately (in the act of reading) rather than witnessed by the speaker. In this sense, reading a novel resembles eavesdropping more than being in direct dialogue with a speaker.

All of this said, a reader may be offended by a novel. Overwhelmingly, that offence is a reaction to the subject matter and language used: a perceived transgression of 'selectional', rather than 'presentational', politeness. This perception of an impoliteness is possible because the actual author is exposing the actual reader to antinarratable information and is (in many cases if not all cases) presumably conscious of doing so: subject matter transcends the relationship between narrator and narratee (and even the relationship between implied author and implied reader) because the offensiveness resulting from exposure does not depend on who it is explicitly addressed towards and in consequence is usually perceived to be intended by the actual author for his or her actual audience. As far as narrative mannerisms and presentation are concerned, the actual reader is less likely to be offended by fictional works because taking offence would involve reacting, on a personal level, to a fictional persona. But the inclusion of antinarratable material is clearly a conscious decision by a real author, and it is a decision to expose the reader to that material. This is

---

[5] Because this work discusses authorial cues that guide the reader's inferences, it focuses on the relationship between actual author and implied reader rather than on the relationship between implied author and actual reader. However, there are exceptions, as when discussing the historically documented reactions of real-life readers to authors' works. Similarly, it is often necessary to distinguish narrators and narratees from implied authors and implied readers. For a more thorough discussion and justification of my chosen terminology, please see the Introduction.

where the ambiguous distinction between paranarratability and antinarratability yet again becomes an issue: there are genres in which antinarratable material would be welcomed. Modern readers seeking a highbrow literary experience might be offended, for instance, by Thackeray's racist characterization of Miss Swartz in *Vanity Fair*; for contemporary readers of Victorian comic and satiric fiction, however, Thackeray's overt racism would have been relatively unremarkable.

This example shows that, despite our uncertain reactions to some of the politeness codes of the eighteenth and nineteenth centuries, politeness in fiction is still an extant issue: there have been substantial shifts concerning what Western society regards as antinarratable, but the antinarratable is still a relevant category. With regard to Victorian literature, the above example illustrates how, despite a lack of articulation concerning how politeness theory relates to the analysis of fiction, previous pragmaticists' core intuitions are correct: politeness theory does apply. However, as with many other subjects of pragmatic study, the fictionality of these texts makes an unaltered application of pragmatics ineffective when analysing them. The fictionality of these texts allows too much leeway for Sell's concept of 'presentational politeness' because the reader is aware that it is a fictional persona with which he or she has interaction and that, because of reader anonymity, the author is incapable of pointed insults towards most readers.[6] Conversely, Sell's concept of 'selectional politeness' is pivotal in that it is the only type of impoliteness that transcends the fictional barrier and is therefore the only impoliteness that the actual reader can react to on a nonfictional, real-life level. In matters of offence stemming from fictional texts, it is the exposure of the reader to offensive material that counts, and not the manner in which the material is exposed.

Consequently, even when a writer is conspicuously obfuscating narrative material, we may be confused or, preferably, entertained, but we are rarely offended. Yet, while presentational impoliteness does not often have the power of offending the actual reader, presentational politeness has the power to ameliorate selectional impoliteness. In contrast to what Sell's theory of politeness predicts, however, this is usually achieved by flouting the Cooperative Principle rather than observing it (or, in Sperber and Wilson's terms, employing 'ostensive-inferential communication').[7]

---

[6] There are obvious exceptions here, such as with Edward and Rosina Bulwer-Lytton's, and Byron and Lady Caroline Lamb's, literary spats.
[7] As discussed in the introductory chapter, 'ostensive-inferential communication' refers to a speaker/writer making his or her communicative intent manifest to a hearer/reader (Sperber and Wilson 1999, 63).

As central as previous pragmaticists have made the Cooperative Principle in their politeness theories, it is relevance theory that best articulates the presentational politeness that authors employ to hedge the communication of selectionally impolite (antinarratable) material. Relevance theory's greater ability to explain the workings of authors' politeness is a consequence of the way in which Sperber and Wilson imagine the Principles of Relevance are 'used': while Grice posits ostensive-inferential communication as the flouting (that is, the wilful disregard) of the Cooperative Principle, Sperber and Wilson characterize ostensive-inferential communication as the manipulation of the Principles of Relevance, which they hold are impossible to disturb (1999, 162).

The (im)politeness with which an author addresses his or her audience (his or her 'presentational politeness') will have a large impact on the audience's perception of the narrative voice and its identification with the narratee, but it is largely incapable of offending readers. The reader's ability to absorb impolite fictional narration without offence connects the possibility of offence solely to the inclusion of antinarratable material. How may an author communicate antinarratable material without alienating readers? These strategies of presentational politeness must rely heavily on implicature because explicit, cooperative strategies would necessarily incorporate only more discussion of the antinarratable material. Moreover, the use of implicatures in these instances effectively communicates antinarratable content while simultaneously being interpreted as what Mark Jary terms 'repair work', in that saliently polite language often communicates the speaker's attempt 'to make up for some prior face-threat in order to re-establish an equilibrium' (1998, 10). Relevance theory is especially useful in analysing how authors communicate antinarratable material, because it shows how readers may be guided towards understanding the relevant meaning of superficially irrelevant scenes and details. The more novelists rely on implicature, the greater relevance theory's ability to explain how we interpret the ideas that they indirectly communicate. Relevance theory will provide considerably more insight into the communication of narrative in *Ruth* and *Adam Bede*, then, than it will for a militantly reformist novel such as *Jessie Phillips*.

JESSIE PHILLIPS: TROLLOPE'S CALL FOR CHANGE

Frances Trollope's 1843 serialized novel *Jessie Phillips: A Tale of the Present Day* makes frequent use of implicature. However, it does so in the main to address less serious subplots and the less antinarratable aspects of Jessie's 'fall'. While Trollope's novel achieved something of the political impact she was seeking, her straightforward narration of Jessie's seduction, pregnancy, and its consequences earned Trollope terrible reviews and solidified her reputation for vulgarity.

In the eighteenth- and nineteenth-century tradition of women writers who wrote only after exhausting other means of financial support, Frances Milton Trollope wrote her first novels for money. At thirty she had married Thomas Anthony Trollope, a barrister who became more likely to quarrel with clients as his chronic headaches became debilitating. After several failed attempts to supplement the family income with various ventures, Frances Trollope began writing novels. She quickly realized she had found a way to support her family, and they moved up several socioeconomic levels as she continued to write steadily throughout her life.

Trollope began writing novels advocating reformation in 1836. By then, she was popular and financially successful, and could branch out from the gothic romances and travel narratives with which she had made her name. As Josephine Guy has noted, the concept of the 'social problem novel' did not exist during Trollope's lifetime; Trollope was not consciously participating in an established authorial tradition (1996, 3, 41). Despite this, however, a clear emphasis on societal reformation in Trollope's writing is well documented (Brandser 2000, 203; Graff 2002, 53–4). Trollope's first such novel, *The Life and Adventures of Jonathan Jefferson Whitlaw*, was an anti-slavery narrative motivated by her friendship with participants in the abolitionist movement and by the years she had spent in the United States (1827–31). Trollope went on to attack various institutions in her literature: she satirized evangelical religion in her 1837 novel *The Vicar of Wrexhill*, spoke out against factory conditions and child labour in *The Life and Adventures of Michael Armstrong, the Factory Boy* (1840), and attacked the New Poor Law in her 1843 novel *Jessie Phillips: A Tale of the Present Day*. Critics were often unsympathetic to her blatant political aims. Helen Heineman writes that Trollope's

> contemporaries were shocked by the harsh bitterness of these novels, and for her pioneering efforts Frances Trollope was much maligned by critics and reviewers.... Unable to dispute her facts, critics directed their venomous attacks to her personality and sex and greeted her unusual subject matter by labeling these novels low, coarse, and vulgar, and her characters hideous, revolting, and repulsive. (1984, 58)

While it is possible that Trollope chose controversial, 'ugly' subject matter to tap a largely undiscovered market (some of her non-reform novels could be slightly bawdy), it is more likely that she was attempting to have an impact on law-making in the most effective way she knew. Kristin J. Brandser writes that Trollope 'had no access to the authoritative language of law. Having much to say about legal issues, however, she entered the dialogue through literary language' (2000, 181–2). As Ann-Barbara Graff notes, Trollope's literary popularity allowed her to write 'purposefully to influence the consciousness of her readers, to enhance the social roles of women, and, in novels like [*Michael Armstrong*] (1840) and *Jessie Phillips: a Tale of the Present Day* (184[3]), to affect the legislative agenda of the House of Commons' (2002, 53–4).

To a certain extent, Trollope's novels can as easily be considered reform documents as examples of early Victorian fiction. This, at least, was what was intended by Trollope: the advertisements for *Jessie Phillips* concentrate largely on its exposition of the New Poor Law, neglecting its quality of writing and plot in favour of emphasizing its political importance. The prospectus extract that was most commonly provided in advertisements for the book read:

> The object the author has had in view in the composition of this work has been to call the attention of her readers to the absolute necessity of some alteration in the law which at present regulates the maintenance and management of the poor. Her own conviction of its tyranny and injustice, of the impracticability of enforcing its provisions with uniformity, and of the cruel hardships which are inflicted on the poor by the attempt to enforce them, is strong, and she conscientiously believes well founded. She is also deeply impressed with the general impolicy and evil tendency of that system of administrative centralization, which seems of late to have been creeping into the practice of our Government. Above all, the author is anxious to declare her detestation of the newly broached doctrine that the poor have no *right* to a sufficiency of necessary food to sustain the life which God has given them; and she hopes and believes that there are still abundantly enough English hearts to join with her in scouting this doctrine as *unchristian*. ('Blasphemous Publications' 1842, emphasis in original)

Another advertisement for *Jessie Phillips* was titled 'THE POOR LAW SYSTEM' and went on to quote the prospectus extract ('Advertisements and Notices' 1842). All early reviews concentrated on the reform aspect of the novel, some defending Trollope's exposé and others condemning it. *The Spectator* compared Mrs Trollope's writing with that of Dickens (whose early pseudonym was 'Boz'), writing that

> perhaps no greater proof of the artistical superiority of Boz to Mrs. TROLLOPE could be given than this, that in the works of Boz the fiction is always most prominent in the mind, whereas with Mrs. TROLLOPE the so-called philosophy attracts the attention of the critic. Her character and story are so obviously framed to forward some theory of the author, that they come to

be considered less in the light of humanities than machines. ('New Fictions' 1843, 17, emphasis in original)

The novel's prospectus and critics' early reviews show that *Jessie Phillips* was intended and considered primarily as a reform document. Correspondingly, Trollope opted to describe the tragedies associated with the New Poor Law relatively directly, using implicature only for the more light-hearted strands of the narrative. The result is a didactic narrative that is far more explicit about seduction, illegitimate pregnancy, and infanticide than most other seduction narratives of the period. This being said, the narration of Jessie's seduction and pregnancy is still oblique by today's standards.

The novel is set in the rural town of Deepbrook, and, contrary to the 'Present Day' setting indicated by the novel's subtitle, the events take place in 1834, the year the New Poor Law was enacted and nine years before the novel's publication date. As Graff writes, 'the story is set in the past to force a contrast between the ways in which dramatic social change is anticipated and the present reality within which the author herself writes' (2008, ix). (Eliot would use the same device decades later for *Adam Bede*.) Because the New Poor Laws have just been passed, the men of Deepbrook devote much of their time to debating how best to implement them. Along with the didactic rendering of this discussion, two plots are narrated, both of which illustrate the pitfalls of the New Poor Law.

The first plot contains the story of the respectable Mrs Greenhill, who is impoverished by the debts of her well-meaning son. With her son in jail and her son's children starving, Mrs Greenhill reluctantly approaches the Board of Guardians to petition for relief. After a lengthy discussion in which Mrs Greenhill is denounced as 'a pestilent, factious, plausible, mischievous old hussy' by the predictably obtuse board, she is granted relief only on condition that her family enters the workhouse (Trollope 2006, 129). Mrs Greenhill even more reluctantly agrees to a condition that will necessarily separate her young grandchildren from their mother and will subject them all to the company of convicts. Luckily, young and wealthy Ellen Dalton hears of Mrs Greenhill's troubles and anonymously donates a sum of money that will tide the family over through the son's imprisonment.

This plot line is central to the first third of the novel and forms the reader's introduction to the New Poor Laws. Despite the relative absence of the novel's eponymous heroine, early reviews concentrated on this plot line, valuing the novel according to the reviewer's politics. While *John Bull* ('Monthly Publications' 1843), *New Monthly Magazine and Humorist* ('Jessie Phillips' Feb. 1843), and *Caledonian Mercury* ('Literature' Mar. 1843) applauded the novel's satirical attack on the New Poor Laws, *The*

Spectator ('New Fictions' 1843) and *Bell's Life in London and Sporting Chronicle* ('Literature' Jan. 1843) both characterized Trollope's portrayal as biased and exaggerated.

Despite her nonappearance in the 'Mrs. Greenhill' plot, Jessie Phillips is introduced early in the narrative as the industrious, virtuous, but only moderately bright village beauty. Unfortunately for Jessie, Ellen Dalton's brother Frederic, the rakish village beau and heir to the Dalton fortune, is determined to seduce her. When Frederic finally obtains Jessie's attention, Trollope describes the incident as 'when the village beauty was beguiled into thus taking her first downward step' (2006, 68). This characterization of an otherwise innocent scene (the two have spoken while gathering flowers with Frederic's sisters) alerts the reader to the tragic and antinarratable nature of the subsequent seduction, which occurs largely 'offscreen'. By this spare use of foreshadowing, Trollope dramatically reduces the antinarratable content which she must explicitly present.

Trollope is, however, explicit regarding Frederic's bad intentions. She writes that, in his view, Frederic

> might indulge himself safely, and with assured impunity, in the gratification of all the wishes and inclinations which destiny, that is to say, his peculiar and individual destiny, suggested to him. In the case of Jessie Phillips, this principle of action was roused into more than ordinary activity by the consciousness that there were some rather strong objections to his pursuing the course his inclination pointed out. In his estimation, the strongest and most obvious of these was the possible obstacle which any discovery of a little *affaire de coeur* with her, might oppose to his views upon any other fair one.... Of this, however, he had little fear. The terror that formerly kept so many libertines of all classes in check was no longer before him, the legislature having, in its collective wisdom, deemed it 'discreetest, best' that the male part of the population should be guarded, protected, sheltered, and insured from all the pains and penalties arising from the crime he meditated. 'No, no,' thought Mr. Frederic Dalton, 'thanks to our noble law-givers, there is no more swearing away a gentleman's incognito now. It is just one of my bits of good luck that this blessed law should be passed precisely when it was likely to be most beneficial to me.'
>
> As to all secondary objections, such as the destruction of the pretty creature who was the object of his passionate admiration, he dismissed them all with a gay smile.   (2006, 108, emphasis in original)

The French phrase '*affaire de coeur*' is the closest Trollope comes to naming 'the crime [Frederic] meditated', but a physical seduction is implicated by the potential consequences mentioned (including the legislation's effect on those consequences) and semantically indicated by such terms as 'indulge', '*coeur*', 'libertines', 'crime', 'destruction', 'pretty', and 'passionate admiration'. Trollope's didacticism regarding the legislation of the 'noble law-givers' also functions as heavy-handed foreshadowing, rendering Frederic's seductive intentions clearer. This is, however, as explicit as Frederic's goals are made, and it is only with the revelation of Jessie's pregnancy that the reader learns he has been successful in his aim of seduction.

Jessie's pregnancy is initially communicated through implicature, although that implicature is soon rendered indefeasible by an explicit announcement of Jessie's being 'in the way to present [Frederic] with AN HEIR!' (2006, 202, emphasis in original). While even this announcement presupposes Frederic's seduction of Jessie by concentrating on the expected issue of a child, the capital letters and exclamation point used make conspicuous information that, in most narratives of the period, would be more delicately and indirectly broached (if broached at all). Three pages earlier, the reader learns that

> Instead of good will, [Jessie] must look for reprobation, and for indignation, and contempt, in the place of respect and esteem. Unhappy creature!... Yet, in the midst of all this anticipated degradation she fondly flattered herself that she was not in reality degraded; for truly did the deluded girl believe that the vows she had exchanged with Frederic Dalton were as sacred in his eyes as in her own, and that she was in spirit and in truth his wedded wife, although the ceremony which was to proclaim their union to the world was delayed till it could take place without injury to the interests of her betrothed husband.... Nevertheless, having once made up her mind to tell her devoted lover, her adoring Frederic, that all considerations of pecuniary interest must give way at once, not only for his sake, and her own, but for that of an unborn treasure more precious than either... her bosom now fluttered more from the anticipation of quickly coming happiness (more quickly coming than she had hitherto ventured to hope for) than from doubt or dread of any kind.   (2006, 199–200)

While the most conspicuous indication of Jessie's pregnancy here is the mention of 'an unborn treasure', that treasure is not identified as *Jessie's* 'unborn treasure', and the indefinite article which introduces it emphasizes the 'treasure['s]' independence and potentially abstract (rather than strictly metaphorical) significance. The reader must seek out the relevance of the utterances by considering the relationships between them; the lines that open the passage function more to indicate communicative intent than they do to communicate concrete information (that is, they function ostensively). Jessie's 'anticipated degradation' is the first piece of superficially unexplained information with which the reader is presented. It is the assumed link between Jessie's 'anticipated' degradation and the unofficial status of her relationship with Frederic Dalton that would have signalled illegitimate pregnancy to most Victorian readers. As noted in the historical section of this chapter, it was widely known that lower-class couples often had intercourse before official marriage ceremonies. However, the implicature still functions clearly without this background knowledge. There are not many occurrences which could link a girl's unmarried status to her 'anticipated degradation', and illegitimate pregnancy is perhaps the most stereotypical of these potential occurrences even today. Jessie's superficially incoherent resolution to tell Frederic that they must marry immediately reinforces the previous utterance's assumed significance and indicates a situation in which immediate marriage would salvage Jessie's reputation. The anticipation of happiness versus the dread of degradation functions similarly. In this context, the word 'unborn' is striking, confirming what the previous sentences have implicated. It is the single word 'treasure' that is semantically irrelevant to the significance of the passage, and causes its meaning to be understood inferentially rather than denotatively.

The description of the child's birth is predictably minimal: only the 'feeble cry of a new-born babe' communicates that the currently unconscious mother has given birth (2006, 403). Conversely, the narration of infanticide is surprisingly direct. When communicating a farmer's suspicion that the newly awakened Jessie has killed her baby and hidden its body, Trollope writes that the 'very darkest suspicions against the unhappy Jessie had taken possession of his mind; he felt not the shadow of a doubt that she had given birth to a child, destroyed, and concealed it' (2006, 409). The narration of the baby's actual murder by Frederic is even less delicate and is clearly intended to shock the reader. In a series of tragic coincidences, Frederic has come across the baby.[8] Trollope writes that

> in an instant the thought suggested itself to Frederic Dalton that Jessie had abandoned her child, with the certainty that a few hours of such abandonment would cause its wished-for death.... 'Confound her idiot folly!' he exclaimed; 'if she had common sense enough to determine that it should perish, why could she not silence this confounded cry?' He had turned as he muttered these words, and was again standing over the spot where the child lay. Again it uttered a sharp piercing cry. He raised his booted foot, and made a movement as in sudden rage, and the piercing cry was heard no more.
>
> Frederic Dalton stood alone in the dark shed, trembling in every limb. He was perfectly aware of the horror that had been perpetrated, yet, with a strangely vehement attempt at self-delusion, he blended the word ACCIDENT with his muttered curses.   (2006, 434–5, emphasis in original)

---

[8] The baby has been taken from Jessie by a minor character while she is unconscious, and later forgotten in an abandoned barn.

While the words 'kill' or 'murder' are not used in the above passage, the narration of Frederic's villainous motivations directly before his violent action shock the reader by emphasizing, rather than deemphasizing, the antinarratable action. The unusual line break between the paragraphs accentuates the gravity of the action, as does Frederic's unexpectedly vulnerable appreciation of 'the horror' of it. Trollope does not let us mistake his vulnerability for innocence, however, and reasserts Frederic's villainy by characterizing his denial of blameworthiness as 'self-delusion'.

It would be wrong to assume that Trollope was unaware of the etiquette prohibiting the narration of such topics; she carefully addresses and defends her shock tactics as an exposition of true practices that could be remedied—that is, as transcending the nonfiction–fiction barrier and making the material relevant to her audience's 'real' lives. In the novel, the workhouse is characterized as having the same effect that negative reviewers characterized *Jessie Phillips* as having: both expose decent audiences to indecent material. This characterization of the workhouse plays a large role in Mrs Greenhill's reluctance to enter it, and is one of Trollope's main arguments against the New Poor Laws: by shutting away the impoverished with the criminal in workhouses, the 'decent' poor are contaminated with the immorality of the 'indecent' poor. Trollope returns to this thread in the *Jessie Phillips* plot, subjecting Jessie to such exposure during her time in the workhouse. In the passage below, the prostitute Caroline Watts embodies the exposure to immorality that Trollope is protesting against but also enacting:

> But the terrible lore of Caroline was not now offered in a way to profit her hearers—the old were shocked and disgusted, while the young, though appalled, were contaminated. To whichever class the reader may belong, the language of the reprobate shall not be recorded to offend him; yet was there one observation made by this same Caroline which had enough of truth and practical wisdom to redeem it from oblivion. 'They pretend to think,' said she, with a bitter sneer, 'that they will save some of their precious parish money by making a poor girl's bad luck too hard for her to bear, and that they shall keep her, that way, from bringing babies to them (kind tender creters!) to be nursed. But they are fools for their pains, and so they will find, whether they are honest enough to say so or no. In the old times, when a boy and a girl wasn't too bad, and too miserable, to be past caring for any thing, both the one and the other had something they were afraid of, that, in two cases out of three, maybe, kept 'em out of mischief. But now our precious gentlefolks have been clever enough to find out that by leaving one to suffer for both, and letting the t'other go free, they have made the girl's share too bad to bear, and so they shall get quit of the paying, either by the poor wench killing herself or her child, or both. A nice charity scheme, isn't it?'
> (2006, 326)

In this passage, Trollope signals that she is obeying decorum: she will not expose her audience to what 'shocked and disgusted...appalled [and] contaminated' her fictional characters. But she defends her own narration of antinarratable content when describing Caroline's similar tirade as having 'enough of truth and practical wisdom to redeem it from oblivion'. The use of Caroline as a mouthpiece allows Trollope to once again offer a didactic condemnation of the bastardy clause but it also, because someone other than the narrator is delivering the condemnation, allows the narrator to comment on why the tirade is permissible.

Jessie Phillips was serialized in monthly parts before being published in three volumes. As a monthly serial the novel received some positive (if short) reviews, but upon volume publication in late 1843 the reviews became lengthier and more negative. While it was overwhelmingly the blatantly political end of the fiction that most irritated reviewers, the antinarratable element of the political problem was also attacked. These reviews echoed the worries first articulated by *The Spectator*, which had rightly predicted the remaining plot of the novel in its early review ('New Fictions' 1843, 17). In an attack that anticipated those later made on sensation novels, *The Spectator* depicted Trollope as 'taking advantage of attractive temporary circumstances, and so working them as to produce their greatest effect at the time of production...she treats her subject cleverly, no doubt, but coarsely, literally, and vulgarly—not so much with vulgarity of manner, but by an appeal to the vulgar prejudices and vulgar cant which animate the ignorant and narrow-minded' ('New Fictions' 1843, 17). *The Spectator's* acknowledgement that there is no presentational impoliteness on Trollope's part is significant: it is the only positive comment on her work. The same thread is carried on in later reviews: a milder review in *The Examiner* notes that 'where a subject is forced and painful in itself, its failings are not likely to be less apparent in Mrs. Trollope's hands. That is the defect of the book before us. There is no relief' ('Literary Examiner' 1843, 675). It is not presentational impoliteness that angered reviewers but Trollope's lack of overt presentational politeness when communicating antinarratable subject matter.

While *The Athenaeum* concentrates primarily on denouncing the reform aspect of *Jessie Phillips* ('Jessie Phillips: A Tale' 1843, 956), it also notes that the novel's 'faults are flagrant and numberless', using as an example Trollope's inability to 'turn away from so tempting a subject as [the law's] dealings with Woman and her Seducer' ('Jessie Phillips: A Tale' 1843, 956). *John Bull*, having published a positive review shortly after *Jessie Phillips* began serialization, later published a second review denouncing the antinarratable content of the novel:

But for the sake of thus having a Poor Law story with which to bleed heavy accusations against the Poor Law itself, Mrs. TROLLOPE has sinned grievously against good taste and decorum. The particular clause of the Act which she has selected for reprobation is the *bastardy clause*—not perhaps the very best subject for a female pen. And then, in order to give dramatic effect to this subject, we have the seduction of Jessie Phillips, her pregnancy, the birth of the child, and its supposed murder by the guilty mother, discussed by two young ladies (Ellen Dalton and Martha Maxwell), of which discussion, the discovery of the body, the probabilities of Jessie being in a condition, just after parturition, to be able to destroy the child, and the enormity of the crime, are the prominent points. We admit that Mrs. TROLLOPE manages these details with as much delicacy and reserve as their nature would admit of, but they are essentially unfit materials.

('Literature' Nov. 1843, 732, emphasis in original)

Again, the manner in which the 'unfit materials' are treated is excused, but the materials themselves pose the problem of audience exposure. In this review, illegitimate pregnancy's antinarratable status is complicated by its inherent paranarratability in yet another way: it is not only that Jessie's illegitimate pregnancy is communicated but also that it is communicated by 'a female pen' and 'discussed by two young ladies' in the novel. The content of the narrative is antinarratable, but it is posed as antinarratable specifically with respect to discussion by women. The contextual dependency of the material's antinarratable status effectively renders it paranarratable. The reviewer's assertion of the material's paranarratability rather than antinarratability demonstrates the variable nature of literary 'decorum': *John Bull*'s specification of the context in which illegitimate pregnancy is antinarratable implies that it would not be antinarratable if, for instance, written by a male author (and consequently approached in a different context). The inherent paranarratability of all antinarratable material (like that presented here) also evidences the selectional character of literary passages which offend: *Jessie Phillips*'s female author and female characters suggest that the novel is likely to command a largely female audience, and the inclusion of illegitimate pregnancy entails that it is a subject not only known to the female author but also deliberately exposed to her female audience. A male-authored text would not convey the same breach of decorum on the writer's part (although of course a similar audience is likely).

It is perhaps even more indicative of *Jessie Phillips*'s offensiveness that, in one of the few positive reviews of the novel, the *New Monthly Magazine and Humorist* felt the need to avoid mention of the 'single incident' that motivates the plot, writing only that the novel 'triumphs over difficulties which perhaps no other female writer would have dared even encounter'

('Jessie Phillips' Nov. 1843, 429). The review goes further, protesting against the exposure in which Trollope's blunt handling of antinarratable information results: the novel is said to busy 'itself with the lowest, the vilest, and the weakest of mankind, and will nevertheless leave the wisest wiser than it finds them, the purest more pure, and the loftiest more fitted for the duties of their lofty sphere' ('Jessie Phillips' Nov. 1843, 429–30).

Most critics believe that, despite negative reviews, Trollope largely accomplished her political goal.[9] While it is difficult to find concrete evidence that illustrates a direct link between the publication of *Jessie Phillips* and subsequent legislation, the first reforms of the bastardy clause of the New Poor Law were passed in 1844, within a year of *Jessie Phillips*'s publication. Considering that Trollope was 'the only novelist who dramatized the disastrous implications of this law for women' and that she was already an established and popular novelist, it is likely that *Jessie Phillips* was partially responsible for the new legislation (Helen Heineman qtd. in Brandser 2000, 202). Unfortunately, the new legislation was inadequate. According to Lionel Rose, women were now allowed to petition for child support, but

> the Poor Law was expressly prohibited from assisting in any action... the government's real objective was not humanitarian at all, but designed really to dissociate a heartily detested Poor Law from one of its most reviled aspects at a sensitive time: for the Act, if anything, made the woman's position worse. Poor ignorant girls were now left entirely to their own devices to start proceedings. The 'corroborative evidence' rule remained.... Allegations of an increase in infanticide, now blamed on the 1844 Act, were to mount sporadically but noticeably into the 1850s, and then reached a crescendo in the 1860s. (1986, 28–9)

If anything, the situation for unwed mothers was made worse by the reforms Trollope had hoped for. It would be decades before their situation improved, and in the meantime more authors felt drawn to protest against unfair laws.

RUTH: GASKELL'S CAREFUL PROTEST

Elizabeth Gaskell had motivations similar to Trollope's when writing *Ruth* (1853). Gaskell had contemplated the novel since 1849, when she helped a young woman emigrate. The girl, 'Pasley', had been seduced by her doctor and incarcerated when (designated 'fallen' and consequently unable

---

[9] Ayres 2002, 4; Brandser 2000, 202; Graff 2008, xviii.

to find employment) she had committed theft (Gérin 1976, 127–8). Gaskell was moved by the girl's story and determined to urge people to reconsider the condemnation with which unwed mothers were treated. Gaskell especially hoped she could move people to consider the negative effect such shame could have on not only the mother but also the infant.

Unlike Trollope, Gaskell was wary of the strong conventional constraints upon handling such a topic in fiction. However, Gaskell was also planning on traversing territory that Trollope had not attempted. While, as Angus Easson writes, the 'fallen woman was a familiar enough character in novels[,] ... Ruth is not only placed centrally, she is also rehabilitated, and both the sexual treatment and the working out of her redemption gave offence' (1991, 26). The 'working out of [Ruth's] redemption' was capable of giving offence on several grounds: not only does it involve the growing idealization of a onetime sinner but it also necessitates the narration of the unwed mother's life, not just her pregnancy. While there is little in the representation of unwed motherhood that would seem to be more offensive than the representation of illegitimate pregnancy (considering, especially, the supposed redemptive qualities of motherhood), the subject's extreme rarity suggests its paranarratability. Jessie Phillips, Esther Barton (*Mary Barton*), Hetty Sorrel (*Adam Bede*), Lady Dedlock (*Bleak House*), and Sarah Leeson (*The Dead Secret*) all disappear from their respective narratives shortly after becoming or being revealed as unwed mothers, and almost all of these disappearances are deaths (the death of Hetty, the only exception, is one of the few things reported of her after her disappearance). While Ruth also dies, she does so a decade later in narrative time. With two thirds of the narrative dedicated to her subsequent life, emphasis is placed on her dedication as a mother and her unfailing piety. Instead of assuming that an unwed (if pious) mother will be unacceptable to her audience, Gaskell's chosen task is one of reconciling the unwed mother to her fictional acquaintances and, simultaneously, to the actual reading public.

Gaskell worried over her novel's public reception from the first. 'An unfit subject for fiction', as Gaskell wrote about it, 'is *the* thing to say about it; I knew all this before; but I determined notwithstanding to speak my mind out about it' (Easson 1991, 202). Many felt that such a subject should not form the central plot of a story written in the 'novel form, which, notoriously, being for amusement in moments of idleness, could not hope to treat seriously a topic suited to morals or theology' (Easson 1991, 26).[10] While the centrality of such an issue was an objection in

---

[10] Margaret Ganz believes that 'a real effort of critical imagination is required nowadays to do justice to Mrs. Gaskell's intentions and artistic execution in *Ruth*. For our attitudes

itself, it would also pose other narrative problems: the seduction of a young girl, an antinarratable topic, would seemingly compose a prominent part of the story. These two problems aside, Gaskell's main objective would be to elicit as much sympathy for her heroine as possible—a goal she could depend on at least some readers to be hostile towards. As Easson writes, '*Ruth* was a "problem" novel' and Gaskell's aim in writing was to work towards a solution' (1991, 26).

The use of implicature alleviated many of the narrative problems Gaskell faced. Implicature allowed her to narrate implicitly rather than explicitly, to maintain presentational politeness while discussing an impolite topic. Implicature's ability to portray various states of awareness is also made heavy use of: Gaskell uses implicature to mimic Ruth's sexual ignorance, emphasizing her vulnerability and making it nearly impossible for readers' sympathies to lie elsewhere.

The first quarter of the novel is dedicated to Ruth's seduction, and, in keeping with Ruth's unawareness, the relationship into which she is entering is never explicitly portrayed as a seduction. However, Gaskell slowly builds a dynamic between Ruth and her seducer, Bellingham, in which Bellingham's unethical sexual intentions and Ruth's innocence are emphasized. This dynamic is introduced in their first interaction, in which Bellingham encounters Ruth working as a seamstress at a local ball. His supposed fiancée's dress is torn, and Mr Bellingham presents Ruth with a camellia by way of thanks for her good work in mending the gown. After an extended passage of free indirect discourse in which Ruth's observations on the ball and on Mr Bellingham are presented, Gaskell writes

> Ruth, then, had been watching him.
>
> Yet she had no idea that any association made her camellia precious to her. She believed it was solely on account of its exquisite beauty that she tended it so carefully. She told [her friend] Jenny every particular of its presentation, with open, straight-looking eye, and without the deepening of a shade of colour. (2008, 17–18)

The first sentence, offset in a paragraph by itself, emphasizes the interest that Ruth takes in Bellingham from the beginning. The proposition that Ruth had 'no idea that any association made her camellia precious to her'

---

toward the "fallen woman" have so greatly evolved that we might minimize Mrs. Gaskell's courage and broad-mindedness in making a then proscribed topic the main subject of a novel' (1969, 105–6). Similarly, Hilary Schor writes that 'Gaskell could be sure of enraging much of her audience through her choice of subject matter alone: in telling the story of an unwed mother, speaking openly of female sexuality and exploited young women, she was challenging accepted notions not just of female behaviour but of what belonged in decent fiction.' (1990, 159) presupposes that an association does make it precious to her, and the gap between the two propositions licenses the reader to infer Ruth's innocence and the danger she is accordingly in. The context of the preceding sentence and the omniscient narration cause the reader to interpret the verb 'believed' as counterfactual, indicating that, although Ruth may be unaware of the fact, it is not 'solely' because of its beauty that she prizes the flower.

The 'deepening... of colour' disnarrated in the last sentence signifies Ruth's unawareness of the romantic import of Bellingham's gift.[11] This signification is one that most readers automatically discern, although the romantic connotations of Bellingham's gift are never explicitly alluded to in the passage. In many ways the 'blush' is a perfect trope through which to discuss implicatures. Always denoting self-consciousness, but varying widely in the origin it designates for that self-consciousness (communicating, for instance, everything between shame and romantic interest), the blush is an ambiguous signal, relying on implicatures to communicate its meaning. Conventionally, it functions as a synecdochic trick, standing in for the embarrassment characters might feel, the hidden knowledge they might possess, or, as in *Ruth*, their growing romantic and sexual awareness. In all instances, the blush signifies feelings that are less likely to be explicitly stated in empathetic narration because they are illicit or not fully realized by the character experiencing them (the character may be 'innocent', or experiencing denial, for instance). Because, conventionally, blushes are ambiguous in the type of self-awareness they express, implicatures are often needed to communicate the origin of characters' blushes. In this case, the romantic import of the scene Ruth is describing (men giving women flowers at balls) provides the context for the described—but disnarrated—blush. That Ruth does *not* blush indicates that she is not aware of these romantic imports, and this achieves Gaskell's aim of portraying Ruth's unusual innocence.

The danger which is introduced into the text with Bellingham is, notably, not made explicit. A sociopathic outlook is indicated in both Bellingham and his mother when the reader is told that his 'boyish tricks annoyed and irritated [his mother] far more than the accounts which reached her of more serious misdoings at college and in town. Of these grave offences she never spoke; of the smaller misdeeds she hardly ever ceased speaking' (2008, 32). This passage also qualifies as disnarration, in

---

[11] Disnarration, or 'terms, phrases, and passages that consider what did not or does not take place', is discussed in the introductory chapter as a concept originated by Gerald Prince and perpetuated by Robyn Warhol in her larger discussion of narrative refusals (Prince 1988, 3).

that it isolates what Bellingham's mother does not discuss. Bellingham's mother's silence mimics that of Gaskell.[12] It is implied that Bellingham's mother subscribes to the hypocritical school of politeness that Sell sees being satirized by Victorian authors. This impression is a result of the generally negative characterization of Mrs Bellingham: she 'hardly ever' stops complaining about her son, but then, as we soon learn, she also rescues him from situations in which he has acted immorally (condemning the victims of his immoral behaviour). And yet Gaskell repeats the pattern of suppressing knowledge of Bellingham's errors: like Mrs Bellingham, she is explicitly vocal about everything except overtly immoral actions. It is the situation in which the reader encounters these figures that dictates whether their silence is perceived as a positive or a negative attribute. Bellingham's mother is a natural guide for her son, and it is disastrous that she does not chastise him for his immoral actions or attempt in some way to stem them.

Gaskell, on the other hand, is excused for her silence by the fictionality of the text. Like the pamphleteers and agitators against the bastardy clause of the New Poor Law, Bellingham's mother is responsible for speaking out against her son's immoralities because that vocalization will have 'real' consequences (that is, consequences on the same fictional plane). Because she is communicating a fiction (and therefore material that is strictly unnecessary), Gaskell is not just exempt from this responsibility but denied it. Gaskell is addressing implied readers, and so the explicit articulation of antinarratable content would not be capable of having a positive impact, but only the negative one of exposure (as Trollope's explicit narration did). While Bellingham's mother's silence is condemned, then, Gaskell's indirectness is read as presentational politeness, as an act undertaken specifically for the benefit of the audience. Context affects the significance of silence: in this case, what has been shown as immoral within the fiction is rendered thoughtfully polite when transcending the fictional plane. This element of thoughtful politeness is precisely what *The Examiner* complained was missing from *Jessie Phillips*.

---

[12] As is indicated by the use of her name, I am referring to Gaskell as the actual author who employs presentational politeness, rather than her narrator. Whereas the presentational impoliteness of narrators has no real-life object, the presentational politeness of actual authors (which often translates into the presentational politeness of the narrator, as well) is in reaction to the presence of selectionally impolite material. Because selectional impoliteness is attributed to the actual author, it follows that presentational politeness used to mitigate selectional impoliteness would be as well. This distinction has less relevance to an analysis of *Jessie Phillips*, in which comparatively little presentational politeness is used to ameliorate the novel's selectional impoliteness.

Bellingham's intentions concerning Ruth are introduced through implicature. Employing free indirect discourse, Gaskell writes that by 'no over-bold admiration, or rash, passionate word, would [Bellingham] startle her; and, surely, in time [Ruth] might be induced to look upon him as a friend, if not something nearer and dearer still' (2008, 33). The first half of this quotation makes Bellingham's awareness of Ruth's ignorance clear—his unwillingness to 'startle' her with his 'rashness' evokes a human/animal interaction in the wilderness, portraying Ruth as almost a 'wild child' in her timidity.[13] The second half of the quote substitutes for the word 'lover' the descriptive phrase 'something nearer and dearer still'. Gaskell's obvious obfuscation ('lover' replaced with 'something', and emphasized by the drawn-out phrase 'nearer and dearer' which follows) qualifies as ostensive-inferential communication in that it relies more on communicating communicative intent rather than on the actual proposition intended. The ostensive-inferential nature of the statement emphasizes that the meaning intended by the utterance is not made explicit and must be inferred (Sperber and Wilson 1999, 49–54). The omniscient narrative voice of *Ruth* is capable of specifying the exact relationship that Bellingham hopes to form with Ruth. Gaskell's unnecessary use of ostensive-inferential communication alerts the reader that the information communicated is better left inexplicit, and correspondingly is illicit. The relationship which the narrative voice is specifying is characterized as 'near' and 'dear' yet also as illicit: two positive concepts that are unusually collocated with a negative one. The unusualness of this description isolates Bellingham's hopes as those of seduction.

A key scene in the narrative follows, and it is one that relies heavily on implicature. Gaskell writes:

> The third [Sunday] he walked by her side a little way, and, seeing her annoyance, he left her; and then she wished for him back again, and found the day very dreary, and wondered why a strange undefined feeling had made her imagine she was doing wrong in walking alongside of one so kind and good as Mr. Bellingham; it had been very foolish of her to be self-conscious all the time, and if ever he spoke to her again she would not think of what people might say, but enjoy the pleasure which his kind words and evident interest in her might give. Then she thought it was very likely he never would notice her again, for she knew she had been very rude with her short answers; it was very provoking that she had behaved so rudely. She should be sixteen

---

[13] Some of Gaskell's early critics speculated that *Ruth* was inspired by one of Wordsworth's poems in his *Lyrical Ballads* (Easson 1991, 208, 219, 235). The poem is about a child, Ruth, who runs away to the forest after suffering neglect from her father. There, she meets a Native American (recently arrived from America) whom she falls in love with and marries. Soon, however, the Native American grows restless and deserts her.

in another month, and she was still childish and awkward. Thus she lectured herself, after parting with Mr. Bellingham; and the consequence was, that on the following Sunday she was ten times as blushing and conscious, and (Mr. Bellingham thought) ten times more beautiful than ever. He suggested, that... she should take the round by the Leasowes; at first she declined, but then, suddenly wondering and questioning herself why she refused a thing which was, as far as reason and knowledge (*her* knowledge) went, so innocent, and which was certainly so tempting and pleasant, she agreed to go the round; and when she was once in the meadows that skirted the town, she forgot all doubt and awkwardness—nay, almost forgot the presence of Mr. Bellingham—in her delight at the new tender beauty of an early spring day in February. Among the last year's brown ruins, heaped together by the wind in the hedgerows, she found the fresh green crinkled leaves and pale star-like flowers of the primroses. Here and there a golden celandine made brilliant the sides of the little brook that (full of water in 'February fill-dyke') bubbled along by the side of the path.... Ruth turned to thank Mr. Bellingham for his kindness in taking her home by this beautiful way, but his look of admiration at her glowing, animated face, made her suddenly silent; and, hardly wishing him good-bye, she quickly entered the house with a beating, happy, agitated heart....

She was not conscious, as yet, that Mr. Bellingham's presence had added any more charm to the ramble. (2008, 39–41)

The free indirect discourse with which this passage begins emphasizes Ruth's childish innocence. It also makes Ruth more sympathetic, inviting readers to follow her train of thought while functioning to contrast her innocence and immaturity with their greater knowledge. The awkwardness of Ruth's reasoning as well as the narrative voice's direct communication informs the reader that Ruth is only fifteen; her youth characterizes her unequivocally as a 'victim' and 'innocent'.

Free indirect discourse functions by way of implicature, in that the primary meaning it communicates is a result of the content's interaction with its context rather than the denotation of a semantically coherent utterance. Specifically, free indirect discourse usually functions by the use of 'foreign words' which articulate a character bias that clashes with the more neutral language of typical third-person omniscient narration (Ginsburg 1980, 551). The meaning of passages using free indirect discourse is not found in the 'foreign words' or in the neutral language of omniscient narration but in the difference that is often evident between the two. In the passage above, for instance, the third-person pronouns used to designate Ruth and the lack of any quotation marks alert the reader that it is the narrative voice that is communicating information. However, because the narrative voice has previously portrayed Mr Bellingham as dangerously immoral, the characterization of Mr Bellingham as 'so kind and good' shows that an opinion at odds with the narrator's is being communicated. On an explicit, superficial level, this characterization of Mr Bellingham is clearly wrong. The only way to resolve the relevance of the characterization to its context (and its coherence) is to understand that the narrative voice is mimicking Ruth's thought process. This conclusion is also substantiated by other 'foreign' phrases that suggest thoughts similarly dissonant with those the audience would associate with the omniscient narrative voice (such as the assertion that 'it had been very foolish of [Ruth] to be self-conscious' when she was walking with Bellingham, and the prediction that 'it was very likely he never would notice her again'). What Gaskell evidently intends to communicate is not that Mr Bellingham is 'so kind and good', or that Ruth should not be self-conscious when taking secrets walks with a bachelor of a higher station, but rather the disconnection between Ruth's worldview and that of the narrator. That this can be communicated inexplicitly shows that Gaskell assumes the reader is able to identify with the narrator's worldview and that Ruth's differing worldview is, in perspective, less informed.

Because of its predominantly mimetic character, free indirect discourse qualifies as echoic discourse.[14] While Sperber and Wilson explain that 'a speaker can use an echoic utterance to convey a whole range of attitudes and emotions, ranging from outright acceptance and endorsement to outright rejection and dissociation' (1999, 240) they also specify that the 'attitude expressed by an ironical utterance is invariably of the rejecting or disapproving kind' (1999, 239). While Dorrit Cohn has rightly described the empathetic capacities of free indirect discourse (1978, 117), it is generally accepted that free indirect discourse functions more commonly as irony, with the true meaning of the utterance lying in the attitude expressed towards the mimicked language. While Gaskell is clearly not 'disapproving' of Ruth, her use of free indirect discourse distances the narrator's opinions from those Ruth espouses, and guides the reader to reject them.

The blush that is disnarrated earlier in Ruth and Bellingham's courtship is enacted in the passage above. However, Gaskell is very thorough in her explanation of Ruth's 'blushing and conscious[ness]', and it is the hefty passage of preceding free indirect discourse that excuses it. While Ruth's previous self-consciousness around Bellingham is explicitly mentioned, it is Ruth's lack of understanding concerning that self-consciousness that is dwelt on. By delineating Ruth's train of thought leading up to her and Bellingham's next meeting, Gaskell aligns Ruth's consciousness and

---

[14] Echoic utterances are those that 'achieve relevance by informing the hearer of the fact that the speaker has in mind what so-and-so said, and has a certain attitude to it' (Sperber and Wilson 1999, 238).

blushing with shame and youthful awkwardness rather than with sexual knowledge. Bellingham, on the other hand, responds to the sexual connotations of Ruth's blush, noting how it enhances her beauty rather than the discomfort it signifies.

Many of the text's implicatures effect dramatic irony by highlighting the implied reader's knowledge of concepts of which Ruth is ignorant. The italicized, typographically foregrounded '*her*' in the passage above functions in this way, characterizing Ruth's knowledge as different from that of the other characters and the reader. When followed by the characterization 'innocent', the phrase '*her* knowledge' communicates that the reader has knowledge which Ruth does not possess. Gaskell's use of dramatic irony here does double duty, creating a suspenseful narrative effect and emphasizing the blamelessness which Ruth's ignorance gives her. She is, in short, a victim of her own ignorance.

The following imagery symbolizes the sexuality that previous implicatures have also communicated. The description of blossoming flowers is especially appropriate in a passage that succeeds free indirect discourse concentrated on Ruth's thoughts, in that it points to the unconscious sexuality of an ignorant girl. These arise among 'last year's brown ruins', which could be related to the death of Ruth's parents the previous year. The passage's spring imagery, then, is symbolic of Ruth's 'budding' sexuality and of her unconscious hopes for a new life, a new source of happiness.

The narrative voice notes that, at the end of their walk, Bellingham's 'look of admiration at [Ruth's] glowing, animated face, made her suddenly silent; and, hardly wishing him good-bye, she quickly entered the house with a beating, happy, agitated heart' (2008, 40). The equivalent of this passage is found in many narratives of courtship; while Ruth may be ignorant of what her body language expresses, the reader is not. This typical scene functions by use of implicature. The awkwardness of Ruth's goodbye silently (and, for her, unconsciously) acknowledges the unspoken romantic element between the two characters. Romantic inclinations often remain inexplicit for an extended period in literary depictions of Victorian courtship (as will be discussed in more detail in Chapter Two). While this is partially due to authors' exploitations of a natural source of narrative suspense, it also reflects the hesitancy with which, in real life as in fiction, many people broach a topic that is potentially face threatening. If nothing unspoken existed between Ruth and Bellingham, there would be no awkwardness. Instead, Bellingham's 'look of admiration' hints at his sexual feelings, and Ruth's consciousness of his gaze results in behaviour that, outside a romantic context, would be incoherent. While my own close reading has worked forward through the sentence (from

Bellingham's 'look' to Ruth's ensuing awkwardness), the reader would be expected to work backwards: Ruth's awkwardness alerts the reader that Bellingham's look made her (if unconsciously) uncomfortable. The scene is reminiscent of many found in less illicit, more encouraging courtship narratives; it alerts the reader to the sexual tension between Bellingham and Ruth.

The narrative voice alludes most conspicuously to the sexual component of Bellingham and Ruth's relationship when explicitly discussing Ruth's innocence. The reader is told that Ruth

> was too young when her mother died to have received any cautions or words of advice respecting *the* subject of a woman's life—if, indeed, wise parents ever directly speak of what, in its depth and power, cannot be put into words—which is a brooding spirit with no definite form or shape that men should know it, but which is there, and present before we have recognized and realized its existence. Ruth was innocent and snow-pure. She had heard of falling in love, but did not know the signs and symptoms thereof. (2008, 44, emphasis in original)

'*The*' subject of the story, 'love', is first explicitly broached here. However, the negative implication of 'love' on which the plot really centres—the seduction Ruth is at risk of because of an absence of 'any cautions or words of advice'—is not made explicit until much later. The above passage is nevertheless clear in its communication. Gaskell imbues the word 'the' with special significance when she foregrounds it by typographical deviation. 'The', in itself, communicates hardly any meaning, in that it is only a definite article (although, importantly, its definiteness isolates 'the' issue that Gaskell means to discuss). Gaskell typographically foregrounds a word that is without explicit content, implicating that '*the* subject of a woman's life' should not be put into words. It is explicitly stated that this 'subject' 'cannot be put into words'; that, like many other concepts which have 'no definite shape or form', this subject is supranarratable and therefore only capable of being narrated indirectly. While this may be true, it is doubtless the case that '*the* subject of a woman's life' is, in this context, antinarratable as well. Gaskell's conspicuously vague terminology and lack of recourse to semantically appropriate words (such as 'seduction', 'sexuality', 'pregnancy', and 'birth') indicate that, while her topic may be supranarratable, its articulation is not being attempted. Instead, the reader is left to relate '*the* subject of a woman's life' to 'falling in love'.

Gaskell makes extensive use of foreshadowing when narrating Ruth's seduction, presupposing the reader's understanding of the relationship between Ruth and Bellingham as an illicit one. Old Thomas, an acquaintance from Ruth's childhood, is filled with a 'tender anxiety' when he witnesses the growing relationship between Bellingham and Ruth (2008, 50). Gaskell's narrative voice is too polite to articulate the nature of Ruth and Bellingham's relationship, but she reports Old Thomas's telling thoughts: 'I misdoubt that young fellow [Bellingham] though, for all [Ruth] called him a real gentleman, and checked me when I asked if he was her sweetheart. If his are not sweetheart's looks, I've forgotten all my young days' (2008, 50). Old Thomas's articulated suspicions, while not as explicit as the circulating pamphlets condemning the New Poor Law, confirm the reader's interpretation of countless implicatures and further evidence Ruth's ignorance. However, as with Mrs Bellingham and Gaskell herself, Old Thomas is kept from giving Ruth 'a [direct] warning of the danger that he thought she was in' by the restrictions that make up polite conduct (2008, 50). His eventual recourse to a quotation from the Bible is so indirect that it gives Ruth 'no definite idea' (2008, 51)—an occurrence which implies Gaskell's criticism of the politeness conventions that her own manner of narration embraces.[15] In this context, Thomas's ineffectual effort to warn Ruth not only foreshadows the future state of Ruth and Bellingham's relationship but also clarifies the present state of it.

The rest of Gaskell's foreshadowing also implicates the present state of Ruth and Bellingham's relationship. As Ruth and Bellingham return from their encounter with Old Thomas, Ruth is described as 'all unconscious of the dark phantoms of the future that were gathering around her' (2008, 51). A little while later, it is noted that Bellingham and Ruth stand 'together at the top of a steep ascent'—an image that is reminiscent of the terminology used in the Victorian era to denote a woman's impending 'fall' (2008, 51). While both of these images are straightforward instances of foreshadowing, they also presuppose the danger and illicitness that necessarily accompany Ruth's actions but that are not explicitly narrated before this point.

The sexual nature of Ruth's relationship with Bellingham is explicitly stated sometime later, when the narrative voice notes that Ruth 'and her lover had rambled in sun and in gladness' (2008, 83). But the one word 'lover' is the only explicit acknowledgement given to the main subject of the book until the presentation of Ruth's pregnancy a few chapters later. The scene of Ruth's actual, physical seduction by Bellingham is omitted. When an abrupt chapter ending is preceded with the information that Ruth 'entered the carriage, and drove towards London', Gaskell implicitly evokes the eighteenth-century perception of London as the British centre of immorality, and communicates that it would be impolite to articulate

---

[15] Old Thomas warns Ruth that 'the devil goeth about as a roaring lion, seeking whom he may devour' (1 Peter 5:8).

the London-based part of the narrative—that it is antinarratable (2008, 61). Gaskell begins the next chapter with a date, 'The June of 18—' and the unusual reference to calendar time compounded with a new, previously unmentioned setting (Wales) alerts the reader that much time has passed (2008, 61). The emphatic silence concerning the activities in the ellipsis foregrounds them, and the reader's background assumptions concerning London implicate the unnarrated activities' antinarratability. The gap in the text that Gaskell makes conspicuous is not representative only of a lapse of time: it signals the illicit, antinarratable activities that occurred during that time.

Ruth and Bellingham's activities are more explicitly referred to later in the text. Ruth's situation is presented by two characters other than herself, with one of them adopting the narratorial role of informant. Mr Benson and his sister, Faith, have been vacationing in Wales when Mr Benson discovers Ruth shortly after she has been abandoned by Mr Bellingham. Ruth is mentally and physically ill with shock, and Mr Benson takes her home for Faith to nurse her. Soon after, they learn that Ruth is pregnant. Gaskell's hesitancy concerning her topic is reflected through her characters' dialogue:

> 'Why, Thurstan, there is something so shocking the matter, that I cannot tell you.'
> Mr. Benson changed colour with affright. All things possible and impossible crossed his mind, but the right one. I said 'all things possible;' I made a mistake. He never believed Ruth to be more guilty than she seemed....
> 'I beg your pardon; but something so shocking has just been discovered—I don't know how to word it—She will have a child. The doctor says so.'
> (2008, 117)

Gaskell's timidity in broaching illegitimate pregnancy, and the immoral sexual act it entails, is evident in her characters' 'shock[ed]' treatment of the information. Because Gaskell momentarily gives over the role of narrator to Faith, her announcement of shock prepares the reader (as it does Mr Benson) for the news of Ruth's pregnancy. One event (the future birth of a child) entails another event that remains unnarrated but becomes clear by inference (that Ruth and Mr Bellingham have engaged in premarital sex). In *Ruth*, then, implicature in character dialogue (that is, implicature 'shown' to us by means of characters' dialogue) is used to bypass the restrictions that social convention places on the communication of antinarratable content.

Gaskell further eases the explicit presence of antinarratable content in her novel by immediately reminding her readers of the content's purpose, and that that purpose is one other than entertainment. In the text succeeding Faith's communication of Ruth's pregnancy, Gaskell uses Mr Benson as a mouthpiece to didactically state her thoughts on the reception of illegitimate children in Britain:

> The world has, indeed, made such children miserable, innocent as they are; but I doubt if this be according to the will of God, unless it be His punishment for the parents' guilt; and even then the world's way of treatment is too apt to harden the mother's natural love into something like hatred. Shame, and the terror of friends' displeasure, turn her mad—defile her holiest instincts; and, as for the fathers—God forgive them! (2008, 120)

The passages of text preceding and succeeding this passage make Gaskell's biographically evidenced views clear: as implied in the above passage, Gaskell believes that the shame people inspire in unwed mothers is the greatest motivator towards infanticide, and that, rather than a 'badge of [an unwed mother's] shame', an illegitimate child should be considered 'God's messenger to lead [the unwed mother] back to Him' (2008, 119). This passage functions primarily to communicate Gaskell's central thesis; however, the didactic explication of her thesis also helps her to maintain presentational politeness. As with similar passages in *Jessie Phillips*, the blatant didacticism acts as an excuse for the presence of the novel's antinarratable content.

Ruth directly portrays Ruth's affair and her subsequent pregnancy as a 'problem': as Faith says, 'there is something so shocking the matter'. Mr Benson and Faith's consequent chapter-long discussion of what to do with the pregnant Ruth emphasizes the approach that Gaskell's novel takes to the 'issue' of the fallen woman. Unlike other Victorian narratives of unwed mothers, *Ruth* depicts a solution to this problem: the ideal rehabilitation of the fallen woman, primarily effected through the characters' (and the narrator's) sympathy for her. Gaskell's solution at work is glimpsed in a late passage of the novel, depicting an unavoidable meeting between Ruth (now known as 'Mrs Denbigh') and Mr Bellingham, about ten years after her seduction:

> Suddenly Ruth felt that his attention was caught by her. Until now, seeing his short-sightedness, she had believed herself safe; now her face flushed with a painful, miserable blush.... He thought this Mrs. Denbigh was certainly like poor Ruth; but this woman was far handsomer.... Poor Ruth! And, for the first time for several years, he wondered what had become of her; though, of course, there was but one thing that could have happened, and perhaps it was as well he did not know her end, for most likely it would have made him very uncomfortable. (2008, 277–8)

This passage has another of Ruth's blushes in it, denoting her self-consciousness and discomfort. Here, Gaskell does not excuse Ruth's blush with alternative explanations (such as the unnecessary social awkwardness Ruth believes has characterized her first interactions with Mr Bellingham) but instead indicates Ruth's lack of control over her blush by characterizing it as 'painful' and 'miserable'. The blush's undesirability signifies Gaskell's 'solution' to the problem of illegitimate pregnancies: acceptance and motherhood create a pious and knowing woman, one who is aware of what a blush signifies and who does not wish to be blushing. An adult woman would not want her sexuality recognized and would not wish to signal her awareness of it. The remainder of the passage is free indirect discourse of Mr Bellingham's thoughts, but his selfish reason for being glad that he does 'not know [Ruth's] end' vilifies him rather than causing the reader to empathize with him: his flinching away from emotional discomfort is plainly inadequate as a moral reaction. This passage also refers, somewhat obliquely, to the 'one thing that could have happened' to a seduced woman—not indicating prostitution necessarily, but portraying Ruth's probable history as unhappy enough to make most people 'very uncomfortable'. It is exactly this discomfort that makes the topic of illegitimate pregnancy a face-threatening, and therefore an impolite, one.

The critical reaction to Gaskell's work was overwhelmingly positive. The animosity which she had predicted was almost unrealized: *Bentley's Miscellany* wrote that *Ruth* was 'better than any sermon' (Easson 1991, 241) and Charles Kingsley reported 'that among all my large acquaintance I never hear, or have heard, but one unanimous opinion as to the beauty, & righteousness of the book.... English people in general have but one opinion of Ruth, & that is, one of utter satisfaction' (Easson 1991, 313).

This is not to say that critics did not respond to the book's 'delicate' subject matter. There were (a very few) negative reviews of the book, all of which objected to its subject matter and one of which condemned the sympathetic manner in which Ruth is treated (Easson 1991, 208, 212, 232, 313). As a minister's wife, Gaskell perhaps felt the relatively little condemnation more than she otherwise would have: she repeatedly mentioned to acquaintances that she had heard of the book being burnt, and reported the disapproval with which some members of her congregation now regarded her (Easson 1991, 203, 246; Gérin 1976, 138–9). Some reviews of *Ruth*, although applauding Gaskell's motives, protested 'against such a book being received into families[;] it would be the certain uprooting of the very *innocence* which is so frequently dwelt upon by the author with pleasure and delight' (Easson 1991, 211, emphasis in original).[16] Gérin reports that Bell's Library withdrew *Ruth* from circulation (1976, 139).

[16] See also Easson 1991, 202, 253.

It is undeniable, however, that *Ruth* achieved Gaskell's aim of raising awareness of the plight of unmarried mothers. Jenny Uglow reports that 'all over the country *Ruth* was debated in drawing-rooms, clubs, churches, chapels—even Oxford colleges' (qtd. in Hughes and Lund 1999, 82). Moreover, some reviewers caught on to Gaskell's larger aim of criticizing 'the traditional opprobrium visited by society on illegitimate children' and explicitly tied Ruth's plight to the occurrence of infanticide (Ganz 1969, 121). One reviewer wrote, 'let us remember that infanticide ... is frequent in England to an extent which few are aware of.... But what has poor Ruth to do with all this vileness? Simply this,—that there is a cant, a notion or a prejudice, false as it is cruel, which, because she once did wrong, would drive her among the outcast' (Easson 1991, 259–60).[17] Gaskell's novel sparked a national conversation that was in the main sympathetic towards the unwed mother. The prominent use of implicature is largely responsible for Gaskell's success in that it politely communicated impolite subject matter, making *Ruth* as authoritative a text as any 'sermon'.

ADAM BEDE: ELIOT'S APPEAL FOR SYMPATHY

George Eliot was a major proponent—arguably *the* major proponent—of classical literary realism, and *Adam Bede* was her first full-length exercise in it.[18] As with all generic categorizations, however, this label is problematically reductive. Eliot believed that there was a strong moral effect to be achieved by realism, and this perceived moral benefit overwhelmingly motivated her writing of fiction (Waldron 'Appendix A' 2005, 577, 578, 580). To Eliot, fiction was attractive primarily because of its ability to broaden the reader's sympathy towards those who might initially seem undeserving of it. A background of Evangelicalism had resulted in the young Eliot's 'wholesale condemnation' of fiction, but the idea that 'in the right hands fiction could teach a moral lesson more effectively than any sermon' later attracted her back to it (Waldron 'Introduction' 2005, 15, 18). By the time she began writing fiction, Eliot 'thought that novelists must finally accept that the representation of a hard line between "the virtuous and the vicious" should be abandoned in favour of what she saw as more important—human sympathy' (Waldron 'Introduction' 2005, 19). A fictional unwed (and even an infanticidal) mother should evoke sympathy rather than antagonism, so that the sympathy could then be extended to real-life unwed mothers.

---

[17] See also Easson 1991, 276.
[18] Chapter seventeen, specifically, is widely regarded 'as the locus classicus of Victorian realism' (Levine 2003, 104).

The degree of Eliot's sympathy for *Adam Bede*'s infanticidal mother, Hetty, has been debated since the initial reception of the novel (Jones 2004, 315–16; Marck 2003, 448; Waldron 'Appendix D' 2005, 610–12). Eliot's ambiguous attitude towards Hetty is frustrating in part because it departs from the fierce sympathy recently extended to unwed mothers in fiction and so problematizes Eliot's otherwise obvious aim of promoting sympathy. Frances Trollope's Jessie Phillips and Elizabeth Gaskell's Ruth are idealized, both novels actively urging the reader's sympathy with a (hardly) faulty human being. This sympathy is understood as an obvious moral good, creating greater tolerance for society's victims and, ideally, spurring those with power into effecting social reform. Hetty, however, is vain, selfish, and 'as unsympathetic as butterflies sipping nectar' (Eliot 2005, 163–4). And yet, as Mason Harris notes, 'Despite Hetty's lack of sympathy and intelligence, we respond more to the nightmare confusion of her aimless journey than to the morally lucid experience of Adam and Dinah' (1983, 191). When it becomes clear that the most sensational passages of *Adam Bede* will follow Hetty rather than the eponymous hero, the nature of the narrative is changed, focusing the reader's attention on Hetty's scenes as consisting of more than just secondary character portraits. In other words, the inclusion of substantial (both in length and content) passages that depart from (and are, in a strict sense, irrelevant to) the novel's eponymous protagonist readjusts the reader's sense of what is most 'relevant' to the story and who, in turn, is the novel's true centre of interest. The narrative prominence created by the extremity of the events depicted leads the reader to identify with the passages' protagonist, creating stronger sympathy with her than would have been generated if the events had not formed so crucial a part of the narrative. The bleakness of Hetty's journey makes her the most pitiable character in *Adam Bede*, and through that pity Eliot manoeuvres the reader into sympathy with someone she has depicted as an unimaginative, materialistic coquette. Hetty's psychological turmoil dominates the description of her plight, and, despite her guilt, it is this turmoil rather than Hetty's blameworthiness that remains uppermost in the reader's mind.

Caroline Levine's reflections on the sympathy Hetty draws are an attractive solution to the seeming disruption of narrative style created by her blameworthiness. Drawing on chapter seventeen of *Adam Bede*, Levine reminds us that Eliot's aim is to represent the true rather than the idealized. How is Eliot's characterization of Hetty's extreme faultiness— even her criminal self-absorption—reconciled with Eliot's greater aim of evoking the reader's sympathy? Levine writes that

> Eliot deliberately prevents us from identifying too closely[;] ... if realism's most urgent aim is to teach us to build responsible relationships with the

alterity of the world, then surely we readers should not learn to assume a perfect identity between our own felt experience and that of the characters we encounter. Rather, we must keep our distance so that we may fashion a relationship of forgiveness and understanding across the gap that necessarily divides us from the other. (2003, 108–9)

In other words, it is Hetty's faultiness that allows us to generalize the sympathy we have felt for her to other real (and equally faulty) human beings outside fiction. Eliot's narrative teaches us to see past Hetty's reprehensible actions and to focus on the pain Hetty has felt, and to feel the sympathy for her that we would more readily feel for more likeable characters and human beings. *Adam Bede* may be classified accurately as realist fiction, but, for Eliot, realism exists primarily to effect social change. For Eliot, realism teaches sympathy for an individual where empathy might not be possible.

As the discussion above shows, interpretation of *Adam Bede*'s narrative style affects the way literary scholars treat the representation of Hetty and the plot that revolves around her. While many social problem novels aim to alert the reader to the ideal social treatment of (potentially) infanticidal mothers, *Adam Bede* concentrates on providing a psychologically probing and plausible representation of illegitimate pregnancy. The novel's historical setting (the story takes place sixty years before the novel was published) supports the conservative aspect of Eliot's representation: instead of highlighting the ideal social climate which the author hopes to urge us towards, it shows a distantly reactionary society, but with aspects that are, embarrassingly, still present in Eliot's day. As discussed in the 'Historical Context' section above, there was widespread feeling that the lack of provision for unwed mothers (such as Hetty) in the 1834 New Poor Law had resulted in a nationwide increase in infanticide. Infanticide was 'punishable by death', but juries' reluctance to convict made these laws difficult to implement and indicated that the villainy assigned to mothers by these laws was viewed as archaic ('Increase' 1867, 8). In 1859, when *Adam Bede* was published, the New Poor Law had yet to be effectively remedied and the rate of infanticide was still high (Brownlow 1864, 19; 'Died' 1843; 'Poor Law' 1843, 6). The historical setting of the novel implicitly invites the reader to compare archaic actions and ideologies with those heavily publicized and debated in contemporary media. The sixty years' difference between the novel's setting and its publication both distances the story from present-day politics and assists its force as social commentary, providing a perfect platform from which to launch a discreet campaign for reform.

In order to make her discussion of an unpleasant topic (one not widely considered appropriate matter for fiction) palatable to polite audiences,

Eliot uses implicature to broach the topic of illegitimate pregnancy gradually and indirectly. This indirectness also allows her to mirror Hetty's gradual realization of her physical condition and its social consequences. Eliot's narration is first notably indirect when describing the growing attraction between Hetty and her seducer, Arthur. Arthur's interest in Hetty is introduced by what is explicitly presented as his interest in dairies:

> 'By the by, I've never seen your dairy: I must see your dairy, Mrs. Poyser.'
> 'Indeed, sir, it's not fit for you to go in, for Hetty's in the middle o'making the butter, for the churning was thrown late, and I'm quite ashamed.' This Mrs. Poyser said blushing, and believing that [Arthur] was really interested in her milk-pans. (2005, 144)

The unnecessary (and therefore subnarratable) emphasis of the word 'really', coupled with the nonfactual verb 'believing', indicates an ulterior motive to Arthur's eagerness to inspect the dairy. The sentence acts as implicature by foregrounding irrelevant, because already stated, information (Arthur's interest in the dairy), and then again by negating the information that it foregrounds. At this point in the narrative, there is no reason to suppose that Arthur is not interested in Mrs Poyser's dairy when he explicitly indicates his wish to see it (as he just has) and so the further reference to Arthur's interest appears redundant. The word 'really' foregrounds this redundancy.

In this context, the narration of nonfactual information (signalled by the verb 'believing') ironizes the semantic import of the sentence. Eliot's use of a particularly intrusive omniscient narrative voice (conspicuous well before this point in the novel) alerts the reader that the focus on Mrs Poyser's beliefs is not the result of limited perspective narration, but is rather a conspicuous selection of information more notable for what it does not articulate than what it does. The narrative voice is pointedly *not* addressing whether Arthur is 'really interested in [Mrs. Poyser's] milk-pans'; it does not provide the reader with information that, because it is omniscient, it is capable of communicating. Although 'believe' is officially categorized as a nonfactive, its use within otherwise omniscient narration could arguably be considered counterfactual.[19]

By both highlighting information as relevant and then pointedly not providing the information signalled as relevant, the narrative defies coded communication, suggesting a correlated reliance on ostensive-inferential

---

[19] The fluctuating significance of the verb 'believe' outlined above should be considered an example of how the fictionality of texts affects utterance meaning (and why pragmatic stylistics needs to take into account the nonfictionality or fictionality of texts when analysing them).

communication. In relevance theoretical terms, an intention to communicate is signalled by the physical text on the page, and here the specific intention that drives the communication is denoted by words that semantically relate to it: Arthur's 'interest... in [Mrs. Poyser's] milk-pans'. Through the use of the nonfactive 'believing', however, the narrative voice withholds the very information it has signalled a wish to communicate. Because, according to the Communicative Principle, hearers assume the relevance of all information that a speaker wishes to communicate, both the explicit reference to the information (Arthur's 'interest') and the withholding of the information are assigned relevance. In this context, the question of Arthur's interest in the dairy is foregrounded, and the most accessible inference for the reader to make is that Arthur is *not* interested in Mrs Poyser's milk-pans. The narrative therefore communicates not that Arthur is interested in Mrs Poyser's dairy but that he is pretending to be interested in her dairy, and that his motivation for pretending to be so is better left unstated.

As with all implicature, the audience is expected to infer the intended meaning of the communication from its context. In this regard the narrative voice is not subtle, and Arthur's real motivation is easily discerned to be the 'distractingly pretty girl of seventeen' standing in the middle of Mrs Poyser's dairy (2005, 145). The inexplicit representation of Arthur's attraction lends it an illicit air. Throughout this initial scene between Arthur and Hetty, their mutual attraction is never stated, but Hetty's 'self-possessed, coquettish air' is reported as if it had no direct object (2005, 145) and Arthur is inexplicably 'determined to make Hetty look at him and speak to him' (2005, 147). The lack of explicit motivation for these actions is enough to communicate to the reader that his motivations are at best suspicious: as relevance theory shows us, readers will actively seek out relevance where it is not explicitly stated, searching for an unwritten connection between two seemingly disparate pieces of information. When Arthur leaves, the narrator makes no reference to his leave-taking of Hetty, only commenting that Arthur had 'exhausted all plausible pretexts for remaining among the milk-pans': this time explicitly stating that he has been employing pretexts and presupposing that he has reason to do so (2005, 155). Eliot's presupposition renders her presentational politeness more conspicuous, further ingratiating her narrative voice with the reader and characterizing Arthur's motivations as clandestine.

The next two chapters provide a franker depiction of Hetty and Arthur's mutual attraction. Eliot writes that 'for the last few weeks a new influence had come over Hetty—vague, atmospheric, shaping itself into no self-confessed hopes or prospects.... Hetty had become aware that Mr. Arthur Donnithorne would take a good deal of trouble for the chance of seeing her' (2005, 162). Meanwhile, Arthur has 'also certain indistinct anticipations, running as an under-current in his mind' (2005, 164). These two passages articulate the 'vague, atmospheric' feelings that implicature communicated in the last scene; implicature lets us understand Arthur's motives, but it also allows Eliot to mimic the 'indistinct', inarticulate feelings of her characters. Just after the above passage, Arthur confesses his feelings to Mr Irwine:

> 'What fascinated you so in Mrs. Poyser's dairy, Arthur? Have you become an amateur of damp quarries and skimming-dishes?'
> Arthur knew the Rector too well to suppose that a clever invention would be of any use, so he said, with his accustomed frankness,
> 'No, I went to look at the pretty butter-maker, Hetty Sorrel. She's a perfect Hebe; and if I were an artist, I would paint her....'
> 'Well, I have no objection to your contemplating Hetty in an artistic light, but I must not have you feeding her vanity.... You needn't look quite so much at Hetty Sorrel then. When I've made up my mind that I can't afford to buy a tempting dog, I take no notice of him, because if he took a strong fancy to me, and looked lovingly at me, the struggle between arithmetic and inclination might become unpleasantly severe. I pique myself on my wisdom there, Arthur, and as an old fellow to whom wisdom has become cheap, I bestow it upon you.' (2005, 164–5)

Despite Arthur's explicit admiration of Hetty, the overall dynamic presented in this dialogue concretizes the illicitness of the attentions he has paid her. In a footnote, Mary Waldron characterizes Mr Irwine's opening as an 'amused, gently sarcastic enquiry. "Amateur" betokened a gentlemanly dilettantism at this date; Arthur might be an amateur in one of the arts, but not in dairying. Here the text suggests that Mr. Irwine knows perfectly well what Arthur finds so fascinating' (Eliot 2005, 164). Arthur's seemingly direct response to his friend's veiled confrontation (which in itself introduces the topic as delicate) is tempered by his dishonesty about the effect Hetty has on him. Arthur downplays his attraction to Hetty by portraying it as purely aesthetic; he does not mention his repeated attempts to interact with the girl he admires, or the lasting, 'indistinct' but palpable effect she has had on him. Mr Irwine sees through Arthur's explanation and conveys a clear warning, couched in terms that superficially belittle the issue. The delicacy with which Mr Irwine treats Arthur's attraction is indicative of the delicacy of the issue: Mr Irwine's comparison of Hetty to a 'tempting dog' might seem light-heartedly derisive, but, by substituting the content of his warning with less antinarratable material, he tactfully acknowledges the potential gravity of the situation. The entire exchange is marked by a jocular presentational politeness that conveys

Mr Irwine's concerns to Arthur while minimizing the necessarily condescending and forbidding nature of the advice-giving. Mr Irwine is, here, perpetrating a face-threatening act, attempting to curb Arthur's ability to flirt with Hetty by reminding him that to do so would be unethical and potentially disastrous. Their dialogue serves as a model of the presentational politeness that Eliot uses throughout the text (which echoes, for instance, Mr Irwine's facetious obtuseness) and introduces Eliot's reasons for treating her topic so carefully: while cross-class romance is not necessarily an antinarratable topic, it can quickly veer into topics that are.

The narration becomes more obscure when Hetty's pregnancy is communicated. The first expression of Hetty's pregnancy is made in a seeming digression bookended by straightforwardly narrated plot. In a chapter conspicuously named 'The Hidden Dread', Eliot writes that

> It was about ten o'clock when Hetty set off.... What a glad world this looks like, as one drives or rides along the valleys and over the hills! I have often thought so when, in foreign countries[,] ... I have come on something by the roadside which has reminded me that I am not in Loamshire: an image of a great agony—the agony of the Cross. It has stood perhaps by the clustering apple-blossoms, or in the broad sunshine by the cornfield, or at a turning by the wood where a clear brook was gurgling below; and surely, if there came a traveler to this world who knew nothing of the story of man's life upon it, this image of agony would seem to him strangely out of place in the midst of this joyous nature. He would not know that hidden behind the apple-blossoms, or among the golden corn, or under the shrouding boughs of the wood, there might be a human heart beating heavily with anguish: perhaps a young blooming girl, not knowing where to turn for refuge from swift-advancing shame....
>
> Such things are sometimes hidden among the sunny fields and behind the blossoming orchards; and the sound of the gurgling brook, if you came close to one spot behind a small bush, would be mingled for your ear with a despairing human sob....
>
> Hetty, in her red cloak and warm bonnet.... (2005, 414–15)

The above excerpt is only half of the narrator's ostensible digression, which protrudes abruptly in between Hetty 'setting off' and Hetty 'turning towards a gate': that is, continuing her journey (2005, 415). The narrator separates the core narrative from the digression by switching tenses (Hetty 'set' off but the narrator 'drives' along valleys) and moving from the third- to the first-person voice, officially entering into extradiegetic territory. This has the effect of generalizing the subject matter to encompass hypothetical situations outside the narrative scope. The narrator then narrows the narrative discourse to a specific narrative trajectory outside Hetty's narrative plane by explicitly moving the discussion away from

Loamshire. This distances the reader even further from the immediacy of Hetty's narrative, and, when conditional markers such as 'perhaps', 'if', 'would', and 'might' indicate that the described scene is hypothetical, the reader is not only focused on a new narrative trajectory but is also not required to suspend disbelief towards that trajectory. The narrator is no longer addressing the reader as if he or she were reading a fictional text.

Symbolism communicates the pregnancy that Eliot cannot state in this non-narrative. The repetitive listing of beautiful fertile landscapes ('clustering apple-blossoms', 'golden corn', and 'blossoming orchards') echoes past characterizations of Hetty's nubile beauty while the 'hidden' nature of the sorrow 'under' and 'behind' that beauty conveys a source of sorrow that is physically both inside Hetty's body and at the source of all things fertile. The imagery can simultaneously be read as depicting Hetty, herself 'under the shrouding boughs of the wood', both a probable source of 'a despairing human sob' and a future source of sorrow to others. In this way the 'human heart beating heavily with anguish' can be interpreted as Hetty's, her future baby's, or (in the more superficial, generalized reading of the passage) anyone's. Lastly, the figuration of the 'agony' as that 'of the Cross' calls to mind a burden physically to be borne as well as the humiliation that the cross was intended to inflict upon Jesus, and that Hetty can expect from public revelation of her condition. However, Eliot's narrative technique of triple displacement (through the diegetic plane, the narrative trajectory, and the crossing of the nonfiction–fiction boundary discussed above) carefully claims no direct link between this humiliation and Hetty.

The passage's implicit importance is marked most effectively by its lack of introduction. Besides the chapter heading (which occurs two pages earlier), there is no explicit transition into this indirect communication of Hetty's pregnancy. It is the absence of any explanation for the passage's presence that attracts the reader's attention to how the passage relates to the narrative around it.

As was discussed in the introductory chapter, the tendency of readers to assume coherence between closely situated passages has been termed the 'assumption of coherence'.[20] Thanks to the 'principles of analogy' ('things will tend to be as they were before') and 'local interpretation' ('if there is a change, assume it is minimal'), Brown and Yule conclude that collocation signals coherence: that is, if two sentences are near each other, it is likely that they will relate to each other (1983, 65–7). By not commenting on the relationship between 'the image of agony' and Hetty, Eliot relates the

---

[20] Gillian Brown and George Yule explain that 'human beings do not require formal textual markers before they are prepared to interpret a text. They naturally assume coherence, and interpret the text in the light of that assumption' (1983, 66).

two to each other implicitly. In turn, the explicit relationship between the two subjects is, superficially, irrelevant, which leads the reader to infer that a relationship is not being directly stated because it would violate social convention, offending the reader. In this way the seeming irrelevance of the passage lends the topic of its communication an illicit air, and the sense that fertility is a source of socially disruptive 'agony' is reinforced.

Hetty's subsequent suicidal thoughts and her resolution to run away are inexplicable without the necessary but inexplicit information of her illegitimate pregnancy. Hetty's motivation is at no point explicitly mentioned, and instead the reader's assumption of coherence leads him or her to draw a connection between two adjacent but superficially distinct paragraphs. Eliot writes that

> No, [Hetty] had not the courage to jump into that cold watery bed, and if she had, they might find her—they might find out why she had drowned herself. There is but one thing left to her: she must go away, go away where they can't find her.
>
> After the first on-coming of the great dread, some weeks after her betrothal to Adam, she had waited and waited, in the blind vague hope that something would happen to set her free from her terror; but she could wait no longer. All the force of her nature had been concentrated on the one effort of concealment, and she had shrunk with irresistible dread from every course that could tend towards a betrayal of her miserable secret. (2005, 416)

The narrative's pointedly obscure references to Hetty's reasons for contemplating suicide and leaving home portray her motivation as socially inappropriate to communicate—which, in turn, further corroborates her shameful state of pregnancy. The description of Hetty's 'great dread' reinforces that impression: we learn that 'all the force of her nature had been concentrated on the one effort of concealment' and that she is terrified of 'a betrayal of her miserable secret'. The use of the term 'concealment' (so strongly related to current laws concerning infanticide), coupled with the characterization of Hetty's unhappiness as 'dread'—as expectancy—lends greater weight to the reader's impression that Hetty is pregnant.[21] Eliot draws on the connotations of words current in her time to relay the unarticulated meaning of her passage: these connotations alert the reader to the text's implicatures, guiding him or her to look beyond the strict denotations of the text.

In the segment detailing Hetty's desperate search for Arthur and her recurrent thoughts of suicide (2005, 418–38), Hetty encounters a character

---

[21] As discussed on page 82, the term 'concealment' denoted the lesser charge of which an ambiguously infanticidal woman could be convicted.

who takes special note of Hetty's 'figure' but is reluctant to articulate that awareness. Eliot writes that

> the good woman's eyes presently wandered to [Hetty's] figure, which in her hurried dressing on her journey she had taken no pains to conceal; moreover, the stranger's eye detects what the familiar unsuspecting eye leaves unnoticed.
> 'Why, you're not very fit for travelling,' she said, glancing while she spoke at Hetty's ringless hand. (2005, 425)

The landlady's observations have a transparent object. The emphasis on Hetty's 'figure', which she has wished to 'conceal' and which has changed so gradually that her condition is only obvious to a stranger, is even today the most established sign of a secret pregnancy. According to Summers (2001), however, concealment of all pregnant bodies (not just those secretly pregnant) was expected in the Victorian era, so the report of the landlady's thoughts not only presupposes Hetty's pregnancy but also highlights an abnormality that signals Hetty's distress to both the landlady and the contemporary reader. The glance 'at Hetty's ringless hand' communicates the landlady's prompt deduction that the pregnancy is illegitimate (that is, that Hetty possesses no wedding ring). The narrative voice excuses the landlady's suppression of her observations: the landlady is reluctant 'to make a remark that might seem like prying into other people's affairs' (2005, 430). Hetty has also just suffered a physical breakdown in the landlady's house; delicacy is understandable. Because the landlady's explicit remarks would constitute a face-threatening act towards an obviously vulnerable person, the continuing inexplicitness of Hetty's pregnancy is justified even in a scene in which all characters, and the implied reader, are aware of it. The reason given for the landlady's silence is identical to the reason Eliot herself has for not articulating Hetty's pregnancy (and that Blackwood, Eliot's publisher, had for being concerned): the delicate handling of a controversial and face-threatening topic. Just as Hetty is expected to conceal her pregnant body, both the landlady and Eliot are expected to avoid explicit reference to her pregnancy. In this scene Eliot forgoes explicit narration of Hetty's pregnancy (and maintains a veneer of delicacy) by her ostensive neglect of relevant information: Eliot highlights the landlady's 'detect[ion]' but conspicuously does not articulate what the landlady detects. The disjunction between the landlady's reaction and (on the explicit, semantically bound plane of the narrative) the apparent lack of stimulus yet again alerts the reader that something more than what has been explicitly narrated is occurring, spurring the reader to seek out the passage's implicatures.

Hetty's pregnancy eventually is made explicit, although through the dialogue of characters who have heard of Hetty's already-passed pregnancy second hand. Mr Irwine tersely alerts Adam Bede that the magistrate from a neighbouring town has just arrested Hetty 'for a great crime—the murder of her child' (2005, 455). Eliot communicates the culmination of Hetty's pregnancy through another character's testimony at Hetty's trial, although emphasis is placed on whether or not Hetty committed infanticide. The witness merely mentions Hetty's 'condition' at the time of their encounter, and the narrative voice notes that the 'witness then stated that in the night a child was born', describing a speech act rather than the speech, or the birth, itself (2005, 476). The statement of the witness has an effect similar to Mr Irwine's communication a few chapters earlier. In both communications, the effect of the information is diminished in comparison to the probable infanticide, and, more importantly, the information is given by someone other than the omniscient narrator, weakening the communication's authority. The trial becomes a narrative tactic by which not only the jury but also the reader must decide whether Hetty committed infanticide. While this debate presupposes Hetty's past pregnancy, it also supplies the reader with little explicit information, requiring that the pregnancy be inferred rather than directly communicating it.

Hetty eventually confesses. However, as with Mr Irwine's communication, Hetty's confession assumes understanding of her illegitimate pregnancy, bypassing an impolite topic to address its unambiguously criminal outcome. And, as Nancy Anne Marck notes, 'Hetty's confession creates the largest "gap" in the narrative as her representation of her experience is marked by uncertainty[;] . . . the fact that she hears [the dead baby's] cry at all suggests that she is still suffering from delusions; her view of this crisis must be moderated' (2003, 466). Even the dispelling 'confession' that acts as the novel's climax fails to directly, unambiguously address the diegetic actions which it concerns.

Eliot's use of implicatures presumably had a dual motive. Implicature communicates through both form and content characters' various states of consciousness concerning Hetty's condition; Eliot's preference for psychological realism led her to mimic what could only otherwise be achieved through lengthy third-person description. It is also doubtless the case, however, that Eliot felt social pressure to represent Hetty's pregnancy as obliquely as possible. While reviews of *Adam Bede* were overwhelmingly favourable, one contemporary response in *The Saturday Review* illustrates a reaction Eliot must have been wary of:

> The author of *Adam Bede* has given in his adhesion to a very curious practice that is now becoming common among novelists, and it is a practice that we consider most objectionable [sic]. It is that of dating and discussing the several stages that precede the birth of a child. . . . Hetty's feelings and

changes are indicated with punctual sequence that makes the account of her misfortunes read like the rough notes of a man-midwife's conversations with a bride. This is intolerable. (Waldron 'Appendix D' 2005, 615)

That the indirect representation of Hetty's pregnancy could be likened to 'the rough notes of a man-midwife's conversations with a bride' shows how great the risk of offence was in handling the topic at all. The distaste pointedly expressed for the material indicates the extremity of the double standard by which Victorian media was judged: while Eliot's writing would have been less controversial if found in a text marketed as political or, for instance, in 'a man-midwife's' communication, it was considered out of place in a novel. In this literary environment it is likely that Eliot would have considered impossible any more explicit representation of Hetty's illegitimate pregnancy than the one she authored. Implicature allowed Eliot not only to avoid impolite language in her novel but also to highlight this avoidance as a mark of respect for her audience—a mark of respect which most of her readers accepted. The publication of *Adam Bede* spurred Eliot's overwhelmingly successful career: from 1860 to 1869, Eliot's works made up 22.2 per cent of the Blackwood titles that generated more that £1,000 and 24.8 per cent of the total profits generated from major titles (Finkelstein 2002, 35).

Although Eliot necessarily employed implicatures to discreetly convey Hetty's illegitimate pregnancy to Mudie's subscribers, a desire for the realistic portrayal of individual and collective psychologies remained at the heart of her work. Without it, readers would have far less motivation to transfer the sympathy inspired by fiction to the world around them. While the mid-Victorian ideas of politeness Eliot faced limited her use of explicit description, her less transparent, more covert methods of narrative are arguably more efficient in portraying character psychologies that are only semi-apparent even to their own agents. Authors' uses of implicature as an efficient method of characterization will be discussed in Chapter Two.

2

Unspoken Desires

Representations of Semiconsciousness and Control

INTRODUCTION

There were momentous developments in the study of the human mind during the eighteenth and nineteenth centuries, and many Victorian-era novelists critically engaged with ideas that were being reported alongside their fiction.[1] Among the most important aspects of the evolution of psychology during this period was the elaboration of the idea of the 'unconscious'. Many novelists capitalized on elements of its contemporary conceptualization in depicting the psychology of their characters. Of course, representations of unconscious thought processes predate the formal theorization of the unconscious in the nineteenth century, and fiction from this period often relies more on popular beliefs about the unconscious than on scientific theorizations of it. Nevertheless, how the idea of the unconscious was publicly debated also affected how fictional psychologies were interpreted. The extent of public interest in the subject makes the examination of fictional representations of unconscious processes from the mid-nineteenth century a particularly fruitful area for pragmatic stylistics. Because the unconscious was identified with unawareness, and consequently with subverbal states of mind, Victorian fiction authors sometimes use implicature to communicate feelings and perceptions that the characters themselves are not fully conscious of. Discussing these implicatures within the context of relevance theory allows for greater insight into how the authors are able to construct representations of their characters' unacknowledged feelings while also allowing us to connect those representations to the contemporary context of psychological debate in which readers would have interpreted them.

---

[1] Many magazines that famously published fiction, such as *Blackwood's Edinburgh Magazine* and *Household Words*, also published popular accounts of current psychological theories and debates. (Taylor 1988, 29; Taylor and Shuttleworth 1998, xv.)

This chapter discusses some of the strategies Victorian authors adopted to implicate romantic feelings or sexual desires of which a character is in denial or only partially aware. I have chosen novels that use characters' semiconscious feelings and thoughts as central aspects of their plots, and have examined various styles of novel in an attempt to explore the variety of purpose, style, and tone with which these implicatures may be used. Because narratives of romantic attachment often portray character feeling and thought as plot, I concentrate on romantic plot developments within these novels. In George Eliot's *The Mill on the Floss* (1860), Stephen and Maggie's illicit feelings for each other are slowly communicated to the reader through narrated actions and occurrences that would otherwise be subnarratable, disjointed from other representations of them, and irrelevant to the overall narrative. As with other conspicuously subnarratable information in fiction, the expected subnarratability of the information in *The Mill on the Floss* foregrounds its presence, emphasizing the information's disjunction from the more obviously significant material that surrounds it and drawing attention to its implicated relevance and significance. In *Orley Farm* (1862), Anthony Trollope concentrates on characters' interpretations of a crime that is communicated through implicature—namely, Lady Mason's forgery of a codicil to her late husband's will. Implicatures also communicate that Lady Mason's lawyer, Mr Furnival, is unconsciously attracted to her, and in turn his transparently biased and vacillating views implicate Lady Mason's guilt.

After a discussion of mid-Victorian discourses concerning the unconscious, I will discuss some current narrative theory on intersubjectivity and consciousness representation in fiction. I will then provide analyses of these fictional narratives of romantic attachment to examine how implicature's role in consciousness representations informs current literary scholarship. The segment 'Victorian Discourses on the Unconscious', found below, is necessarily superficial; limited space dictates that only the most prominent aspects of contemporary readers' likely background assumptions be discussed. This segment is not meant to indicate that the fiction authors discussed afterwards had minute knowledge of the reviewed concepts; instead, it is intended to introduce popular discourses which likely impacted both the creation and reception of the implicatures found in these authors' writings.

VICTORIAN DISCOURSES ON THE UNCONSCIOUS

From the eighteenth century, many philosophers interested themselves in the idea of a reservoir of psychological experience that was inaccessible from conscious states. Henri F. Ellenberger claims that the concept originated with Gottfried Wilhelm Leibniz in 1704 (1970, 329), writing that it 'was Leibniz who proposed the first theory of the unconscious mind supported by purely psychological arguments. He pointed to the small perceptions, that is, those that are under the threshold of perception even though they play a great part in our mental life' (1970, 312). Conversely, Edwin G. Boring, 'psychology's most influential historian' (Richards 1996, 25), aligns the origination of the concept with Johann Friedrich Herbart's 1816 proposal of a 'limen' model of consciousness (Boring 1957, 257). It was Herbart's studies that had a greater impact on the Victorian conceptualization of the unconscious and that made the concept a locus of contention throughout the century. Jerome Bruner and Carol Fleisher Feldman explain that, for Herbart,

> forms of knowing or awareness were held to exist at some level below consciousness and to need some kind of impetus to be boosted above the threshold.... the force that impels content from the unconscious 'apperceptive mass' over the threshold into awareness is the strength of an 'associative connection' with something already in consciousness, which is an accident of the historical circumstances that have led particular ideas to be contiguous in time or space. (1994, 232)

The role of the unconscious in cognition—namely, as an unquantified store of information that may be only haphazardly tapped into—would reappear throughout the nineteenth century as one of the primary hypotheses of associationism. Associationism developed from the writings of John Locke, David Hume, and others and was prominently carried on into the nineteenth century by James and John Stuart Mill. According to Graham Richards, the 'central tenet of this school was that all psychological phenomena originated in atom-like or "corpuscular" sensations which were built up into complex ideas by a few simple "laws of association"' (1996, 13). In these theories emphasis is placed on the ways in which 'psychological phenomena' become associated with each other (hence 'associationism'). Jenny Bourne Taylor and Sally Shuttleworth add that associationism includes the 'idea that the mind spontaneously links ideas in chains of thought—that it was the mental representations themselves which somehow recognized their affinity with each other' (1998, 67). Herbart expanded the role that the unconscious played in associationist theories, emphasizing the dynamic upheavals that routinely occur in our thought. Ellenberger writes that

> Herbart thought of the threshold as a surface where an everchanging multitude of perceptions and representations constantly fight against one another.

The stronger ones push the weaker ones down under the threshold, the repressed representations strive to reemerge, and for that reason often associate themselves with other representations. Under the threshold, the obscure representations constitute a kind of chorus that accompanies the drama being played on the conscious stage. (1970, 312)

Herbart hypothesized an unconscious which affected and was affected by the conscious mind. While Jenny Bourne Taylor has explained that Victorian concepts of the unconscious did not include the repression associated with psychoanalytic models (1988, 256), there was believed to be 'repression' occurring of a different sort. This repression centred on our finite attention span and the consequent need to be conscious only of what is relevant to our immediate situation. Above, Ellenberger outlines a model of consciousness in which unconscious perceptions are competing with others, actively associating themselves with other perceptions and 'striv[ing]' to gain our attention. This model of consciousness foregrounds the role of the unconscious, positing it as powerful and a largely unknown repository of responses.

By the mid-nineteenth century, the idea of unconscious cerebration had become widely accepted in England (Richards 1996, 18), with experiments designed as early as 1850 to detect and analyse unconscious states of activity (Ellenberger 1970, 312–13). Throughout the rest of the century, debates centred on the nature of the unconscious rather than the existence of it. For instance, the completeness of 'perceptions and representations' within the unconscious was contested. While the term 'perceptions' may be extended to include other inexpressible phenomena such as unconscious impulses, the term 'representations' indicates value-laden (if unconscious) reactions to perceptions and urges. William Benjamin Carpenter believed that only perceptions could be housed in the unconscious, writing in the second half of the nineteenth century that 'since, in the systems of Philosophy long prevalent in this country, *consciousness* has been almost uniformly taken as the basis of all strictly *mental* activity, it seems convenient to designate as Functions of the Nervous System all those operations which lie below that level' (1998, 99). However, other philosophers had different views. In her book *Shock, Memory, and the Unconscious in Victorian Fiction*, Jill L. Matus claims that '[George Henry] Lewes had long disputed the idea that all conscious behaviour was mental, and all unconscious physical. That is, he understood "unconscious" as a term to be applied to far more than reflex action' (2009, 145). Lewes's stance can be observed in his determination to discuss both sensations and thoughts in a section of *The Physiology of Common Life*. After discussing the automatic return of habits learned by rote (an occurrence analogous to the more physiological concept of 'muscle memory'), Lewes turns his attention to 'old associations, old beliefs, [which] are not to be displaced. A man may be thoroughly convinced to-day by the logic of his opponent, and yet to-morrow he will be heard uttering his old convictions, as if no one had ever doubted them. His mind cannot move except in the old paths' (1998, 88).

Most nineteenth-century debates about the unconscious centred on the degree to which it affects one's conscious mind and behaviour and on the possibility of controlling the influence of unconscious processes on both. Herbart's writings had changed the way philosophers conceptualized not only the unconscious mind but also the origin of the conscious mind; scholars were understandably disconcerted by the possibility that the known, seemingly controllable sphere of the conscious was only the visible output of the uncontrollable unconscious. Taylor writes that the debates on 'consciousness were marked by an extraordinary ambivalence, and mid-century psychology continually wavered between a fascination with the apparently irrational workings of the mind, and the urge to regulate and control them' (1988, 46). This discourse of control developed over the century, growing in reaction to the idea of the mind as a source of potential irrationality.

William Carpenter and Herbert Spencer were two philosophers who helped to popularize, from the 1840s through to the 1870s, the idea of the unconscious as an uncontrollable source of impulse (to which later philosophers would respond with theories of control).[2] Although Carpenter eventually revised his position, his stance prior to the 1840s indicated that it was impossible to control the formation of unconscious urges, so that 'an individual committing a crime reflexively or automatically could not be held responsible' (Matus 2009, 36). Spencer propounded similar views in 1855, claiming

> That every one is at liberty to do what he desires to do (supposing there are no external hindrances), all admit; though people of confused conceptions commonly suppose this to be the thing denied. But that every one is at liberty to desire or not to desire, which is the real proposition involved in the dogma of free-will, is negatived [by] the internal perception of every one.... Thus it is natural enough that the subject of such psychical changes should say that he wills the action; seeing that, psychically considered, he is

---

[2] I concentrate on Carpenter and Spencer because they were both active and highly influential during the timeframe in which the novels under discussion were published (1857–62). The views I discuss here were also held by others, and were partially developed by earlier scholars. Helen Small notes that James Ferrier, for instance, assigned a discriminatory and controlling function to the conscious mind in the late 1830s (2012, 491).

at that moment nothing more than the composite state of consciousness by which the action is excited. But to say that the performance of the action is, therefore, the result of his free-will, is to say that he determines the cohesions of psychical states by which the action is aroused; and as these psychical states constitute himself at that moment, this is to say that these psychical states determine their own cohesions: which is absurd. (1998, 85–6)

Herbert Spencer is remembered primarily for his prominent role in the popularization of evolutionary psychology. The semideterminism inherent in his understanding of evolution is evident in the above passage (Richards 1996, 21–3). He posits, in effect, a universal characteristic that would be reflected in many of the psychological dilemmas presented in Victorian fiction: an inability to control what we desire. Within the context of romantic fictional plots, this hypothesis often manifests itself as characters' frustrations over being attracted to and in love with those they know they should not or do not want to be attracted to. While these issues predate Victorian fiction, their depiction in Victorian fiction draws from the uniquely Victorian discourse concerning the unconscious and one's inability to control what originates in it. Importantly, Spencer's writing distinguishes between the will to act (or desire) and the act itself. Although the overall tenor of the passage is deterministic (in accordance with his main thesis concerning the origin of desires in the unconscious), Spencer supplies an implicit loophole by which the will to act may be resisted by the reacting, conscious mind and therefore controlled.

Many other psychologists debated this point. Sir William Hamilton, working within the 'Common Sense school of Scottish Enlightenment Philosophy', posited a wholly deterministic unconscious (Rylance 2000, 44).[3] His posthumous 1859 publication posited 'three degrees of... mental latency', each of which performs different functions and consequently illustrates different levels of unawareness and power over the conscious mind (W. Hamilton 1998, 81). The first degree of latency consists of all of a person's 'acquired habits' and knowledge that he is not consciously

---

[3] The term 'Common Sense' in Rylance's quotation is used more literally than it is often used today: it denotes ways of thinking that Hamilton and the school's founder, Thomas Reid, considered universal. Reid posited a 'universal predictability of the faculties of the human mind' (Rylance 2000, 44). Hamilton combined Reid's propositions with insights from Immanuel Kant, concluding that humans are 'compelled to believe that we possess free will, that the soul is immortal, and that God exists' (Ryan 2004). During the period with which this chapter is concerned, Hamilton was considered the main proponent of this school, known as 'intuitionism'. In 1865, John Stuart Mill successfully discredited Hamilton's theories, causing his popularity to dwindle (Ryan 2004). Previously to this, however, Hamilton was one of the 'most celebrated philosophical thinkers in Britain' (A. Hamilton 1998, 142).

thinking of at the moment; as Hamilton explains, 'I know a science, or language, not merely while I make temporary use of it, but inasmuch as I can apply it when and how I will' (1998, 81). The second degree of mental latency is made up of

> certain systems of knowledge, or certain habits of action, which [the mind] is wholly unconscious of possessing in its ordinary state, but which are revealed to consciousness in certain extraordinary exaltations of its powers. The evidence on this point shows that the mind frequently contains whole systems of knowledge, which... may [show themselves] in certain abnormal states, as madness, febrile delirium, somnambulism, catalepsy, &c. (1998, 81)

This conceptualization of the unconscious depends heavily on contemporary experiments concerning 'double consciousness'. While Taylor and Shuttleworth more generally refer to 'double consciousness' as the 'notion that the dreaming and waking state might correspond to two parallel mental worlds, each separate from the other', they report that it was 'discussed through the second half of the nineteenth century as an extreme state of disordered association and disrupted memory', probably approaching what we would now term dissociative identity disorder (1998, 70). Several cases were documented throughout the nineteenth century, exhibiting the mind's ability to retain skill sets that the conscious mind was unaware of (Taylor and Shuttleworth 1998, 123–40).

William Hamilton believed that his third degree of mental latency would be controversial, and it was in fact more extreme than Carpenter's or Spencer's hypotheses. In his argument, Hamilton does not limit the role of the unconscious to only the origin of urges, but claims that it is the source of all knowledge. Hamilton 'affirm[s]' that there are 'mental activities and passivities, of which we are unconscious, but which manifest their existence by effects of which we are conscious' (1998, 82). Hamilton goes on to specify 'that our whole knowledge, in fact, is made up of the unknown and the incognisable [sic]' (1998, 82). While aspects of Hamilton's other writings lessened the superlative nature of the hypothesis presented here, Taylor and Shuttleworth report that this 'theory of latent mental modification remained a central influence on later psychological writing' (1998, 80). However, it influenced later scholars by propelling both agreements and disagreements with the views expressed above.

Frances Power Cobbe was among those who disagreed. While she was primarily interested in positing the 'entire *separability* of the conscious self from its thinking organ, the physical brain', she characterizes the difference between self-awareness and more automatic knowledge as evidence of an external 'Conscious Self' which oversees our behaviour (Cobbe

1998, 93, emphasis in original). In her 1870 text 'On Unconscious Cerebration', she wrote:

> there are two kinds of action of the brain, the one Automatic, and the other subject to the will of the Conscious Self; just as the actions of a horse are some of them spontaneous and some done under the compulsion of his rider. The first order of actions tend to indicate that the brain 'secretes thought;' [sic] the second order (strongly contrasting with the first) show that, beside that automatically working brain, there is another agency in the field under whose control the brain performs a wholly different class of labours. (1998, 95)

While Cobbe acknowledges that unconscious processes do occur, she argues for a 'meta' level of cognition that regulates the self's reaction to the conscious output of these processes. The idea of inner regulation of the unconscious has important consequences for how one conceives of will and responsibility for one's actions. Cobbe points out that people only take responsibility for conscious actions:

> When our brains perform acts of unconscious cerebration (such as dreams), they act just as our hearts do, *i.e.* involuntarily; and we ought to speak of them as we always do of our hearts, as of organs of our frame, but not our Selves. When our brains obey our wills, then they act as our hands do when we voluntarily strike a blow; and then we do right to speak as if 'we' performed the act accomplished by their means. (1998, 94, emphasis in original)

While Cobbe assigns the unconscious an active, creative role (as opposed to a passive and merely receptive one), she also understands it as something to be reacted against rather than irresistibly obeyed.

In his later career, William Carpenter agreed with Cobbe's assignment of limited power to the unconscious. Carpenter famously retracted some of the views he proposed in the 1840s, and in their stead claimed that self-discipline could control otherwise destructive unconscious tendencies (Matus 2009, 36). His 1875 writing seemingly doubles as a how-to manual:[4]

> In regard to every kind of Mental activity that does *not* involve origination, the power of the Will, though limited to *selection*, is almost unbounded. For

---

[4] The timeline given for this section's publications is somewhat less clear than it appears. I have quoted the original dates of documents as they appear in Taylor and Shuttleworth's *Embodied Selves*; however, much of the information contained in these documents was published earlier in circumstances less relevant to the arguments presented here. Hamilton's papers were published posthumously, and presumably reached their largest audience at that time; however, he had previously presented them as lectures from 1836 onwards at University of Edinburgh (Taylor and Shuttleworth 1998, 80). Carpenter's 1875 writing is an extensive revision of his 1852 publication *Human Physiology*, which also made a

although it cannot directly bring objects before the consciousness which are not present to it, yet, by concentrating the Mental gaze (so to speak) upon any object that may be within its reach, it can make use of this to bring in other objects by associative Suggestion. And, moreover, it can virtually determine what shall *not* be regarded by the Mind, through its power of keeping the Attention fixed *in some other direction*; and thus it can subdue the force of violent impulse, and give to the conflict of opposing motives a result quite different from that which would ensue without its interference.

(Carpenter 1998, 97, emphasis in original)

In this passage, Carpenter moves beyond telling his audience that control of unconscious output is possible into telling them how they might practice it themselves. It is Carpenter's explanation of how to 'determine what shall *not* be regarded by the Mind' that is most relevant to this chapter. Carpenter appears to be advocating denial as a method of quashing undesired thoughts and impulses. Carpenter implies that those lacking the necessary self-control should still be held accountable for their actions, adding a moral component to the scientific discussion.

Victorian discussions concerning the unconscious and how best to control its output were vigorous and widely publicized, and the considerable influence of contemporary psychological theories on the writing of many Victorian fiction authors is well documented (Matus 2009, 36; Taylor 1988, 29; Taylor and Shuttleworth 1998, 22). Authors engaged these models of unconsciously developing desire and conscious attempts at control, reflecting and sometimes providing implicit arguments against them in their representations of characters' romantic dilemmas. At times, this resulted in the communication of psychological processes through implicature.

NARRATOLOGICAL DISCUSSIONS OF REPRESENTED INTERSUBJECTIVITY AND CONSCIOUSNESS

Narratives of romantic desire often represent consciousness as profoundly intersubjective—that is, as 'existing between conscious minds' (OUP 2011). In other words, consciousness is seen as involving an interplay

---

considerable impact on the wide audience it reached (Taylor and Shuttleworth 1998, 95). As noted, however, Carpenter's views changed considerably over this period, and the 1875 edition may be read as the most reliable source of his later (although still extremely influential) views.

between awareness of others and awareness of the self in relation to others. As used here, 'intersubjectivity' denotes the impact that the awareness of one's immediate social context has on one's thoughts and actions. The ensuing close readings of romantic plot developments are designed to show that intersubjectivity may be represented (and perceived) as occurring on semiconscious levels. Fiction and literary criticism have long assumed this aspect of intersubjectivity, but relatively little has been written about it. Instead, literary criticism often describes represented semiconscious intersubjectivity as if it indicated fully conscious intersubjectivity. The criticism on represented intersubjectivity discussed below offers little on the various levels of consciousness at which intersubjectivity can take place; however, the narratological discussion of how intersubjectivity is represented in fiction is relatively rare, and the critics acknowledged here have made important contributions upon which I hope to build.

There has been a recent surge of scholarship on the fictional representation of intersubjectivity, although its prevalence in the novel has been commented on for decades. In his classic 1977 study of free indirect discourse, Roy Pascal comments on the deeply intersubjective nature of Jane Austen's plots, tying the emergence of free indirect discourse to plots that consist 'almost entirely of the changing attitudes of the characters to one another, so that their thoughts and feelings are the structural elements of the story' (1977, 45). More recently, Alan Palmer introduced his intersubjective approach to the analysis of fictional minds by explaining that the study of separate, unique subjectivities 'has become the dominant paradigm for the study of consciousness within narrative theory', so that the bias contained in his book 'is intended to redress the balance a little' (2004, 5). Palmer believes that an emphasis on the intersubjectivity of fictional consciousnesses captures a pervasive phenomenon that explains much about the way authors represent and readers perceive characters. It would, in effect, shed light on the amount of textual space that is dedicated to showing 'when a character is anticipating, speculating on, reconstructing, misunderstanding, evaluating, reacting to, and acting upon the thought of another' (2004, 174).

Like Alan Palmer, George Butte was one of the first narrative theorists to emphasize the force of represented intersubjectivity. Tracing scholarly commentary on fictional intersubjectivity to Bakhtin (2004, 27), Butte's *I Know That You Know That I Know: Narrating Subjects from Moll Flanders to Marnie* articulates a history 'not only of consciousness, but also of consciousne*sses*, of a newly framed intersubjectivity, which Jane Austen's novels are among the first in English to speak of clearly' (2004, 26, emphasis in original). For Butte, it is 'Austen's ability to articulate the frightening interiority of the intersubjective' that distinguishes her from her predecessors, creating a fictional emphasis on interiority that would change how the representation of consciousness functioned within fictional narratives (2004, 25). Austen's emphasis on character interiority and the intersubjectivity that frames it is part of her legacy to the fiction discussed here. The nineteenth century added to that legacy by creating a discourse which observed the less conscious aspects of interiority and intersubjectivity.

While some believe that literature in general 'is a record of human consciousness, the richest and most comprehensive we have' (Lodge 2002, 10), other theorists differentiate more 'psychological' novels from other fiction genres and date their emergence to the beginning of the nineteenth century, aligning an emphasis on character interiority with the Romantic and Victorian eras. Many theorists attribute the first substantial use of free indirect discourse in the English language to Jane Austen, and cite specifically her interest in character interiority as the reason for its deployment (Cohn 1978, 113; Lodge 2002, 46; Pascal 1977, 34). Dorrit Cohn believes that the growth of free indirect discourse is tied to 'the moment when third-person fiction enters the domain previously reserved for first-person (epistolary or confessional) fiction, and begins to focus on the mental and emotional life of its characters' (1978, 113). It is interesting that Austen was active directly before Herbart's theories of the unconscious were first introduced into Britain: the new fictional emphasis on interiority anticipates the newly discovered level of interiority depicted in contemporary psychological theory. The analysis of consciousness representation, then, may be considered as especially appropriate for the fiction of an age in which theories of interiority were influential to an unprecedented degree, although the emphasis on interiority in Austen's writing shows how little of both readers' and writers' thinking about the psyche need be explicitly formalized.

The early nineteenth century's new-found emphasis on interiority may be witnessed in the representation of characters' thoughts as action affecting the development of plot. Pascal writes that, in Austen, the 'main issue is the establishment or dislocation of true, sincere, personal relationships; what [characters] do is only important in relation to the intentions and feelings that promote and accompany the actions' (1977, 45). Pascal's comments also apply to later narratives of romance in which desires, conceptions of others, and (both failed and successful) schemes are in themselves noteworthy and are considered plot even if they result in no physical action by the characters.[5] Characters' desires and emotions may

---

[5] This characterization is dependent on one's definition of 'plot'. Because the issue of what constitutes 'plot' is not central to my argument, I am using, somewhat uncritically, David Herman's cursory distinction between what can and cannot be considered plot in his

act as plot in other ways: Palmer points out that represented emotions and thoughts can be regarded as 'action tendencies', or potentials for character actions that are then either carried out or resisted (2004, 174).

Character thought and character action are further blurred by fiction authors' tendencies to indicate the former by mention of the latter. Many critics note the frequency with which authors use character actions to communicate character psychology: in describing the third-person novel of the nineteenth century, Cohn writes that authors 'dwelt on manifest behaviour, with the characters' inner selves revealed only indirectly through spoken language and telling gesture' (1978, 21). Palmer writes that 'just as in real life the individual constructs the minds of others from their behaviour and speech, so the reader infers the workings of fictional minds and sees these minds in action from observation of characters' behaviour and speech' (2004, 11). Palmer further institutionalizes this common authorial practice, coining the term 'indicative description' to denote authorial 'descriptions of actions that appear to indicate an accompanying state of mind' (2004, 172). In *Language and Characterisation: People in Plays and Other Texts*, Jonathan Culpeper invokes Sperber and Wilson on relevance theory in order to explain why character actions are interpreted as relevant to the rest of the narrative, and often as representative of the character:

> As a result of the fact that character interaction may be described as a discourse level embedded within that of the author and reader... we are in a position to make a much stronger assumption that [character] behaviour will be interpretatively significant. Any character behaviour is part of an act of communication between the playwright and the audience/reader, and as such we can assume that character behaviour has additional significance or relevance.... In relevance theory terms, any character behaviour is part of an ostensive act of communication between the author and the reader, and as such 'communicates the presumption of its own optimal relevance' [Sperber and Wilson]. (Culpeper 2001, 145–6)

Although his discussion concentrates on drama, Culpeper makes explicit the pragmatics of textual representation here: just as all information that is included in a text 'communicates the presumption of its own optimal relevance' simply because of the 'ostensive act of communication between

---

introduction to *The Cambridge Companion to Narrative*. 'Delete or add to the kernel events of a story and you no longer have the same story,' Herman explains; 'delete or add to the [satellite events] and you have the same story told in a different way' (2007, 13). In a courtship plot, a difference in a lover's desire would change the story: it is a 'kernel' event in the courtship.

the author and the reader', so any action on the part of a character will be deemed particularly significant to the development of the narrative, and also to how we view the individual character (who constitutes part of the narrative). The same is true of thought representation: just as any narrated action of a character will be interpreted as relevant to the overall plot, so any narrated thought will be interpreted as relevant. It is this assumed relevance that allows seemingly incongruous character actions and thoughts to be read as implicatures of inexplicit, possibly unconscious character thoughts and desires.

The omniscience exhibited in some narratives generates perhaps the most significant aspect of the reader's interpretations of fictional characters: the belief that he or she can know them completely. As Cohn notes, in fiction there are characters that 'we know most intimately, precisely in ways we could never know people in real life' (1978, 5). Culpeper phrases the same concept somewhat differently: 'character behaviours are complete.... By reading the whole text we have access to that character's whole life—complete and finite' (2001, 145). Culpeper's phrasing highlights a further difference between the interpretation of fictional and nonfictional (or real-life) people: when reading fiction, readers 'have access to [a] character's whole life'—they can be sure that the character thoughts they have access to are representative of the character. Several theorists rightly add the qualifying claim that only characterizations and thoughts reported by a third-person omniscient narrator are perceived as unqualified assertions rather than as probabilities; Margolin, for instance, writes that 'only individuation claims made by an authoritative narrating voice are universally valid, and they too can be weakened by modifying them as "possibly" or through an ironic tone' (2007, 73).[6] Readers' assured access to a character's 'action tendencies' (Palmer's concept denoting perceived potentials for character action) allows them to witness either the congruity or the incongruity with which that action tendency is carried out. A character such as William Dobbin in *Vanity Fair*, for instance, is shown to be excessively reticent by the extreme disjunction between his narrated action tendencies and his narrated actions. It is disjunctions such as these that allow readers to infer character thoughts and desires without any explicit, textual representation of them. Because they are not explicitly represented, such disjunctions are commonly used to communicate subverbal or latent character states. Such implicatures are possible without the aid of third-person description of character thoughts: just as action tendencies may be inferred, so may be the psychologies that either allow or

---

[6] Culpeper (2001, 114) and Palmer (2004, 33) make similar points.

restrain characters from following through with them. By exploiting the reader's assumption of narratorial omniscience, then, Victorian fiction authors were also able to communicate their characters' less conscious psychological states. Contemporary readers' interpretations of these implicatures would have been informed by their background assumptions concerning popular discourses about control and the unconscious; both the discourse techniques and social contexts of these novels would have guided readers towards graduated understandings of characters' consciousnesses and desires.

An examination of the implicature used to represent subverbal psychological states would be of benefit to narrative studies. Monika Fludernik and Alan Palmer have both expressed the belief that the 'more unaware a character is of the thought content described, the more [an author] reverts to an external description of that consciousness' (Fludernik 2001, 431). This chapter's examination of the use of implicatures in representations of unconsciousness and semiconsciousness will show that this is not always the case. While the verbally mimetic quality of quoted thought and free indirect discourse often poses problems in the representation of thoughts that are not themselves articulated in a character's mind (Palmer 2004, 13, 56), implicature is often heavily mimetic as well, reflecting a character's inability to verbalize the thoughts and emotions that are implied in the text. By incorporating implicatures into their mimetic representations of character consciousness, authors were able to expose latent feelings and thoughts that must otherwise be narrated through third-person omniscient report of thoughts. By implicating rather than explicating these feelings, authors were offering more sympathetic portrayals of character consciousnesses as well as avoiding didactic or unduly technical discourses concerning their own and other contemporary ideas about human psychology.

Narratives of romantic attachment are primarily records of intense intersubjectivity; by definition they chronicle the developing relationship between two characters. Fictional representations of these intersubjective experiences both influenced and were influenced by mid-Victorian philosophical discourses on the unconscious; to differing extents they engaged with popular discourses in their representations of the unconscious and semiconscious processes that affect, motivate, and result from these interactions. A further complication of these narratives is produced by the discourse of moral or social control that often enters when, for reasons of modesty or illicitness, a potential lover is torn between semiconscious urges and the perceived need to maintain an appropriate distance from the loved one. The vocabulary which a pragmatic stylistic analysis provides is capable of articulating how contemporary discourses influenced these uniquely Victorian emphases on the unconscious origination of desires and issues of control. A pragmatic analysis of these narratives also allows us to isolate implicatures that mimic and communicate semiconscious character states—states that propel and result from actions that in themselves are often minute, inexplicit, and only semiconsciously performed. Relevance theory provides a terminology with which to explicate the strategies authors use to communicate actions and psychological processes that remain inexplicit throughout large portions of narrative, allowing us to discuss how it is that readers infer psychological states that are not explicitly narrated.

THE MILL ON THE FLOSS: ELIOT'S NARRATION OF RESISTED ATTRACTION

On a first reading of George Eliot's *The Mill on the Floss*, the passages that communicate Maggie Tulliver and Stephen Guest's mutual attraction may seem too straightforward to contain much implicature. The narration of *The Mill on the Floss* does not call attention to its implicatures by ironically posing them as incongruous; there are very few utterances that explicitly contradict their context. Instead, the relative inconspicuousness of the implicatures creates an effect of narratorial frankness. Upon closer inspection, however, it becomes evident that Maggie and Stephen's attraction is made explicit only belatedly; before this explication, only indicative and conventionally subnarratable behaviour is narrated, leading the reader gradually to perceive the attraction as it is gradually perceived, and then resisted, by Maggie and Stephen themselves. The text's implicatures, then, communicate the intense but semiconscious intersubjective activity that results from and further impels Maggie and Stephen's growing mutual attraction.

The Mill on the Floss follows the short life of Maggie Tulliver, the daughter of a miller in rural, early nineteenth-century England. The early portions of the novel concentrate on Maggie's childhood, with emphasis on her youthful waywardness, her intelligence, and her love for her older brother, Tom. The family encounters immense hardship when Maggie's father is suddenly bankrupted. During this period, Tom begins to work (and eventually recovers his father's debts) while Maggie turns first to religion and then to literature to quell her dissatisfaction with her life. Maggie's love of literature is encouraged by Philip Wakem, the hunchbacked son of a lawyer who played a key role in bankrupting Maggie's father. Tom eventually puts a stop to their clandestine meetings, but not before Philip persuades Maggie to return his love for her. Upon her father's death, Maggie leaves her hometown, St Ogg's, to become a schoolteacher.

The portion of the narrative with which this section is concerned occurs two years later, when Maggie comes back to St Ogg's in an interval between teaching jobs. While staying with her cousin, Lucy Deane, she meets Stephen Guest, the young man with whom Lucy is 'in that stage of courtship which makes the most exquisite moment of youth, the freshest blossom-time of passion—when each is sure of the other's love, but no formal declaration has been made' (1994, 296). Maggie and Stephen are instantly attracted to each other, and, despite the reluctance both feel to hurt Lucy, their attraction grows and ultimately results in the start of an elopement that is, on Maggie's side, only semiconsciously performed. At the first opportunity, Maggie leaves Stephen and returns to St Ogg's. Soon after her return there is a flood, and Maggie dangerously steers a boat through the disaster to rescue Tom from the siblings' childhood home. They both drown while attempting to join the rest of their family.

The attraction between Maggie and Stephen may be considered more than just a romantic subplot of the novel. While contemporary critics (and modern-day scholars) are almost unanimous in deploring Eliot's choice of a love object in the egotistical and shallow Stephen Guest, many readers see Maggie's illicit attraction to him as the central venue through which Eliot explores the primary themes of the novel. Eliot herself wrote that

> Maggie's position towards Stephen—is too vital a part of my whole conception and purpose for me to be converted to the condemnation of it.... If the ethics of art do not admit the truthful presentation of a character essentially noble but liable to great error—error that is anguish to its own nobleness—*then*, it seems to me, the ethics of art are too narrow, and must be widened to correspond with a widening psychology.   ('George Eliot' 1994, 430–1, emphasis in original)

The extent of Eliot's informed engagement with Victorian psychology has been well documented. Besides being widely read in her own right, Eliot was the long-term partner of George Henry Lewes, who wrote extensively on the subject.[7] She was also a good friend of Herbert Spencer, whose unpublished work she sometimes discussed with him (Paxton 1991, 8; Eliot 1998, 83) and who was close enough to her to know her pseudonym before her real identity was made public (Paxton 1991, 69). In her book *George Eliot and Herbert Spencer: Feminism, Evolutionism, and the Reconstruction of Gender*, Nancy L. Paxton shows that elements of *The Mill on*

---

[7] See this chapter's introduction for a discussion of Lewes's contributions.

the Floss reflect Eliot's engagement with Spencer's writing, concentrating on aspects of the novel that, she argues, pointedly repudiate some of Spencer's postulations about sex and gender (1991, 70). However, while Eliot was often critical of Spencer's work, it is also undeniable that it greatly influenced her. Michael Davis notes that 'Eliot's writing suggests parallels with, and criticisms of, Spencer' and bases this fluctuating relationship on the writers' sometimes similar and sometimes differentiated views on human psychology (2006, 70).

As was discussed in the introduction to this chapter, Spencer's belief in the controlling power of the conscious mind was widely shared. While Eliot was very familiar with his work (Spencer repeatedly dined with her and Lewes during the period in which she was writing *The Mill on the Floss* (Eliot 1998, 81, 83)), she was equally well versed in the work of William Carpenter, whose later writing comes closer to Spencer's view of the relationship between the unconscious and the conscious mind (Davis 2006, 121; Shuttleworth 1986, 75). Sally Shuttleworth attributes much of Eliot's characterization of the unconscious in *The Mill on the Floss* to Lewes and Carpenter, rather than to Spencer—although the characterizations of the unconscious that she attributes to Carpenter's writing are sufficiently general that they could also be attributed to Spencer's. These characterizations concern the manner in which the unconscious might act as a potential 'threat and possible source of moral weakness' (Shuttleworth 1986, 75). In this section I claim that implicatures in *The Mill on the Floss* cause the novel to be interpreted as gesturing towards celebrating the general terrain of Carpenter's and Spencer's accounts of unconsciousness and conscious control, rather than contesting the details of their theories. However, I believe that Eliot's engagement with contemporary psychology is, in this instance, only gestural; Eliot's representations of character consciousnesses and unconsciousnesses are far more nuanced than a simple application of contemporary psychological theories will allow. The 'unconscious', the 'conscious', the 'will', and 'desire' are not completely discrete categories in *The Mill on the Floss*; instead, there is a complex rendering of them in which consciousness and unconsciousness are shown as both antagonistic and cooperative.

Previous readers, including some of the earliest, have discovered similar themes in Eliot's novel. The *Saturday Review*, for instance, believed that, in writing *The Mill on the Floss*, Eliot 'set herself to describe the triumph of principle over feeling' ('From *Saturday Review*' 1994, 447). This general proposition can be seen throughout the historical evolution of critical reactions to Eliot's work: George Levine, for instance, proposes that, while 'all the major themes of *The Mill on the Floss*... are related to determinism', Eliot argues 'that determinism does not entail belief in inefficacy of the will' (1994, 490).[8] These theses pursue different aspects of the same theme, namely the socially sanctioned, rational resistance to biologically rooted and irrational desires. The fact of resistance is what makes these desires particularly amenable to communication through implicature: through implicature, unconscious, and indeed unwanted, desires are shown to slowly fight their way into characters' consciousnesses. Eliot's use of implicature, then, allows her to enact the central themes of her novel. More importantly for my argument, Eliot's use of implicature allows her to mimetically represent psychological processes that culminate in one of the text's climaxes (the elopement). Without the reader's recognition of the text's implicatures, the climax appears abrupt and inexplicable.

Maggie and Stephen's mutual attraction is introduced by the narration of their extreme reactions to each other. Although their attraction is clear, it is not explicitly stated and is partly obfuscated by a playful trick that Lucy has played on Stephen: when Stephen incorrectly surmises that Lucy's cousin will be 'a fat, blonde girl, with round blue eyes, who will stare at us silently', Lucy agrees, laughing at the surprise which Stephen is bound to endure (1994, 296). This context provides an 'excuse' for the strong reactions which ensue and which more conventionally signal immediate attraction. Eliot writes that

> For one instance Stephen could not conceal his astonishment at the sight of this tall dark-eyed nymph with her jet-black coronet of hair; the next, Maggie felt herself, for the first time in her life, receiving the tribute of a very deep blush and a very deep bow from a person towards whom she herself was conscious of timidity. This new experience was very agreeable to her—so agreeable, that it almost effaced her previous emotion about Philip. There was a new brightness in her eyes, and a very becoming flush on her cheek, as she seated herself. (1994, 304)

The surprise that the reader expects Stephen to experience does much to explain Stephen's 'astonishment', and the 'very deep blush' that could, potentially, be associated with it. Similarly, although timidity does not

---

[8] Other readings include that of U. C. Knoepflmacher, who interprets the narrative as illustrating the struggle between 'inner' and 'outside' forces (1994, 515). Hao Li argues that the novel explores the universal struggle between 'internalized communal feelings' and those that are more innate (2000, 50). In her reading of how Eliot repudiates Spencer's postulations in her novels, Paxton switches the 'inner' and 'outside' forces which Knoepflmacher discusses, claiming that, in giving up Stephen, 'Maggie acts on particular inward commands of the "mind and heart," which are dictated by the "divine voice within." This "divine voice" authorizes Maggie's resistance to the demands of a passion that, Stephen insists, are determined by "outward law"' (1991, 91). Shuttleworth believes that 'the central moral issue of the novel' concerns the clash between 'the promptings of egoism' and a socially influenced memory of the 'past' or, put another way, 'the disjunction between the prompting of Maggie's unconscious and her social conscience' (1986, 52).

usually characterize Maggie, it is fitting that she would feel so when first introduced to the wealthiest, most influential young man in town.

The exchange of blushes is the most conventionally telling sign of Maggie and Stephen's mutual attraction. However, although the blush is commonly considered in association with romantic self-consciousness, in fiction it is often more complexly context-dependent, causing the reader to infer the self-conscious character emotion which is most relevant and suitable to the passage. Blushing as a fictional occurrence was briefly discussed in Chapter One, where its potential for implicated significance was suggested. Although narrated blushes almost uniformly represent some form of self-awareness, that self-awareness varies greatly from, for instance, embarrassment to romantic interest to indignation. The ambiguity of this image makes it especially suitable for communicating implicatures: although the blush may be said to function as code for self-awareness, its ambiguity regarding the type of self-awareness it poses foregrounds the blush's context. As with all implicatures, the metonymic substitution of a blush for the narration of the feelings from which it originates implies a need to keep the non-narrated information hidden.

Margaret Homans and Caroline Levine have noted the use of the blush to communicate self-conscious sexuality, but, in *The Mill on the Floss*, as in other fictional works, it is used to indicate a wide spectrum of emotion (Homans 1993, 168; Levine 2003, 115). Two pages after the above quote, for instance, the blush is used to unambiguously signal Lucy's embarrassment at Maggie's allusion to her own poverty (1994, 306). In light of the ambiguity inherent in represented blushes, then, Maggie's and Stephen's 'blush[es]' and 'flush[es]' imply sexual attraction but do not communicate it as a certainty. Instead, it is the context in which the blushes occur that dictates their significance.

It is implicature that securely communicates the romantic nature of Maggie's and Stephen's reactions and that provides the context in which the reader can decode the blushes' significance. Maggie's new, blush-worthy encounter is only vaguely termed an 'experience'. This vagueness is foregrounded by the repetition with which it is described as 'agreeable', and is only dispelled by its association with 'her previous emotion about Philip'. This is a straightforward case of implicature—so straightforward, in fact, that the passage might easily be mistaken as explicitly expressing Maggie's attraction to Stephen. However, it is only because of the passage's context (a section which details Maggie's romantic relationship with Philip, placed 150 pages previously) that the reader associates romance with Philip and can, in consequence, associate that romance with Maggie's current feelings.

The passage may also be said to implicate, rather than explicate, Maggie's romantic feelings because the communication of that romantic

Unspoken Desires

quality is defeasible. As noted in the introductory chapter, implicatures are uniquely defeasible; more explicit language may not be contradicted with the coherence of the utterance maintained. While it is assumed that the 'previous emotion' mentioned refers to Maggie's romantic feelings for Philip, it would not lower the coherence of the passage if another aspect of Maggie and Philip's relationship were later specified. However, Maggie only becomes self-conscious with Philip when their relationship becomes a romantic one; prior to his confession of love, her behaviour is consistently 'unconstrained and indifferent' (1994, 271–2). In this way, various contexts coalesce to form an implicature: in the passage above, the emphasis on self-consciousness (indicated by Maggie's 'flush') combines with information concerning her 'previous emotion about Philip' to communicate her attraction to Stephen.

Stephen's attraction to Maggie is reinforced by the direct report of a conscious thought, which functions primarily to implicate the inexplicit feelings which motivate it. After Maggie and Stephen have exchanged their first introductory (and somewhat combative) statements, Stephen's conscious reaction is provided: '"An alarming amount of the devil there," was Stephen's first thought. The second, when [Maggie] had bent over her work, was, "I wish she would look at me again"' (1994, 304). Stephen's two represented thoughts oppose each other: the first provides a negative assessment of Maggie and the second implicates a disjointed wish to further attract Maggie's attention. The disjunction between these two narrated thoughts implicates a further emotion of which Stephen is not yet conscious; his desire to gain Maggie's attention, coupled with his previous blushes, indicates that this unknown emotion may be identified as sexual attraction. This interpretation suggests that not just narrated actions but also narrated thought quotations are capable of functioning as a deeper kind of indicative description. Here, it is a 'state of mind' that is narrated, but it is narrated only to indicate another, semiconscious state of mind. By limiting her text to the narration of only verbalized thoughts, Eliot creates a temporary appearance of limited omniscience for her narrative voice, simultaneously shielding Stephen's attraction while communicating it through the disjunction of Stephen's conscious thoughts. The temporary nature of this limited omniscience indicates that the limitation (and the narration's consequent reliance on implicature rather than on explicit language) is intended, rather than an insignificant by-product of the generic limitations of the narrative. In fact, it is the text's assumed fictionality (and specifically the assumed potential for omniscient narration) that permits the intent behind the temporary limitation to be discerned by the reader and that communicates the second-order implicature concerning the illicitness of Stephen's attraction to Maggie (the first-order, more local implicatures act to establish Stephen's attraction to Maggie).

The significant contribution of implicature in these passages is attested to by Lucy's continued obliviousness to Maggie and Stephen's mutual attraction. Lucy is present and attentive for both of the above passages; aside from the second half of Stephen's conscious thought ('I wish she would look at me again'), Lucy is aware of all that is narrated in these passages. Lucy is presented as a fairly intelligent character, and is adept at reading people (she later effects a chain of manipulations that restores the mill to the Tullivers). However, the narrative voice notes that, far from registering the sudden attraction building between Maggie and Stephen, 'Lucy was rather alarmed: she thought Stephen and Maggie were not going to like each other' (1994, 305). This dramatic irony confirms the use of implicature in the text: if an astute character who is privy to the same information as the reader cannot interpret that information correctly, it is clear that the real meaning of the information is communicated through its relationship with a narrative context that the character (Lucy) is not privy to. It is only the reader who is urged to compare Maggie's present experience with her previous one with Philip and who is subject to Stephen's conflicting thoughts; it is the context of Maggie and Stephen's actions which causes them to be read as indicative description, signifying a semiconscious attraction.

Telling, but superficially incoherent, utterances continue to appear throughout the text. Later in the same scene, the reader is notified that Stephen 'was so fascinated by [Maggie's] clear, large gaze, that at last he forgot to look away from it occasionally towards Lucy' (1994, 308). While 'fascinat[ion]' does not necessarily equate with sexual attraction, it does often imply it. A few paragraphs later, however, Eliot writes

'And you *will* like Maggie, shan't you?' [Lucy] added, in a beseeching tone. 'Isn't she a dear, noble-looking creature?'

'Too tall,' said Stephen, smiling down upon her, 'and a little too fiery. She is not my type of woman, you know.'

Gentlemen, you are aware, are apt to impart these imprudent confidences to ladies concerning their unfavourable opinion of sister fair ones. That is why so many women have the advantage of knowing that they are secretly repulsive to men who have self-denyingly made ardent love to them. And hardly anything could be more distinctively characteristic of Lucy, than that she both implicitly believed what Stephen said, and was determined that Maggie should not know it. But you, who have a higher logic than the verbal to guide you, have already foreseen, as the direct sequence to that unfavourable opinion of Stephen's, that he walked down to the boat-house calculating, by the aid of a vivid imagination, that Maggie must give him her hand at least twice in consequence of this pleasant boating plan, and that a gentleman who wishes ladies to look at him is advantageously situated when he is rowing them in a boat. What then? Had he fallen in love with this surprising daughter of Mrs Tulliver at first sight? Certainly not. Such passions are never heard of in real life. Besides, he was in love already, and half-engaged to the dearest little creature in the world; and he was not a man to make a fool of himself in any way. . . . It was perfectly natural and safe to admire beauty and enjoy looking at it—at least under such circumstances as the present. And there was really something very interesting about this girl, with her poverty and troubles: it was gratifying to see the friendship between the two cousins. Generally, Stephen admitted, he was not fond of women who had any peculiarity of character—but here the peculiarity seemed really of a superior kind; and provided one is not obliged to marry such women, why, they certainly make a variety in social intercourse.   (1994, 308–9, emphasis in original)

The spirit of Stephen's response to Lucy is, of course, in contradiction to the 'fascinat[ion]' narrated so shortly beforehand. Eliot takes the opportunity to interject one of her famous narratorial commentaries, matching Stephen's 'impruden[ce]' with the narrator's own equally disingenuous discussion of 'that unfavourable opinion of Stephen's'. The sentence beginning 'That is why' introduces a heavily sarcastic tone in which the narrator communicates a meaning other than what is explicitly stated (that is, not that the women are 'secretly repulsive' but that the gentlemen are often hypocrites), implicitly providing a commentary that derides Stephen's behaviour. As discussed in the introductory chapter, this type of utterance is described as 'echoic' by Daniel Sperber and Deirdre Wilson, and more specifically as ironic. The irony of the utterance continues to function significantly throughout the paragraph: two sentences later, it is only by attributing an ironic tone to the narrator that the reader is able to reconcile Stephen's 'unfavourable opinion' of Maggie and the characterization of the 'boating plan' (with its attendant contact with Maggie) as 'pleasant'. Importantly, this sentence explicates its use of implicature, in that the narrator baldly recognizes that the attraction he is communicating is discerned only through 'a higher logic than the verbal'. This comment further foregrounds the text's previous implicatures by pointing out the method through which they have been effected—the narrator, here, is commenting on the pragmatic inferences expected of his readers. The reader is in need of this pragmatic inference to understand the rest of the sentence as well as the significance of the paragraph as a whole.

While the first half of the paragraph presents a heavily sarcastic commentary on Stephen's fickleness, the second half functions as free indirect discourse concerning Stephen's thoughts. The shift occurs between the previous ironized sentence and the short ejaculation, 'What then?'. Mixed in with the numerous clauses of the narrator's self-reflexive sentence is a thought report of Stephen's 'calculating'. This thought report segues between utterances that function as pure commentary and the free indirect discourse signalled by 'What then?', in which psychological representation takes precedence over the now-backgrounded commentary. With the transition into free indirect discourse, the 'certainly not' (now attributed to Stephen) is partially voided by Stephen's lengthy attempt to excuse his (unarticulated) attraction. Stephen quiets his conscience by characterizing the indulgence of his attraction as 'natural and safe', then displacing his interest in Maggie's looks onto an interest in her 'poverty and troubles', and then by assuming a charmed amusement at 'the friendship between the two cousins'. These non sequiturs emphasize Stephen's lack of reliance on his one previously mentioned and uniquely valid excuse: that 'he was in love already, and half-engaged to the dearest little creature in the world'. Stephen's last 'excuse' proves most effective, by locating the source of his interest in a 'peculiarity' that he characterizes as negating Maggie's marriage potential. It is the unnecessary repetition of explanations regarding why Stephen's interest in Maggie is 'safe' that indicates a semiconscious awareness on his part that it might not be. The free indirect discourse of Stephen's thoughts does not explicitly communicate the extremity of Stephen's attraction to Maggie, then, but implicates it through the unnecessary repetition of disjointed verbalized thoughts that, together, function as indicative description.

While Eliot continues to rely primarily on implicature to communicate Maggie and Stephen's growing mutual attraction, she soon introduces a nominal element of explicitness. Although the growing romance is semantically represented in the text, it is fashioned so that it does not provide indicative, factual descriptions of Maggie's and Stephen's emotional states. The narrator carefully precedes the introduction of this semantic dimension by commenting

> Had anything remarkable happened?
> Nothing that you are not likely to consider in the highest degree unimportant.
> (1994, 311)

After unravelling the triple negation of the narrator's answer to his own question, it becomes clear that the narrator is posing the subnarratability of what he is about to communicate. With that, he narrates that

> It was not that [Maggie] thought distinctly of Mr Stephen Guest, or dwelt on the indications that he looked at her with admiration; it was rather that she felt the half-remote presence of a world of love and beauty and delight, made up of vague, mingled images from all the poetry and romance she had ever read, or had ever woven in her dreamy reveries.' (1994, 311)

Importantly, this quotation communicates Maggie's lack of consciousness of a carefully distanced, 'half-remote... world' beneath its lexical associations with conventional narratives of romance ('admiration', 'love', 'beauty', 'romance')—for all of the utterance's seeming explicitness, it repeats and plays out the triple negation of Eliot's warning, communicating only that Maggie is not fully conscious of a romantic world that she is not explicitly included in. While the text's implicatures portray romantic developments that include Maggie, the message implicit in the above quote is significant in a context in which Maggie is only a visitor in a house filled with material 'beauty and delight' and the onlooker to her cousin's unspoken engagement.

From this point onwards the implicated narrative of Maggie and Stephen's growing love is replaced by an explicit narrative of Maggie and Stephen's growing consciousness of each other. Semantic indications of the romantic character of this self-consciousness are rarely invoked; instead, these passages function as didactic substitutions for narrative blushes, foregrounding the context that their self-consciousness must result from. It is the consciousness of each other's physical presence that is narrated; the significance of this spatial consciousness (Maggie and Stephen's attraction to each other) remains unarticulated. In a chapter whose title, 'Illustrating the Laws of Attraction', is one the of few available semantic clues, Eliot writes that Stephen's

> personal attentions to Maggie were comparatively slight, and there had even sprung up an apparent distance between them.... If Stephen came in when Lucy was out of the room—if Lucy left them together, they never spoke to each other: Stephen, perhaps, seemed to be examining books on music, and Maggie bent her head assiduously over her work. Each was oppressively conscious of the other's presence, even to the finger-ends. Yet each looked and longed for the same thing to happen the next day. Neither of them had begun to reflect on the matter, or silently to ask, 'To what does all this tend?' Maggie only felt that life was revealing something quite new to her, and she was absorbed in the direct, immediate experience, without any energy left for taking account of it and reasoning about it. Stephen wilfully abstained from self-questioning, and would not admit to himself that he felt an influence which was to have any determining effect on his conduct. And when Lucy came into the room again, they were once more unconstrained. (1994, 326)

This passage effectively acts as disnarration: Maggie and Stephen do *not* speak to each other; they do *not* look at each other.[9] These narrative actions are more than subnarratable; they are disnarrated: they do not

---

[9] For a discussion of disnarration, see the section 'Narratological Discussions of Gaps'.

happen. However, it is not their nonexistence that is significant (non-action could be considered the springboard from which narratable actions are produced) but the studied nonexistence of these actions—the consciousness with which they are avoided. Stephen 'seem[s]' to be examining books, and Maggie has her head bent over her work; the otherwise omniscient narrative voice refuses to comment on whether or not Stephen is actually examining, or Maggie is actually working. Quintessentially subnarratable elements are manipulated into expressing the romantic drama that is developing between Maggie and Stephen.

Instead of narrating through relevant thought report or through conventional indicative description, the narrative concentrates on the thought report of feelings that have only limited relevance: as has been stated, Maggie's and Stephen's self-consciousness is relevant only because it results from a semiconscious desire that is not explicitly indicated. Eliot further highlights this unexplained self-consciousness by problematizing its significance; just as it is emphasized that Maggie and Stephen do *not* engage in narratable behaviour when Lucy is away, it is also emphasized that Maggie and Stephen do *not* reflect on what their self-consciousness means.[10] Eliot is making explicit the semiconsciousness which her implicatures mimic; however, those implicatures are held in place by the evasiveness concerning what it is that Maggie and Stephen are semiconscious of. Here again, then, Eliot's thought report (or, in this case, lack-of-thought report) is more significant for what it implicates that the character is experiencing than what it directly tells the reader the character is experiencing. By temporarily employing a limited omniscience that is perceived as ironic, Eliot transforms thought report into indicative description, implicating rather than explicitly reporting the contextual effects (that is, the meaning) of her characters' consciousnesses. These implicatures, in turn, communicate the information of which these characters are only semiconscious, and the result is a multilayered presentation of Maggie's and Stephen's psychologies.

As indicated above, many scholars have discussed Eliot's use of Maggie and Stephen's mutual attraction as a platform on which to discuss self-control and the power of unconscious drives. Almost all scholars focus on the climactic scene between Maggie and Stephen, in which Maggie exhibits a (to most critics) highly suspect passivity and lack of consciousness while Stephen effects their elopement. This occurs when circumstances unexpectedly leave only Maggie and Stephen free to partake in a boating trip that has been planned. Maggie has had 'fits of absence' while Stephen

---

[10] As noted in the introductory chapter, one of the conditions of narratability is that the information 'is worthy of being told' (Warhol 2006, 22).

purposely rows too far to allow them to return home within the expected timeframe (1994, 376–7). Maggie is only able to return home the next day, but is so flustered that she accidentally boards a coach going in the wrong direction (1994, 388). It takes Maggie five days to return home, by which time word has spread about her elopement with Stephen (1994, 391).

It is the initial scene on the river, in which Stephen is rowing and Maggie is daydreaming, that scholars often concentrate on. This scene occurs after both the narrative voice and the characters have articulated the characters' love, and draws comparatively little on implicature to communicate Maggie's and Stephen's inner lives. Both, however, have remarkably little conscious inner life to communicate. Unlike in the passages marked by the multilayered, semiconscious thoughts and emotions that have propelled the narrative to this point, Maggie, here, experiences a lull in which her passivity within her own situation allows for little narrative information that is worth telling: there is simply no narratable information to communicate.[11] As Eliot later writes, 'All yielding is attended with a less vivid consciousness than resistance; it is the partial sleep of thought' (1994, 378). The reader is told that

> Some low, subdued, languid exclamation of love came from Stephen from time to time, as he went on rowing idly, half automatically: otherwise, they spoke no word; for what could words have been but an inlet to thought? and thought did not belong to that enchanted haze in which they were enveloped—it belonged to the past and the future that lay outside the haze. Maggie was only dimly conscious of the banks, as they passed them, and dwelt with no recognition on the villages: she knew there were several to be passed before they reached Luckreth, where they always stopped and left the boat. At all times she was so liable to fits of absence, that she was likely enough to let her way-marks pass unnoticed. (1994, 376)

The thought report that describes Maggie as 'dimly conscious' indicates that the previous sentences are not free indirect discourse but earnest narratorial commentary: Maggie really is in a haze and has few articulated thoughts. The remark which ends the passage justifies her passivity, characterizing 'fits of absence' as characteristic of her. She has, as she thinks, harmlessly given in to her attraction, and the emphasis placed on her unconsciousness seems less an ironic assertion of denial (regarding feelings of guilt towards Lucy) and more a straightforward account of her dreamlike state. The passage straightforwardly presents the lack of

---

[11] With the primary conflict of the narrative (Maggie and Stephen's mutual attraction) momentarily resolved (they have temporarily and—as far as Maggie knows—harmlessly given in to their feelings), there is little that is 'worthy of being told'.

conscious self-control that is enacted by her physically accompanying Stephen into the boat; both instances present a lapse from the self-control advocated by Carpenter and Spencer.

With respect to my argument, the passage is structurally significant, functioning as the climax of the novel. The climactic force of the scene substantiates the centrality of Maggie and Stephen's evolving emotions, and specifically their attempts to resist their mutual attraction; the scene temporarily resolves the narrative 'problem' of their attraction. Implicature, rather than more explicit narration, is used to communicate this central drama of the narrative. Eliot's heavy reliance on implicature illustrates its ability to withstand significant narrative responsibility, and the enduring popularity of the text evidences the modern reader's ability to appropriately interpret texts that rely heavily on implicatures. The novel's trans-generational popularity also serves to isolate the effectiveness of the text's implicatures, as opposed to its other techniques of discreet narration: current readers may be less likely to recognize era-bound codes such as euphemism and the symbolism of the period. The continued success of the novel is, partly, the continued success of its implicatures.

ORLEY FARM: INTERPRETATIONS, INFATUATIONS, AND CRIME

Slightly more than half way through the 800 pages of *Orley Farm*, Anthony Trollope provides one of his famous narratorial intrusions:

> I venture to think, I may almost say to hope, that Lady Mason's confession at the end of the last chapter will not have taken anybody by surprise. If such surprise be felt I must have told my tale badly. I do not like such revulsions of feeling with regard to my characters as surprises of this nature must generate. That Lady Mason had committed the terrible deed for which she was about to be tried, that Mr. Furnival's suspicion of her guilt was only too well founded, that Mr. Dockwrath with his wicked ingenuity had discovered no more than the truth, will, in its open revelation, have caused no surprise to the reader;—but it did cause terrible surprise to Sir Peregrine Orme. (2008, 2: 42–3)

The narrator's comments on the expectation with which he hopes readers will have viewed Lady Mason's confession refer to the heavy use of implicature within the text. For the first half of the novel, Lady Mason's guilt—the narrative fact around which the plot revolves—is communicated through implicature, and Trollope fashions the surrounding novel into a discourse on the vagaries of interpretation.

Complicating characters' skewed understandings of Lady Mason's guilt is the attraction she holds to both the reader and other characters in the novel; two of the novel's central characters, Sir Peregrine Orme and Mr Furnival, have romantic feelings for her. Mr Furnival's feelings are of especial interest to this chapter: his thought processes concerning the likelihood of Lady Mason's guilt are much of what causes the reader to infer that she is guilty, and they are coloured by his unconscious attraction to her. These two facets of Mr Furnival's presentation reinforce each other: just as his obvious bias towards Lady Mason allows the reader to interpret his hesitant suspicions as obvious truths, the hesitancy with which he accepts Lady Mason's blatant guilt indicates his unconscious inclination towards her. These indications work to advance earlier implicatures in the text: the articulated suspicions of other characters function as nonfactual reports of Mr Furnival's attraction, simultaneously communicating the unconscious character of his attraction by verbalizing it only in other characters' words. The nonfactiveness of these passages is rendered pronounced by an absence of clarifying narratorial commentary. With these narrative possibilities highlighted for the reader, succeeding passages function to establish the truth of the otherwise nonfactive assertions regarding Mr Furnival's attraction to Lady Mason. In these passages Mr Furnival's attraction is portrayed through indicative behaviour that is often focalized through Lady Mason's perception, superficially rendering the implicated conclusions concerning his behaviour nonfactual as well. Together, these narrative occurrences remove much of the uncertainty that each one would communicate alone.

As indicated in the preceding discussion, the novel centres on the beautiful Lady Mason, the young second wife of the established and elderly Sir Joseph Mason. When Sir Joseph refuses to leave his newborn son an adequate inheritance (leaving all to his older son, Mr Mason), Lady Mason forges a codicil to Sir Joseph's will, claiming his lesser property, Orley Farm, as her son's. When Sir Joseph dies, Lady Mason is taken to court by his older son and found innocent.

Twenty years later, Lady Mason's son Lucius upsets their tenant, Mr Dockwrath, by abruptly revoking his right to use their land. In revenge Mr Dockwrath unearths papers implicating Lady Mason's guilt, and, on presenting them to Mr Mason, a new accusation of perjury is levelled against Lady Mason. Lady Mason relies heavily on her lawyer, Mr Furnival, who secured her acquittal twenty years earlier and, at the time, strongly believed in her innocence. Lady Mason is presented as having lived a mostly solitary life: her guilt has caused her to isolate herself from close friendships with others. Her closest friends are Sir Peregrine and his widowed stepdaughter, Mrs Orme. When Lady Mason's legal troubles recommence, the Ormes offer closer friendship as support, and Sir Peregrine soon proposes to her. Lady Mason initially accepts out of respect but is soon convinced by Mr Furnival and others that the match would be inappropriate and harmful to both her reputation and that of Sir Peregrine. In her successful attempt to break off the engagement, Lady Mason resorts to confessing her crime to Sir Peregrine, devastating him with the revelation of her immoral activities. Lady Mason's confession introduces the first factive, explicit discussion of her guilt. As the opening quotation shows, however, her guilt has previously been communicated through the persistent use of salient and sustained implicatures. Despite his own growing misgivings concerning Lady Mason's innocence, Mr Furnival does his best to secure a second acquittal, and she is eventually found not guilty.

Mrs Furnival is introduced into the narrative in the context of the Furnivals' marital problems. While little of the marriage's status is discussed in relation to Mr Furnival, the first the reader learns of Mrs Furnival is that she is 'not quite so happy as she had been when watching beside [Mr. Furnival] in the [early] days of their poverty' (2008, 1: 99). Her unhappiness is largely attributed to the assertion that Mr Furnival, 'at the age of fifty-five, was now running after strange goddesses! The member of the Essex Marshes, in these his latter days, was obtaining for himself among other successes the character of a Lothario' (2008, 1: 99). However, an assertion that initially (if ambiguously) is attributed to the omniscient narrative voice is soon characterized as 'supposed' and pointedly attributed to Mrs Furnival (2008, 1: 100).[12] 'That he did wander afield', the narrator notes, 'poor Mrs. Furnival felt in her agony convinced; and among those ladies whom on this account she most thoroughly detested was our friend Lady Mason of Orley Farm' (2008, 1: 100). It is noteworthy that it is a character, rather than the omniscient narrative voice, who is 'convinced' of Mr Furnival's affairs: the attribution of the feeling to a character rather than the narrator designates the information as nonfactive. The uncertainty of the information discussed is further highlighted by the addition of the word 'felt', which conveys less certainty and a greater dependence on emotional, rather than rational, bases for the conclusion reached. A similar emphasis on emotions is carried through to the next sentence, in which Lady Mason is not 'detected' so much as she is 'detested'. Nonetheless, although Mr Furnival's romantic feelings are not

---

[12] Although the passage is dedicated to the portrayal of Mrs Furnival's reflections, its tone and vocabulary are consistent with those adopted by the narrator generally, diminishing the likelihood that Trollope intended the assertion to act as free indirect discourse. The exclamation point placed after 'goddesses' is the one exception to this tonal homogeneity, communicating an exasperation unlikely to be portrayed by a worldly narrator but potentially attributable to an adulterer's wife.

indicated, the possibility of their existence is made salient, and these emphatically nonfactive statements create a context in which Mr Furnival's interactions with and thoughts concerning Lady Mason are rendered conspicuous. In other words, the backdrop against which Mr Furnival and Lady Mason's interactions are placed (Mrs Furnival's suspicions) foregrounds the possibility that Mr Furnival's actions will act as indicative description with regard to whether or not he has romantic feelings for Lady Mason. With Mrs Furnival's suspicions in mind, the reader is likely to pay attention to what Mr Furnival's recorded thoughts and actions indicate about his feelings for Lady Mason, rather than any other narrative fact they might communicate either about him or the other conditions under which the characters meet.

It is significant that the possibility of Mr Furnival's attraction to Lady Mason is verbalized only in the free indirect discourse of another character, rather than in any passage where the assertions could be attributed to him. As discussed in the introduction to this chapter, many narratological theories of the representation of character psychologies are somewhat limited in that they tend to focus on techniques, such as free indirect discourse, which depict only the articulated thoughts of characters. Less articulated character states (including those that are less conscious) are often neglected by these narratological frameworks, and when they are discussed it is often assumed that they must be depicted through third-person narration. Implicature provides a mimetic alternative for the presentation of less conscious character states, and the accumulation of Mrs Furnival's suspicions, Mr Furnival's indicative behaviour, and the narration of his (non-romantic) thoughts implicates his romantic attachment to Lady Mason. Because his attraction is only verbalized through other characters, it retains the possibility of being unconscious. The indicative description and third-person report of conscious thoughts (which themselves function as indicative description) further implicate Mr Furnival's attraction and cement the unconscious status of his desires.

The narration of Mrs Furnival's suspicions runs throughout most of the novel and culminates in a meeting between Mrs Orme and Mrs Furnival that quiets her jealousy permanently (2008, 2: 115). Trollope foregrounds Mrs Furnival's suspicions, however, by applying them explicitly to the first meeting narrated between Mr Furnival and Lady Mason. After being alerted that her husband will unexpectedly return to London that evening, Mrs Furnival learns, by chance, that Lady Mason will be shopping in London the next day. Trollope writes that

> Now if it were an ascertained fact that he was coming to London merely with the view of meeting Lady Mason, the wife of his bosom would not think it

necessary to provide for him the warmest welcome. This of course was not an ascertained fact; but were there not terrible grounds of suspicion? Mr. Furnival's law chambers were in Old Square, Lincoln's Inn, close to Chancery Lane, and Lady Mason had made her appointment with her son within five minutes' walk of that locality. And was it not in itself a strange coincidence that Lady Mason, who came to town so seldom, should now do so on the very day of Mr. Furnival's sudden return? She felt sure that they were to meet on the morrow, but yet she could not declare even to herself that it was an ascertained fact. (2008, 1: 107)

Because this passage is narrated in free indirect discourse (as is evident from the use of question marks, repeated phrases, and redundant phrases such as 'of his bosom') the narrative information meditated upon—Mr Furnival's appointment with Lady Mason—is presented as uncertain; the passage narrates a character's thoughts, rather than what is happening or will happen within the narrative. The uncertainty of this information is emphasized by the repeated phrases in this passage, which depict the narrative information as 'not an ascertained fact': even within Mrs Furnival's mind, the information is uncertain.

Nonetheless, the passage is the text's first indication that Lady Mason has indeed made an appointment to see Mr Furnival (she is shown considering the necessity of it earlier in the novel) and Mrs Furnival's general suspicions remain relevant when it is shown that the specific ones presented in the passage are correct. Both Mr Furnival and Lady Mason have travelled to London solely with the purpose of meeting each other (2008, 1: 111). Mrs Furnival's more general suspicions, however, remain unconfirmed: Mr Furnival is incapable of informing his wife of their intended meeting, and the narrative voice clarifies that 'this deceit was practised, not as between husband and wife with reference to an assignation with a lady, but between the lawyer and the outer world with reference to a private meeting with a client' (2008, 1: 111–12).

The neutrality implied in this last observation by the narrative voice is negated by a parallel observation which opens the narration of the meeting. 'Had [Lady Mason] given way to dowdiness', the narrator claims, 'or suffered herself to be, as it were, washed out, Mr. Furnival, we may say, would not have been there to meet her;—of which fact Lady Mason was perhaps aware' (2008, 1: 117). This narratorial statement asserts a certain element of appearance-related interest Mr Furnival has in Lady Mason, and implicates Lady Mason's awareness and manipulation of that interest. However, the interest asserted here is little more than the intangible effect Lady Mason's appearance has on her attractiveness as an acquaintance generally, and one which she is previously shown to be conscious of in front of all acquaintances (2008, 1: 46). As the passage develops, however, the romantic tenor of Mr Furnival's interest is emphasized by indicative description, and a series of em dashes (like the one in the quote above) communicates that an unspoken affection might motivate his eagerness to help his client. The em dash, here, characterizes the comment that succeeds it as a hesitant aside, portraying its content as suspect (which the use of 'perhaps' reinforces) and, more importantly, illicit. In the context of Mrs Furnival's suspicions and the emphasis on Lady Mason's pleasing appearance, this illicitness implicates the adulterous feelings which Mrs Furnival attributes to Mr Furnival and which his succeeding indicative behaviour communicates.

At the opening of their interview, Mr Furnival is shown to sit 'rather close to [Lady Mason],—much closer to her than he ever now seated himself to Mrs. F' (2008, 1: 117). The implication of illicit motivations enacted by the em dash recalls the jealousy attributed to 'Mrs. F' in earlier passages and characterizes Mr Furnival's proximity to Lady Mason as indicative description, specifically indicating the romantic feelings Mrs Furnival attributes to him. In the next paragraph the narrator notes that Mr Furnival 'again took [Lady Mason's] hand,—that he might encourage her. Lady Mason let him keep her hand for a minute or so, as though she did not notice it; and yet as she turned her eyes to him it might appear that his tenderness had encouraged her' (2008, 1: 117). As with the previous two em dashes employed, the one used here renders the narratorial commentary which follows it suspect. It is not that it ironizes the commentary (although, in the last example, that claim is arguable)[13] but that it functions as a pronounced ellipsis, drawing the reader's attention to the possibility that the narrator is only narrating Mr Furnival's more professional motivations and is not disclosing his more illicit ones.

The indicative description outlined here affects the reader's interpretations of succeeding passages which detail Mr Furnival's thoughts, and specifically those concerned with the possibility of Lady Mason's guilt. As mentioned previously, however, the hesitancy and idealization of Lady Mason that are evident in these succeeding passages also reinforce the reader's conclusions regarding Mr Furnival's attraction to her. The narration of his

---

[13] When followed by the pause that the em dash indicates, the phrase 'that he might encourage her' could be read as echoic of Mr Furnival's thoughts: the utterance could be interpreted as free indirect discourse, and, in a denial similar to that practiced by the characters in *The Mill on the Floss*, Mr Furnival could be excusing his inappropriate actions with inadequate justifications. In order to be categorized as 'ironic', a derogatory attitude towards the utterance must also be detectable; in 'that he might encourage her', this derogatory attitude results from the excuse's apparent inadequacy. However, the end of the quote shows that Mr Furnival's actions do indeed 'encourage' Lady Mason when she is hesitant and troubled; this outcome problematizes the characterization of Mr Furnival's excuse as 'inadequate' and, consequently, the categorization of the utterance as ironic.

suspicions begins during his first conversation with her about the possibility of a new trial. Lady Mason's main object is to learn how likely it is that she will be taken to court. Trollope writes that

> She was trying to gather from his face whether he had seen signs of danger, and he was trying to gather from her words whether there might really be cause to apprehend danger. How was he to know what was really inside her mind; what were her actual thoughts and inward reasonings on this subject; what private knowledge she might have which was still kept back from him?... Could it be possible that anything had been kept back from him? Were there facts unknown to him, but known to her, which would be terrible, fatal, damning to his sweet friend if proved before all the world? He could not bring himself to ask her, but yet it was so material that he should know!... he sat, thinking, not so much whether or no she had been in any way guilty with reference to that will, as whether the counsel he should give her ought in any way to be based on the possibility of her having been thus guilty. Nothing might be so damning to her cause as that he should make sure of her innocence, if she were not innocent; and yet he would not ask her the question. If innocent, why was it that she was now so much moved, after twenty years of quiet possession? (2008, 1: 118–19)

Trollope delicately balances Mr Furnival's willed disbelief in the possibility of Lady Mason's guilt with his professional acknowledgement of suspicious circumstances. The intense intersubjectivity with which the passage opens is immediately backgrounded as the narrative voice slips into free indirect narration of Mr Furnival's thoughts. Lady Mason is attempting to 'read' Mr Furnival's mind, but he unconsciously retreats from intersubjective engagement as he attempts to reconcile her as she presents herself with the Lady Mason he idealizes. His explicit characterization of a probable criminal as a 'sweet friend' and his unwillingness to question her illustrate the influence that she has over him; it is an influence that causes his line of questioning to concentrate on her relationship with him ('Could it be possible that anything had been kept back from him?') and on how best he may help her, rather than on whether or not she is guilty. The perceptible influence of his admiration on his line of thought creates a narrative irony in which Lady Mason's actions indicate her guilt to the reader but not to Mr Furnival: for the reader, Lady Mason's agitation 'after twenty years of quiet possession' is paramount, while for Mr Furnival it is an afterthought. The discrepancy between Mr Furnival's thoughts and his failure to reach the same conclusions as the reader implicates the influence of his romantic feelings on his reasoning.

Mr Furnival's suspicion deepens as Lady Mason unwittingly further suggests her guilt. When Mr Furnival resumes questioning her, he is struck by how quickly she recalls incidents that occurred twenty years prior: 'how was it that she knew so accurately things which had occurred before the trial,—when no trial could have been expected? But as to this he said nothing' (2008, 1: 121). Occurrences that would not be suspicious if narrated differently are portrayed as indicative of Lady Mason's guilt: it could be argued that, having gone through a traumatic trial, it is only natural that Lady Mason would remember details she had dwelt on excessively twenty years prior. Mr Furnival's suspicions are shown, here, and guide the reader to a deeper suspicion of Lady Mason's guilt. The last sentence, however, indicates a willing passivity in response to raised suspicions: a deliberate semiawareness indicates Mr Furnival's professional acuity as well as his attempts to ignore it.

Despite Mr Furnival's conclusion, the passage encourages the reader to infer Lady Mason's guilt by echoing his or her possible deductions in the text. The novel contains many lengthy passages of free indirect discourse communicating Mr Furnival's ruminations, most of them regarding the possibility of the omitted action that is central to the narrative:

> What was the real truth of all this? . . . Nothing could be more natural than her anxiety, supposing her to be aware of some secret which would condemn her if discovered;—but nothing more unnatural if there were no such secret. And she must know! In her bosom, if in no other, must exist the knowledge whether or no that will were just. If that will were just, was it possible that she should now tremble so violently, seeing that its justice had been substantially proved in various courts of law? But if it were not just—if it were a forgery, a forgery made by her, or with her cognizance—and that now this truth was to be made known! How terrible would that be! But terrible is not the word which best describes the idea as it entered Mr. Furnival's mind. How wonderful would it be; how wonderful would it all have been! . . . Had not she been a woman worthy of wonder! . . . But it was impossible. So said Mr. Furnival to himself, out loud.   (2008, 1: 130–1)

The beginning of the above excerpt isolates the 'truth' as its object of inquiry and echoes many of the novel's primary themes. The trial that ensues interests not only the neighbouring gentility but also 'the London world, especially the world of lawyers' (2008, 2: 207). Trollope writes that men 'about the Inns of Court speculated as to the verdict, offering to each other very confident opinions as to the result, and offering, on some occasions, bets as well as opinions' (2008, 2: 207). *Orley Farm* is emphatically more concerned with interpretation than with narrative fact; its sustained omission of the narrative's central act foregrounds the various interpretations offered concerning the likelihood of the act having taken place (and almost every character within the novel does offer a view, however cursory). As minute and lengthy as Mr Furnival's interpretations are, however, they are only interpretations: the defeasible nature of all inferences allows Mr Furnival to maintain his illogical conclusions concerning Lady Mason's innocence. Mr Furnival's feelings for his client skew an interpretation that otherwise mirrors the reader's own inferences, reinforcing the novel's message concerning both the fickleness and primacy of interpretation (it is, after all, the court's mistaken interpretation of past events that leads it to conclude that Lady Mason is not guilty).

The passage also self-reflexively echoes the suspended omniscience of the narrative voice. Mr Furnival's evident preoccupation with Lady Mason's evasiveness mirrors the reader's reaction to the narrative voice's conspicuously selective silence. The passage moves from exclamations of Lady Mason's sure knowledge ('she must know!'), to a rehearsal of deductions the reader is likely to have made, to conclusions of her guilt. Mr Furnival's repetition of the reader's likely inferences legitimizes them, as does the implicit acknowledgement of the narrative voice's conspicuous omissions. Unlike the reader, however, Mr Furnival is driven back from his conclusions, and his characterization of Lady Mason's probable criminal activities as 'wonderful', making her 'a woman worthy of wonder!', adds to the accumulating evidence of his infatuation with her. Although readers' views of Lady Mason have generally been sympathetic, the extremity of Mr Furnival's enthusiasm further distances his conclusions from the reader's, adding to the general impression of his romantic regard for her. The free indirect discourse detailing Mr Furnival's deductions further implicates the unconscious status of his romantic feelings because they are perceived as having a decisive effect on his thoughts. Mr Furnival is incapable of recognizing the emotion which controls his inferences, and it is this lack of recognition which grants his feelings for Lady Mason control over his perceptions of her.

Romance's complete absence from textual representation in these passages from *Orley Farm*, coupled with the implicatures communicating it in preceding passages, leads the reader to infer that Mr Furnival's romantic interest has not been consciously realized on any psychological level. The wholly unconscious status of Mr Furnival's attachment is eventually made explicit alongside the explication of the attachment itself. The articulation of this previously implicated information appears after Mr Furnival finally concludes what the reader has concluded long before him: 'that that codicil had been fraudulently manufactured by his friend and client, Lady Mason' (2008, 1: 340). In describing Mr Furnival's extended reaction to Lady Mason's engagement with Sir Peregrine, Trollope writes

> he thought of the woman herself, and his spirit within him became very bitter. Had any one told him that he was jealous of the preference shown by his client to Sir Peregrine, he would have fumed with anger, and thought

that he was fuming justly. But such was in truth the case. Though he believed her to have been guilty of this thing, though he believed her to be now guilty of the worse offence of dragging the baronet to his ruin, still he was jealous of her regard.... And what reward did he expect? None. He had formed no idea that the woman would become his mistress. All that was as obscure before his mind's eye, as though she had been nineteen and he five-and-twenty. (2008, 1: 405)

Trollope pointedly negates the immorality of a married man's infatuation with a client by positing it as unconscious: Mr Furnival can honestly show outrage (he can 'fume justly') at the imputation of adulterous feelings because he is, despite their existence, innocent of them. Accordingly, he cannot attempt control of his desires because he is unaware of them. Trollope's complete exclusion of the generally pervasive discourse of control is motivated: even a portrayal of the psychological control on the terms suggested by Carpenter and Spencer would have repelled readers and would have dictated that Mr Furnival be viewed as an antagonist (because of the implied indifference towards his wife) rather than the sympathetic protagonist's primary support. By posing Mr Furnival's romantic attachment as wholly unrealized, Trollope creates a realistic basis for the otherwise shrewd lawyer's skewed interpretation of his client's past, while maintaining his sympathetic standing within the novel. Trollope's portrayal echoes Cobbe's claim that humans intuitively are not blamed for acts of 'unconscious cerebration' but only those in which 'our brains obey our wills' (1998, 94). As in the Victorian schemas discussed in this chapter's introduction, however, these unconscious drives affect Mr Furnival's conscious thoughts and actions: his unceasing appreciation of Lady Mason's better qualities and his illogical determination to have her acquitted of a crime he believes she has committed. The unconscious status of Mr Furnival's infatuation is just as necessary to the conveyance of the novel's primary theme as the infatuation itself: it is Mr Furnival's lack of awareness that allows the infatuation to cloud his judgment, skewing the novel's primary example of fallible deductive processes.

In January 1863, *National Magazine* printed an appreciative discussion of *Orley Farm*'s realist cast: 'Here, for once, we have a break in the smooth landscape, a cloud on the calm horizon: a lady forger, and a perjurer to boot, is a character which might well become a "sensational" feature in other hands; but the author, who disdains all clap-trap or stage-trickery, softens even this down' ('Unsigned Notice' 1969, 164). Trollope's reputation as a 'realist' fiction writer was widely recognized. Nonetheless, the reviewer's comparison of *Orley Farm* with sensation fiction is apt, although most scholars today would argue that this (always fuzzy) generic categorization relies more on the narrative's discursive presentation than on its content. *Orley Farm*, begun in 1860 and initially serialized in 1861, was written as the sensation movement was gaining recognition throughout the United Kingdom (Hamer 1987, 90). The salient, sustained use of implicature played a role in distinguishing sensation from other fiction modes at the time, and its inherent emphasis on information kept secret could have played a role in *National Magazine*'s ability to identify similarities of content between *Orley Farm* and the sensation mode. The central use of implicature in the sensation novel forms the subject of the next chapter.

3

The Narrative Tease

Open Secrets in Sensation Fiction

INTRODUCTION

The Dead Secret, an 1857 novel by Wilkie Collins, begins with a conspicuous discussion of an event that is not explicitly communicated until near the end of the novel (and then only through character dialogue). The event is 'not narrated' in a way that foregrounds its importance:

> 'Have you told my master?'
>
> 'No,' was the answer. 'I sent for him, to tell him—I tried hard to speak the words—it shook me to my very soul, only to think how I should best break it to him.... But I should have spoken in spite of that, if he had not talked of the child.... and that silenced me.... Get my writing-case, and the pen and ink....'
>
> Sarah peered anxiously over her shoulder, and saw the pen slowly and feebly form these three words:—*To My Husband*.
>
> 'O, no! no! For God's sake, don't write it!' she cried....
>
> 'Don't!' reiterated Sarah, dropping on her knees at the bedside. 'Don't write it to him if you can't tell it to him. Let me go on bearing what I have borne so long already. Let the Secret die with you and die with me, and be never known in this world—never, never, never!'
>
> 'The Secret must be told,' answered Mrs. Treverton. 'My husband ought to know it, and must know it. I tried to tell him, and my courage failed me. I cannot trust you to tell him, after I am gone. It must be written. Take you the pen; my sight is failing.... Take the pen, and write what I tell you.'
>
> (2008, 15–18)

The 'Secret' under discussion is, of course, the 'Secret' of the title, foregrounded before the narrative itself begins. Emphasized by nonstandard capitalization, the word is also repeated numerous times throughout the passage. More striking than even this, however, is the characters' discussion of an occurrence that is consistently left unidentified: the repeated references to communication ('tell[ing]' and 'writ[ing]') presuppose that there is information to communicate. The explicit discussion of a secret foregrounds the narrator's refusal to communicate the 'Secret' information, emphasizing both the omission of the information and the information's probable antinarratability. This practice differs from instances of ostensive-inferential communication in *Jessie Phillips*, *Ruth*, and *Adam Bede*, in which more earnest narrators concentrate on communicating antinarratable information (illegitimate pregnancy and illegitimate birth) politely rather than teasingly withholding and thereby emphasizing it. The 'Secret' of the novel is that Mrs Treverton's supposed daughter Rosamond is actually the illegitimate daughter of the maid Sarah. The melodramatic exclamations Mrs Treverton and Sarah's discussion produces ('For God's sake!') and the contention surrounding even the mode in which the 'Secret' should be communicated elevate its perceived antinarratability. While Frances Trollope, Gaskell, and Eliot seek to minimize the effect their antinarratable subject has, Collins maximizes it.[1]

The above excerpt from *The Dead Secret* functions primarily to foreground the presence of a mystery, but clues regarding the character of that mystery are also present. It is revealed that the 'Secret' is relevant to the husband and to the child—both of whom, we learn, are ignorant of the secret's existence. Collins conspicuously avoids explaining the relevance of succeeding, superficially irrelevant scenes (such as Sarah's overwhelming emotion when she sees 'Little Rosamond' (2008, 27–8)), and the narrator's manifest abdication of omniscience alerts the reader that they must primarily infer rather than 'decode' the significance of the narrative information that Collins does present. These incongruous scenes guide the reader's inferences so heavily that, as *The Saturday Review* noted, the

---

[1] The content of *The Dead Secret* is unlikely to have been as inflammatory as that of *Jessie Phillips*, *Ruth*, or *Adam Bede*. *The Dead Secret* focuses far less on illegitimate pregnancy (which it excuses by way of the mother's formal engagement to the father) and instead emphasizes what was popularly recognized as a less controversial topic: the stigma attached to bastardy. When Collins wrote *The Dead Secret* in 1857, bastardy was a far from original topic in literature: Jessica Cox writes that 'Charles Dickens's *Oliver Twist* (1838) heralded a new wave of illegitimate children in literature.... Dickens's attitude to Oliver is typical of that of many Victorian writers. The narrative condemns the illicit relationship that led to the child's birth, but sympathizes with the child himself' (2004, 151). The conspicuous presentational politeness that communicates Rosamond's illegitimacy, then, appears to enlarge the presence of its borderline antinarratable content rather than minimize it. Not only does Collins appear to be exploiting the antinarratability of illegitimate pregnancy for entertainment purposes, but (unlike Trollope, Gaskell, and Eliot) he does not truly tackle what his readers might be too offended to read. While Collins's conspicuously muted narration is also characteristic of these earlier renditions of illegitimacy, then, in *The Dead Secret* Collins renders the unstated more conspicuous, using implicature to not only communicate the antinarratable but also exploit it as a source of suspense.

secret is 'plainly discernible in the very opening of the book [and] the interest of the story hangs not upon the nature of the secret, but upon the mode in which it is discovered' ('Dead Secret' 1857, 188). 'The secret', *The Athenaeum* archly noted, 'is buried (not dead), but its coffin is of crystal' ('New Novels' 1857, 788). Assumptions of relevance force the reader to search out the narrative significance of the communicated material, implicating an unwritten plot in which all seemingly superfluous material is formed into a coherent storyline.

The effect of Collins's plot communication through unnecessary implicatures was debated in contemporary reviews, but there is no doubt that *The Dead Secret*, and specifically its style of narration, was a success. While the transparency of the 'secret' brought Collins's skill as a writer into question (*The Athenaeum* noted that 'it is doubtful how far the intentions of a novelist should be impenetrable' ('New Novels' 1857, 788)), all critics agreed that it was the style of narration that saved the novel. The success of the novel, if not as great as that of *The Woman in White*, is undisputed: popular as a serial in *Household Words*, the volume form of the novel did not sell as well as Collins had hoped, but a new edition was proposed by 1860 (Collins 1999, 163, 190).[2] In the preface to the 1861 edition of the novel, Collins directly addressed the perceived 'critical objection' to his 'construction of the narrative' (2008, 5). He wrote:

> I was blamed for allowing the 'Secret' to glimmer on the reader at an early period of the story, instead of keeping it in total darkness till the end. If this was a mistake (which I venture to doubt), I committed it with both eyes open. After careful consideration, and after trying the experiment both ways, I thought it most desirable to let the effect of the story depend on expectation rather than surprise; believing that the reader would be all the more interested in watching the progress of 'Rosamond' and her husband towards the discovery of the Secret, if he previously held some clue to the mystery in his own hand. So far as I am enabled to judge, from the opinions which reached me through various channels, this peculiar treatment of the narrative presented one of the special attractions of the book to a large variety of readers.
>
> (2008, 5–6)

This passage contains one of the few explicit references to the purposeful construction of inexplicit 'glimmer[s]' in Victorian fiction. It evidences

---

[2] Collins's use of implicature should be considered partially responsible for *The Dead Secret*'s success as a serial. The serial form naturally depends on almost immediate plot development, so as to attract the reader's attention. By immediately communicating the presence of a 'secret' to his reader, Collins catches the reader's attention without exhausting his dramatic resources; instead, his narrative indirectness provides a resolution that the story can work towards.

the presence of implicature in Collins's novels as an entertaining end in itself, rather than, as in the previous novels discussed, a means of communicating information more politely and efficiently. *The Dead Secret*'s publication precedes the vogue for sensation fiction which would result from Collins's 1860 publication, *The Woman in White*. The 'peculiar treatment of the narrative' detailed above, however, echoes the heavy use of implicature that would appear in many of the era's iconic sensation novels.

This chapter discusses implicatures that are intentionally central to mid-Victorian texts, concentrating on those in the 'sensation' school of fiction. These implicatures are, superficially, unmotivated: unlike those discussed in Chapter One, they do not seem to be motivated by social considerations such as propriety and politeness. In fact, these implicatures often exaggerate, rather than diminish, the disreputable quality of the actions which they communicate. Moreover, while supplementary characterization is sometimes effected by the implicatures discussed in this chapter, the obtrusiveness of these implicatures and the amount of textual space devoted to them is not warranted by their relatively slight impact on characterization.

These implicatures often have a metafictional function, drawing attention to the narrative voice and, many times, foregrounding its assumed omniscience (and, in conjunction, its fictionality). In these cases, the 'trick' of the narrative's subversiveness is almost more striking than the content that is being communicated subversively: the narrator is providing the reader with a puzzle to be solved, and the inferential processes involved in solving that puzzle are highlighted. While pragmatic stylisticians have noted the resulting sense of readerly collaboration in creating the story, there has been little discussion of the manner of entertainment that these salient implicatures (themselves the blueprints of the reader's expected collaboration) provide.

While the puzzles that these implicatures afford are entertaining in themselves,[3] the echoic nature of the fictional prose that tends to adopt them complicates the nature of the entertainment that the reader is experiencing. As has been discussed in previous sections of this work, echoic utterances are not always ironic but may be used for various reasons. Sensation fiction is known for plots that rely heavily on events that had previously been uncovered in newspapers (Pykett 2006, 52); sensation authors' mimicry of newspaper-style objectivity is, in the novels

---

[3] Furlong notes that 'successful interpretations of witty utterances flatter the reader in much the same way that puzzle-solving does: the more quickly he arrives at the intended interpretation and resolves the momentary quandary posed by the text, the more highly he rates his intellectual powers' (2011, 7).

discussed, often carried to a humorous extreme that results in the implicatures that the reader is called upon to piece together. In the above passage from *The Dead Secret*, the primary information is implicated through character dialogue rather than communicated through narratorial commentary. The communication of the 'secret' information's antinarratability results largely from this lack of narratorial commentary, which persists despite the vagueness of Mrs Treverton and Sarah's discussion. Because it is antithetical to communicative norms (and, more specifically, repeatedly flouts Grice's maxims of quantity and manner), the extent to which this vagueness dominates the passage takes on humorous overtones. The question is, primarily, whether this humour is intentional or simply bathetic. If it is intentional, the echoic nature of the passage then reads as ironic: the ignorance pretended to by the otherwise omniscient narrative voice becomes a transparent act, as does the ease with which the reader can infer information that the omniscient narrative voice 'cannot' provide. However, it is necessary to identify the teasing quality of these narratives before their authors' ironic intentions can be assumed. Pragmatic stylistics provides a vocabulary with which to articulate a kind of narrative tease that scholars of sensation fiction have mostly neglected: a tease dependent on salient implicatures that are only made explicit midway through, or sometimes near the end of, the novels. A discussion of specific examples of such implicatures will help to define the distinctively tongue-in-cheek manner of the genre.

After a preliminary discussion of sensation fiction, this chapter will examine the historical context of literary realism (broadly conceived) within which scholars usually situate the sensation movement, and which is often considered to have been the default mode of mid-nineteenth-century literature. Specifically, the relationship between these two movements will be discussed. It is not a new observation that they are interrelated; however, pragmatic analyses of these texts provide conclusions that are not common in scholarship on the sensation mode, and it is consequently hoped that pragmatic stylistics may be able to provide a more nuanced account of sensation's relationship with realism. In particular, the arguments presented in this chapter (and supported by the case studies) will build on Patrick Brantlinger's and George Levine's conceptualizations of narration in the sensation novel. Brantlinger's 'What Is "Sensational" About the "Sensation Novel"?' (1982) is now a classic piece of scholarship, providing definitive characterizations of sensationalism that are still valid for Levine's *How to Read the Victorian Novel* (2008). Both authors provide nuanced discussions of sensation fiction, but their analyses do not articulate the role that implicatures play in some iconic sensation narratives. In accordance with Levine's proposals, this chapter adopts a definition of sensation fiction that characterizes it as a subgenre of nineteenth-century realism: sensation fiction both participates in and self-consciously distinguishes itself from the more dominant realist mode. A discussion of the implicatures in these novels illustrates one previously unarticulated way in which sensation fiction self-consciously sets itself apart from the dominant realist mode: the obtrusive use of implicatures places an emphasis on the act of narration, calling attention to exaggerated realist conventions and so 'echoing' and exposing realist conventions *as* conventions. The metafictional emphasis on narration (often when detailing borderline antinarratable content) is the source of many narrative 'puzzles' in sensation fiction and causes the narrative to be perceived as non-serious and, at times, irreverent. These last characteristics of sensation fiction were commonly noted in contemporary reviews, and it is hoped that pragmatic stylistic analyses of these texts will shed light on this popular view of them.

The three case studies that form the remaining sections of this chapter are designed to provide evidence for these claims. As with the case studies that make up the previous chapters, those offered here are intended to demonstrate the inferential processes involved in reading these novels. More specifically, they are meant to offer evidence concerning how salient implicatures are interpreted within fictional contexts. The three novels focused on are Mary Elizabeth Braddon's *Lady Audley's Secret*, Charles Dickens's *Our Mutual Friend*, and Wilkie Collins's *Armadale*. These novels have been chosen as representative texts of the sensation movement that make prominent, sustained use of implicature in referring to the principal activities on which their plots centre. As noted previously, the salience of the implicatures in these novels disrupts the 'transparent' feeling of much classic realist narration, calling attention to the narration and encouraging metafictional readings of key passages in their narratives.

SENSATION FICTION AND LITERARY REALISM

The 1860s tradition of sensation fiction is known for having placed significantly more emphasis on detection than the fiction that preceded it. Stephen Knight notes that 'detection was a recurrent element in these first major sensational novels, and in some it can dominate' (2010, 43). Brantlinger provides an extended analysis of the extent to which sensation fiction relies on secrets and their detection, claiming that the 'best sensation novels are also, as Kathleen Tillotson points out, "novels with a secret," or sometimes several secrets, in which new narrative strategies were developed to tantalize the reader by withholding information rather than divulging it. The forthright declarative statements of realistic fiction are, in a sense, now punctuated with question marks' (1982, 1–2). In *Victorian Sensation Fiction*, Andrew Radford agrees with Knight's and Brantlinger's emphases on detection, noting that 'the typical sensation narrative has been assessed as a "novel with a secret" in which the solving of puzzles becomes a principal ingredient in its extraordinary commercial impact' (2009, 6). The element of detection which pervades sensation fiction, then, is perceived as one of the characteristics that differentiate it from more 'realistic fiction'.

While the sensation mode's emphasis on detection has been described as one of its definitive components, there is generally more scholarly attention paid to its content (which was, historically, perceived as far more 'sensational' than that of realist fiction) and to the conditions of its historical emergence. There are notable precursors (such as *The Dead Secret*) that blur the exact era to which sensation fiction belongs, but it is primarily identified with the 1860s.[4] *The Woman in White* (1860) is often described as the watershed novel of the movement (Knight 2010, 40; Law 2006, 97; Levine *How to Read* 2008, 100; Pykett 2006, 50). It was followed closely by *Lady Audley's Secret* (1861) and Mrs Henry Wood's *East Lynne* (1861) (Knight 2010, 41–2; Radford 2009, 19). Together, these three novels were perceived as defining and leading the sensation movement.

Although sensation fiction was hugely popular, it was regularly criticized for its perceived deviations from realism. This criticism tended to concentrate on sensation novels' content, claiming that much of it (such as representations of multiple murders, bigamous marriages, and hidden identities) was both immoral to depict and depicted unrealistically (Radford 2009, 2; Levine *How to Read* 2008, 102). Sensation fiction became derogatorily associated with the lower reaches of the press;[5] however, sensation authors often rebelled against the association and against the implication that the novels were lurid reading for the working classes (Knight 2010, 31; Radford 2009, 1). On the contrary, sensation authors claimed that the similarities between their stories and those in the

---

[4] After Radford writes, for instance, that 'the sensation novel burst onto the literary scene at the start of the 1860s', he notes that Winifred Hughes's *The Maniac in the Cellar* (1980) provided a 'seminal construction of a seemingly self-contained sensational decade' and that John Sutherland later perpetuated Hughes's claim (Radford 2009, 18–19). George Levine's historical blurb claims that it 'all began—the story goes—in 1860 . . . when Wilkie Collins' *The Woman in White* began weekly serialization . . .' (*How to Read* 2008, 100).

[5] Brantlinger notes that, 'disparagingly, Henry Mansel complained about the emergence of "the criminal variety of the Newspaper Novel, a class of fiction having about the same relation to the genuine historical novel that the police reports of the 'Times' have to the pages of Thucydides or Clarendon"' (1982, 10).

press were indicative of sensation fiction's faithful representation of reality (Brantlinger 1982, 10). The mode declined in popularity near the end of the decade (and critics perhaps lost interest in disparaging certain fictions as 'sensational') but it is thought to have been an important precursor to the more 'decadent' literary movements that would characterize the end of the nineteenth century.

That the sensation mode was heavily reliant on narrative secrets is generally accepted by literary scholars. However, scholars often fail to differentiate between characters' secrets that are nonetheless communicated to the reader (those which create dramatic irony, for example) and narrative secrets that keep information from the reader for a significant portion of the narrative (true omissions). Narratives of the former kind may employ the type of pronounced implicature that has been discussed here; the presence of implicatures naturally emphasizes information's secret status by communicating it inexplicitly. The novels discussed in this chapter use implicatures in this manner.

These sensation novels readily lend themselves to pragmatic analysis—that is, an analysis of how readers interpret the texts and what cues authors may provide to trigger specific interpretations of them. Pragmatic stylistics is, essentially, the study of reader inference, and it is fitting that it should be used to analyse a narrative mode in which detection is known to play a key role. Such analyses are less especially suited to the study of detective narratives that do not make obtrusive use of implicature. In novels where information is omitted rather than implicated, the reader's inferences do not usually parallel, and are not as pronounced as, those of the narrative's detective (who, like Sherlock Holmes, is often designed to impress the reader with his unusually powerful skills of deduction). When 'novels with a secret' make obtrusive use of implicature, however, the narrative is often designed to encourage the reader's inferences to parallel those of a protagonist or detective; in the absence of a detective figure, it is the reader's inferences which may be said to form the detection with which the narrative mode is closely aligned. Although he does not comment on how the presence of salient implicatures affects readers' interpretations of sensation's detection motif, Brantlinger notes the narrative responsibility acquired by the 'detective' character in many sensation novels, writing that

> The detective—in the sensation novel, often the protagonist... appears to fill the vacuum created by the at least partial abdication of authority by the narrator. Even when the conventions of third-person omniscient narration are maintained, as in *Armadale* and *Lady Audley's Secret*, once detection begins the information supplied to the reader tends to be reduced to the information possessed or discovered by the detective.
> (1982, 18)

While Brantlinger's discussion identifies the narrative role that detectives often fill in tales that rely heavily on omission of central information, his analysis does not acknowledge the possibility of the reader's 'detection' without the straightforward guidance of a detective figure; Brantlinger describes only narration that is focalized through a character. This is not what occurs in either *Armadale* or *Lady Audley's Secret*. In *Lady Audley's Secret*, the narrator's reliance on implicature to convey the primary elements of the plot begins before the reader is introduced to Robert Audley (the protagonist and eventual 'detective figure' of the narrative). Moreover, Brantlinger's comment implies that the detective figure's reflection on 'information supplied' is necessary to the coherence of the plot, in that it is needed to articulate the significance of the 'information' presented; in *Lady Audley's Secret*, the narration of Robert's reflections is in fact kept to a minimum, yet the significance of the 'information supplied' is clear to the reader. Salient implicatures are responsible for many of these narrative effects: without their articulation, it is difficult to explain how 'detection' results from the narrator's 'partial abdication of authority'.

Sensation fiction's emphasis on detection also allows it to be the perfect mode through which to explore, more generally, readers' interpretations of salient implicatures in fictional texts. In the three novels discussed in this chapter, the 'secrets' which form the key to the novels' plots are communicated only through implicature for hundreds of pages at a time. As with the implicatures explored in other chapters, readers must recognize them in order to interpret the text as coherent. Because of this, the novels (and generations of readers' interpretations of the novels) provide evidence that readers are able to follow narratives in which the central actions of the plot are communicated through implicature.

By contrast with the implicatures explored in other chapters, those discussed in this chapter call more attention to the narration of the texts than to the nature of the content which they communicate. The implicatures discussed in Chapter One, for instance, are used to ameliorate the offensiveness of the content that they communicate, and those discussed in Chapter Two emphasize the character psychology that is often also communicated in explicit language. Uniquely, the implicatures discussed here seem to function primarily as tools to emphasize the art of the text's narration. In the excerpt from *The Dead Secret* discussed in the introduction to this chapter, for instance, the characters' dialogue creates an implicature that communicates the familial importance and antinarratability of the undisclosed 'Secret', both of which relate to the content of that 'Secret'. But the more pronounced implicature that the passage creates concerns the persistence with which it does not communicate what Mrs Treverton has not told Sarah's 'master', does not communicate what Sarah has 'borne so long already', and does not communicate what Mrs Treverton dictates in her letter to her husband: while the passage narrates the act of dictating (and Sarah's writing of) the letter, it does not communicate the information within it. Everything about the characters' discussion is recorded except for the subject of the discussion, and the persistence with which this omission is repeated implicates an emphasis on narrative reticence that differs from the less obtrusive politeness implicatures discussed in Chapter One and the passages which approach free indirect discourse discussed in Chapter Two. The implicatures discussed in the previous two chapters are not communicated in so markedly inexplicit a way as the implicature which drives *The Dead Secret*; while perceived authorial intentions form a component of all recognized implicatures, the implicatures discussed here function more to illustrate the author's control of the narrative and less so other, content-related intentions the author might have for employing implicature. This teasingly, conspicuously withheld information draws attention to the author's ultimate control of what is communicated and how it is communicated. In *The Dead Secret*, the emphasis put on the text's narration calls attention to the exaggerated use of realist conventions, highlighting the fact that the ideal objectivity of realist narration has, in the sensation mode, been transmogrified into incongruous abdications of omniscience.

This discussion is partially inspired by the connection that scholars have made between what is often taken to be sensation fiction's non-serious tone and its poor moral standing. While the classic definition of sensation fiction concentrated on its 'sensational' content (Brantlinger 1982, 1; Radford 2009, 1–2), scholars have long remarked that it was more authors' treatment of this content, rather than the presence of it, that was controversial (Brantlinger 1982, 7). The discussion of impolite material in Chapter One might seem antithetical to these scholars' claims, in that it argues that it is the presence of impolite material, rather than the manner in which it is communicated, that is potentially offensive to readers. However, the two claims go hand in hand: it is the silent commentary on the conventionality of face-saving implicatures that characterizes sensation authors' treatments of serious topics as offensive. The exposure of these implicatures as conventional undermines the 'realist' objective of the works in which they are found and implicitly satirizes previous authors' attempts at presentational politeness.

The content of sensation fiction is, in practice, often hard to differentiate from that of decisively 'realist' fiction from the same era. George Levine notes that the 'sensation/realism distinction doesn't hold because the central qualities of the sensation novel—its emphasis on intrigue, its focus on behaviour beyond the bounds of ostensibly decent social order, its revelation of dirty secrets, its suspenseful registration of mysteries—are virtually always also aspects of the realist novel' (*How to Read* 2008, 102). He goes on to note that self-defined realist author Anthony Trollope's novel *The Eustace Diamonds* 'could easily pass for a sensation novel' (*How to Read* 2008, 104)[6] and that Elizabeth Gaskell's famously realist (and social problem) novel *Ruth*

> is the story of an illegitimate sexual relationship, and an illegitimate child, and while Gaskell relentlessly pursues Ruth, most particularly for allowing herself to lie about her past, the book once again depends on material that would become grist for sensation fiction.
>
> Yet even the great Victorian theorist and exemplar of moral realism, George Eliot, who criticized silly women novelists for filling their books with romance and the extraordinary, filled her novels with sensational material. We have illicit sex and baby murder in *Adam Bede* (1859) [and] violent death and quasi-adulterous behavior in *Mill on the Floss* (1860). (*How to Read* 2008, 105)

Levine's discussion exposes the content-based definition of 'sensation fiction' as problematic: as we have seen, the realist novels discussed by Levine do in fact contain 'sensational' content, so much so that the authors named used implicatures to ameliorate the offensiveness of their novels' contents. The obvious content-based similarities between the two modes also spur questions about why sensation fiction was considered fodder for criticism when more realist fiction generally was not.

Partly in recognition of the above similarities, scholars today often attribute sensation fiction's 'immoral' reputation to its non-serious tone, specifically in relation to its serious, and even controversial, subject matter. Radford notes that 'reviewers frequently branded sensation fiction the genre of emotional excess, not only for its dependency on heightened incident and unbalanced protagonists, but also for its stylistic mannerisms' (2009, 3). Brantlinger discusses how the manner of these novels fed their reputation; he explains that 'subjects were broached in sensation novels that many good Victorians thought inappropriate, and the fact that these subjects seemed not to be addressed seriously but merely "sensationally" made them all the more disreputable' (1982, 7). This perceived lack of seriousness is, essentially, what differentiated sensation fiction from more realist fiction in contemporary readers' eyes. The same failing is perceived by scholars today: Brantlinger notes that 'rather than striking forthright blows in favour of divorce law reform and greater sexual freedom, sensation

---

[6] Other scholars believe that *The Eustace Diamonds* may be a parody of the sensation mode in general and *The Moonstone* in particular (Brantlinger 1982, 15; Radford 2009, 152).

novels usually tend merely to exploit public interest in these issues' (1982, 6). Sensation fiction's perceived lack of political and moral responsibility appears to translate into a purely 'entertaining' experience and is both the source of much of the pleasure it gives readers and the source of sensation fiction's historically disreputable status.

As this work has shown, both mainstream realist and sensation fiction authors made central, salient uses of implicatures in their texts. In *Jessie Phillips*, *Ruth*, and *Adam Bede*, however, implicatures are used to introduce potentially offensive material indirectly, ameliorating (or intending to ameliorate) any offence given. In the novels discussed in this chapter, the uses of implicatures are as salient but more varied: while implicatures are used to communicate uncomfortable subject material such as bigamy and murder, they are also used to communicate characters' social identities ('who' they are, without referring to their names), girlish crushes, petty grudges, and the performance of mundane tasks (such as sending telegrams and reading newspapers). In effect, the same technique used to communicate mundane actions is also used to communicate serious and controversial issues, complicating implicatures' face-saving qualities by employing them when not required. The sensation novels discussed here echo the realist convention of face-saving implicatures, consequently ironizing them and highlighting their conventionality.

The unnecessary use of implicatures may be interpreted as metafictional commentary, but many of these implicatures also function as dysphemism, causing otherwise 'innocent' events and activities to be interpreted with suspicion. In consequence, the implicatures used to communicate central issues are often communicated through the presence of several less central implicatures that build upon one another. These high-order implicatures emphasize a narrative technique (implicature) that usually functions invisibly (that is, with readers automatically inferring the information that the implicatures are meant to communicate). In other words, implicatures which build upon one another call attention to the reader's inferential process in deducing the implicatures, highlighting the relative absence of explicit communication. This salience effectively puts a premium on the author's method of communication, emphasizing the 'style' (that is, the techniques used) in which the narrative has been written. It is the unusual overtness and number of these implicatures that lead readers to consider sensation fiction as excessive in its 'stylistic mannerisms' and to note especially the entertaining 'feeling of narrative wilfulness' and 'narrative hide-and-seek' that results (Brantlinger 1982, 14).

While Brantlinger's discussion of sensation fiction is especially articulate about the 'feeling of narrative wilfulness' that arises in readers, he only cursorily speculates as to its source. Much of Brantlinger's analysis of 'narrative wilfulness' focuses on sensation authors' uses of third-person omniscience, and specifically the temporary renunciation of it in some sensation texts. His discussion informs the one presented here, but I argue that it underestimates the pivotal role that implicatures play in these sensation narratives. Brantlinger does not distinguish between narratives that omit central information and those that use implicature to communicate it inexplicitly. His articulation of 'Braddon's narrative hide-and-seek' in *Lady Audley's Secret* is sharp: he notes that one passage of the novel's early foreshadowing seems 'abrupt, gratuitous, shocking, like its subject matter' (1982, 13), so articulating the passage's salience but not commenting on the ostensive quality of the passage, and specifically its ostensive communication of a narrative mystery. Brantlinger goes on to describe the general tenor of Braddon's implicatures, although without acknowledging that they are implicatures:

> Sensation novels involve not radically new techniques but manneristic extensions of features from earlier novels. Braddon's key jingling is a case in point. Without any consciously experimental intention, she pushes third-person omniscient narration to its logical limits. The narrator, even while foreshadowing with fatalistic implications, ceases to convey all information and begins to disguise much of it as hints, clues, hiatuses.... The central mystery, the disappearance of George Talboys, involves the same pattern. We sense that the narrator is being willful and even capricious when George and Robert view Lady Audley's portrait, but George—and the narrator—give no sign of recognition.   (1982, 14)

> At the same time that the narrator of a sensation novel seems to acquire authority by withholding the solution to a mystery, he or she also loses authority or at least innocence, becoming a figure no longer to be trusted.... From a presiding mentor, sage, or worldly wise ironist guiding us through the story as in *Middlemarch* or *Barchester Towers*, the narrative persona must now become either secretive or something less than omniscient, perhaps slipping back into the interstices of the story as unobtrusively as possible.   (1982, 15–16)

This chapter's discussion of *Lady Audley's Secret* will endorse, and build on, Brantlinger's characterizations of the narrative voice's indirect style of communication in the first paragraph excerpted above. However, I disagree with some of Brantlinger's other characterizations of the narrative voice. Brantlinger believes that the narrative voice 'disguise[s]' information when, in contrast, it shares that information with the reader. Information may be only partially given in a fictional text, but it may not be 'disguise[d]': it is either (perhaps partially) on display for the reader to perceive or is nonexistent. Characterizing the narrative voice as 'secretive' is equally problematic because it detracts from its sly and playful undertone and (again) erroneously characterizes the indirectly communicative narrative voice as withholding. If a narrative voice truly 'cease[d] to convey all information', there would be no narrative. Far from being secretive, the narrative voice echoes the cant of obtuse yet hyperbolically 'objective' report; if anything, the narrator is a 'figure no longer to be trusted' because it does not recognize secrets *as* secrets.

Brantlinger believes that sensation fiction's problematic use of omniscience 'marks a crisis in the history of literary realism' (1982, 27). He believes that the 'early, naïve development of omniscient narration in fiction breaks down partly from the intrusion of mystery into it, but partly also from the recognition of the conventional—and logically preposterous—nature of omniscience' (1982, 17). Despite Brantlinger's doubts concerning 'the secretive or somehow remiss narrator-author' in *Lady Audley's Secret* (which stem largely from his conflation of narrative omission and implicature), he characterizes sensation fiction as a subversive subgenre of the dominant realist mode, and its 'undoing [of] narrative omniscience' as indicative of this subversion (1982, 26).

In *How to Read the Victorian Novel*, George Levine characterizes sensation fiction similarly, as 'not so much an aberration from as it was a particular inflection of the dominant realist mode' (2008, 101). While his discussion of the similarities between sensation and realist fiction's content (given above) is integral to his argument, he also notes, like Brantlinger, that the 'sensation novel, particularly in Collins' hands, calls into question the epistemological authority that the omniscient narrator of most Victorian novels implies' (*How to Read* 2008, 122). Both Brantlinger and Levine, then, characterize sensation fiction as a short-lived evolution of the realist novel, claiming that narrative omniscience is perceived somewhat ironically in the sensation mode, but not articulating why.

Levine's own characterizations of realist fiction recount narrative omniscience's historical alliance with it and point towards possible explanations for the perceived differences and similarities between the way omniscience is presented in the sensation and realist modes. According to Levine, both realism and omniscient narration are dominant features of Victorian fiction, although the exact natures of both concepts are controversial and variable from author to author (*How to Read* 2008, ix, 33). Levine believes that realism 'aspires, above all, to truth-telling' (*Realism* 2008, viii). This objective necessarily complicates processes of representation: realism, Levine writes, 'makes the difficulties of the work of representation inescapably obvious to the writer; it makes inevitable an intense self-consciousness, sometimes explicit, sometimes not' (*Realism* 2008, 189). That self-consciousness motivates but also complicates 'objective' modes of writing, such as those which employ omniscient narration. Levine explains that the 'objective,' third-person mode of writing novels that tended to dominate in the nineteenth century would seem to be a way of ducking the epistemological problem. But there are inescapable authorial 'intrusions' even in the most objective and apparently unselfconscious rendering of narratives, and a great part of the history of Victorian fiction relates to the various efforts and devices by which narrators registered their self-consciousness about the partialness of *any* representation, about the threatened opacity (of the writing self) blocking real entrance into otherness. (*Realism* 2008, 8, emphasis in original)

Levine's discussion of Victorian realist fiction emphasizes authors' attempts at objectivity, and equates objectivity with 'truth-telling' (adding a moral urgency to the pursuit). However, because authors, unlike their narrative voices, are never omniscient, it is a pursuit that sets standards for itself which it cannot meet—at least not within the framework of an earnestly narrated fiction. 'Ironically', Levine writes,

> realism, the Victorian novel's primary method, whose determination to get at the truth entailed at least an overt rejection of merely literary forms, is thoroughly literary. It is so in two ways, primarily: first, it sets itself up as rejecting earlier literary representations and thus frequently re-enacts satirically aspects of more traditional literature. Satire is intrinsic to realism, and satire depends in part on knowledge of that earlier literature. (*How to Read* 2008, 12)

Following and expanding upon an influential claim by Ian Watt, Levine asserts that realist fiction must continuously break previous literary conventions in order to evoke an objective reality.[7] That 'objective reality' can be, simply, the exposure of previous literary conventions as subjective cants. Whether or not 'objective', or even new, information is presented, this effect is simulated by the reader's realization that the debunked conventions are merely conventions. Essentially, irony effects the revelation with which the realist mode is ideally associated. As Levine notes

---

[7] In his classic study *The Rise of the Novel*, Ian Watt notes that

> it is surely very damaging for a novel to be in any sense an imitation of another literary work: and the reason for this seems to be that since the novelist's primary task is to convey the impression of fidelity to human experience, attention to any pre-established formal conventions can only endanger his success. What is often felt as the formlessness of the novel, as compared, say, with the tragedy or the ode, probably follows from this: the poverty of the novel's formal conventions would seem to be the price it must pay for its realism. (2000, 13)

One of Watt's claims is that the rise of the novel correlated with the rise of literary realism; the 'fidelity to human experience' that novels are preoccupied with is also a main objective of realist fiction. While his examples include only structural conventions, his overall discussion indicates that it is the perceived lack of literary convention that allows a work to be considered more 'realistic'.

elsewhere of *Vanity Fair*, 'it creates its reality by satirizing conventional literary form' (*Realism* 2008, 195).

While both Brantlinger and Levine characterize sensation fiction as an evolution of, rather than a separate school from, realist fiction, neither considers the possibility that sensation fiction's problematic relationship with more realistic fiction might be explained by ironic elements in sensation fiction's narration. Similarly, while they both note the subversive use of omniscient narration in sensation novels, they do not specify why the 'fluid' omniscience found in sensation fiction seems subversive.

A relevance theoretical discussion of the omniscient narration found in sensation novels might help to clarify these issues. While 'fluid' omniscient narration (or, the occasional abdication of narratorial omniscience) is not found in all sensation fiction, its acknowledgement could enrich the ongoing debate concerning sensation fiction's relation to more realist fiction. The concepts provided by relevance theory allow us to articulate the implicatures which communicate the central narrative acts of these novels. These implicatures are what identify these novels' narrative omniscience as echoic: it is only with the inconsistent, incongruent use of a literary convention that it may be recognized as ironic, and consequently as both participating in and building on the realist conventions of the past.

READING FOR SUBVERSIVE MESSAGES: TONAL AMBIGUITY IN *LADY AUDLEY'S SECRET*

It is only since the 1980s that much non-contemporary critical attention has been given to *Lady Audley's Secret*.[8] This attention was largely shaped by new historicism, and the resulting scholarship concentrates almost exclusively on the cultural discourses which would have motivated Braddon's depictions of gender dynamics, insanity, class boundaries, and homosocial relations. In each case, subversive messages are often attributed to the novel.

Whether or not they attribute conscious intentions to Braddon, these readings often begin by articulating authorial intentions (however weak) that are then bolstered by biographical, cultural, and textual evidence. In effect, these readings view Braddon as a communicator and her text as a communication, and attempt to explicate various views of hers made

---

[8] Braddon's immense success during the latter half of the nineteenth century begged critical attention, and many literary critics (including Henry James) published essays on her writing.

manifest in the text. The narratorial manner of *Lady Audley's Secret* is sometimes drawn upon, in passing, as evidence of her subversive intentions.[9] In general, the emphasis on plot-related issues in *Lady Audley's Secret* has resulted in relatively little attention to the novel's narratorial style (with Brantlinger's analysis being an important exception). While Braddon's ability to represent Lady Audley 'subtly and incrementally as a crazed killer' (Knight 2010, 41) is almost universally noted, little has been said about how Braddon achieves the narrative effect of 'subtl[e] and incrementa[l]' communication. Still less has been written about how this means of communication might be tied to the (as yet unsubstantiated) subversive intent that scholars often detect.

Lady Audley's Secret is often described as one of 'the' iconic sensation novels, helping to found the mode it participated in. The novel brought Braddon literary fame and defined the rest of her career: although she wrote over eighty novels, she continued to be known as 'the author of *Lady Audley's Secret*' for the rest of her life (Taylor and Crofts 1998, vii, xi). The work was an early success: when its serialization halted with the folding of its journal, *Robin Goodfellow*, readers protested until the remainder of the serialization appeared in the *Sixpenny Magazine* (Taylor and Crofts 1998, vii). As has been indicated in the above discussion, the narrative has an unusually strong reliance on non-coded communication, using implicature to convey much of the narrative information that motivates the plot. Much of this implicature is achieved through the distanced report of narrative details, the relevance of which is uniformly unexplained. Together these details implicate a plot in which a deserted wife ('Helen Talboys', née 'Maldon') has changed her name (to 'Lucy Graham') and bigamously married the established and wealthy Sir Michael Audley (becoming 'Lucy Audley'). When her estranged first husband, George Talboys, returns from Australia, his chance encounter with his schoolmate and close friend Robert Audley (Sir Michael's nephew) places George within the social sphere of his bigamous wife, whom he has been told is dead. Lady Audley is intent on avoiding exposure and subsequently pushes George down a well with the intention of killing him. Upon the disappearance of his friend, Robert actively occupies the role of amateur detective, following various leads until

---

[9] In Richard Nemesvari's exposition of homosocial dynamics in the novel, for instance, he describes the final reinstatement of the status quo as 'so overdetermined that it can only be read as an ironic statement' (1995, 526). In her examination of 'The Discourse of Madness in *Lady Audley's Secret*', Jill L. Matus is more hesitant, writing that at 'times the narrator seems to favour Robert Audley and appears to look upon his final marriage and assumption of career with approval, but the narrative tone also encourages us to see him as misogynistic and self-righteous' (1993, 336).

'circumstantial evidence' leads him to confront Lady Audley about her guilt. As Matus notes, one 'true' secret of the novel, one of the few narrative twists not hinted at in advance, is the madness Lady Audley confesses to at the end, blaming her criminal actions on hereditary insanity (1993, 334). In an attempt to deal with her humanely (and to save his family from scandal), Robert has Lady Audley committed to a Belgian asylum. In a last narrative twist, George suddenly reappears, having fled to New York after his wife's murderous attempt. As this synopsis suggests, the novel rewards the new historicist slants with which current critics often approach it.

This section will discuss some of the most implicature-heavy passages of the novel, although the context described is built up steadily through seemingly irrelevant details mentioned on almost every page. After the title of the narrative (which entails that Lady Audley has or will develop a 'Secret'), the existence of Lady Audley's true identity is first suggested to the reader in her own soliloquy: after she ruminates about 'every clue to identity buried and forgotten—except these, except these', the reader is told that she keeps 'a ring wrapped in an oblong piece of paper' hidden under her dress (1998, 17). Lucy's rumination is in reaction to Sir Michael's marriage proposal, which is narrated on the same page. In this context, the ring (defeasibly) signals a prior marriage and, correspondingly, Lucy's bigamous intentions towards Sir Michael (she has accepted his proposal). How the reader is meant to detect that Lady Audley is George Talboys's deserted wife is less easy to articulate, partly because the communication of the information spans most of the novel, until Lady Audley confesses to having pushed him down a well. The information is partly communicated through persistent alternations between scenes which primarily follow Lady Audley and scenes which primarily follow George Talboys: these alternations are in place before any explicit connection has been made between their social spheres, so that the ostensive lack of narrative coherence between the passages implicates an inexplicit connection between the two characters. In this context, Braddon employs foreshadowing to cement the reader's expectations of the mystery that is already forming: after Robert receives a letter from Sir Michael's daughter by his first marriage, Alicia, the reader is informed that

> If any one could at that moment have told the young barrister that so simple a thing as his cousin's brief letter would one day come to be a link in that terrible chain of evidence afterwards to be slowly forged in the one only criminal case in which he was ever to be concerned, perhaps Mr. Robert Audley would have lifted his eyebrows a little higher than usual. (1998, 54–5)

Although the criminal nature of the ensuing plot is made explicit, it is telling that it is framed within a conjecture based on the mention of the future crime, the discussion of which is itself hypothetical: the narration of the future 'criminal case' is at several removes from factual report. It is not only that the information is found within a counterfactual conditional but also that it is the nonfactual information (the presence of a 'criminal case') on which the counterfactual (telling the 'young barrister' about it) of the conditional operates. Moreover, it is noteworthy that the crime already communicated through implicature (bigamy) is unmentioned, with only the mention of a 'criminal case' to indicate the serious and mysterious quality of the unfolding plot. Like the 'Secret' that is present in the novel's title (and much like the 'Secret' mentioned in the title of *The Dead Secret*), the foreshadowing explicitly communicates the mysterious quality of the plot; this emphasis on mystery alerts the reader that the narrative's incoherence is indicative of as yet 'secret' information. In effect, it acts to turn otherwise irrelevant, incongruous narrative details into ostensive communicators of the inexplicit storyline.

While narrating the 'gradual discovery—or, better, recovery—of knowledge' of Lady Audley's crime, Braddon simultaneously employs implicature to communicate Alicia Audley's attempts to ensnare her cousin Robert (Brantlinger 1982, 19). Alicia's attempts are comically transparent, and similar narrative strategies are used to communicate 'serious' and this relatively 'light' subject matter. While similar nonfactive statements are used to communicate certain events, the tone adopted is less formal and echoes the insincerity of a gossip who communicates delicate facts but, out of mock politeness, refuses to verify their truth:

> I am afraid, if the real truth is to be told, there was, perhaps, something of affectation in the anxiety [Alicia] expressed in making George's acquaintance; but if poor Alicia for a moment calculated upon arousing any latent spark of jealousy lurking in her [cousin Robert's] breast by this exhibition of interest, she was not so well acquainted with Robert Audley's disposition as she might have been. (1998, 63)

The first sentence in this passage implicates Alicia's romantic feelings for her cousin Robert: the feigned interest shown in another man is conventionally linked with coquetry, and the 'latent spark of jealousy' that she hopes to arouse is explicitly mentioned. This information's factuality is initially asserted by being linked with the tautologically insistent phrase 'real truth'. However, the individuated narrator introduces this information with a hedge ('perhaps'), and the modality of the latter half of the sentence only presupposes Alicia's attachment to Robert. The phrase 'I am afraid' is also telling, although ambiguous: while it would normally act as narratorial commentary on the 'real truth' that the sentence communicates, when used in conjunction with 'perhaps' it can be read as further hedging the information presented: the narrator is only *afraid* that Alicia may be attempting to make Robert jealous, not sure of it. In this passage, the narrator seems truly individuated, employing the first-person 'I' and exhibiting an archness foreign to the ideal neutrality found in third-person narration. The perception of that archness, however, depends on the reader's recognition of the passage's implicatures, which themselves rely on their ironic echoing of 'objective' report.

A similar mockery of the ideal of objectivity is discernible in the unexplained details which, together, implicate Lady Audley's guilt. The inability of Brantlinger's schema to explicate the effect of these narrated details is evident in his treatment of a scene in which

> Lady Audley orders her maid to send what would be, if revealed, an incriminating telegram: '"And now listen, Phoebe. What I want you to do is very simple." It was so simple that it was told in five minutes, and then Lady Audley retired into her bed-room' (ch. 7, p. 39). The central mystery, the disappearance of George Talboys, involves the same pattern. (Brantlinger 1982, 14)

Brantlinger uses this scene as an example of how the narrative 'ceases to convey all information and begins to disguise much of it as hints, clues, hiatuses' (1982, 14). He rightly compares the tactic Braddon uses to communicate Lady Audley's request with the tactic Braddon uses to communicate what happened to George Talboys (although Brantlinger does not mention that it is the accumulation of scenes such as these that implicate what has happened to George; in effect, the described scene is a microcosm of the way implicature operates in the narrative as a whole). However, Brantlinger's specification of the 'hints, clues, [and] hiatuses' Braddon uses to 'disguise' narrative information is misleading. The narrative information presented here is not, and cannot be, disguised, but is rather only partially given: Braddon's narration carries distanced 'objective' report to a satirical degree, reporting only what can be 'overheard' and providing none of the usual narrative commentary that accompanies such report. This narratorial restraint functions as a purer form of narrative objectivity than is found in most texts (including, as Brantlinger points out, that found in *Middlemarch*), but also satirizes the narrative distance that is often entangled with that objectivity. While narrative omniscience and the aim of objectivity do not necessarily entail narratorial distance, they do often consist of an element of narratorial restraint, in that 'intrusions' (in the form of commentary) are frowned upon. In many passages in *Lady Audley's Secret*, Braddon takes this philosophy to an extreme by refusing to comment on the significance of narrated acts. Although the context of this scene allows the reader to reconstruct the missing narrative information, the very information that the narrative voice omits is the most interesting and relevant to the narrative: Lady Audley has ordered Phoebe to send a telegram, requesting that Lady Audley visit London on the same day that George Talboys is expected at Audley Court. The passage implicates not only these concrete details of the plot but also the lengths to which Lady Audley will go to avoid meeting George. Instead of explicitly disclosing this significant information, the distanced narrative voice narrates only a relatively immaterial conversation that could realistically be 'overheard'. In *Lady Audley's Secret*, narrative 'distance' equates with obtuseness, and that obtuseness both satirizes the broad aims of realist fiction and highlights the 'mystery' which the passage is instrumental in (inexplicitly) dispersing.

Brantlinger's analysis does not consider that the reader draws on textual context in interpreting the passage quoted in this last excerpt, and in effect does not describe how the reader infers that 'Lady Audley orders her maid to send what would be, if revealed, an incriminating telegram'. An examination of the passage's context clarifies how that implicature is constructed (from what contextual information it arises). A few sentences prior to giving the instruction, Lady Audley introduces her request by saying, 'I want you to go to London by the first train to-morrow morning to execute a little commission for me. . . . I shall give you a five-pound note if you do what I want, and keep your own counsel about it' (1998, 61). From these sentences we learn that the task requires Phoebe's presence in London and that it is incriminating or at least delicate enough to warrant a substantial bribe. The larger context and succeeding paragraphs of the passage communicate the task's relevance to the narrative: the reader has previously been made aware that George Talboys's initial visit is expected at Audley Court the next day (1998, 58), and soon afterwards learns that a telegraph has reached Lady Audley from London, asking for her immediate presence at the side of an ill former employer (1998, 61–2). Because Lady Audley's absence will conveniently allow her to avoid George, the reader deduces that it has been prearranged by Phoebe's dispatch of a telegraph.

Other key passages in the text work similarly to evoke a picture of Lady Audley's secret guilt. George's first recognition of Lady Audley is spurred not by meeting her but by viewing her portrait while she is in London. Braddon writes that

> strange as the picture was, it could not have made any great impression on George Talboys, for he sat before it for about a quarter of an hour without uttering a word—only staring blankly at the painted canvas, with the candlestick grasped in his strong right hand, and his left arm hanging loosely by his side. He sat so long in this attitude, that Robert turned round at last.
> 'Why, George, I thought you had gone to sleep!'

'I had almost.'

'You've caught a cold from standing in that damp tapestried room. Mark my words, George Talboys, you've caught a cold; you're as hoarse as a raven. But come along.'

Robert Audley took the candle from his friend's hand, and crept back through the secret passage, followed by George, very quiet, but scarcely more quiet than usual. (1998, 72–3)

The phrase 'it could not have made any great impression on George Talboys' is clearly facetious, as the context of the passage confirms (as well as the length of time George spends in front of the portrait and the immediate physical changes witnessed in him). Brantlinger writes that 'we sense that the narrator is being willful and even capricious when George and Robert view Lady Audley's portrait'—but how does the reader sense this wilfulness? (1982, 14). The feeling of narrative wilfulness that Brantlinger identifies is most likely a result of the incongruence between the display of the narrative voice's powers of clarifying commentary in the first paragraph and the converse lack of narratorial clarification in the dialogue underneath and afterwards. As in other key passages of the text, the narrator remains playfully silent as to the factive status and significance of the assertions depicted in the latter half of the passage: whether or not George had almost fallen asleep, and whether or not he caught a cold, is never explicitly resolved; the assertions explicitly stated in these sentences hold only arrested relevance. But the information they entail—that George spent an unexpectedly long time in front of the portrait and that his voice is now hoarse—provides evidence for the reader (who has narrative context to draw upon) that George has recognized his wife. In this passage's dialogue, Robert plays the role of the unreliable commentator, voicing an obvious misconstruction of narrative information. Brantlinger's analysis does not capture the dramatic irony which arises from Robert's (and the narrative voice's) obtuseness. Robert, of course, is not privy to as much context as the reader possesses. He has not followed the scenes which sharply alternate between George Talboys and Lady Audley; more importantly, his interpretation is not subject to the conventions of fiction which allow the reader to perceive the markedness with which certain narrative details are presented. The silence with which George's response is communicated, then, not only depicts Robert's obtuse perception of the situation but also functions as a narrative joke of which Robert is the butt: he has been unable to solve a narrative puzzle which is clear to the reader.

Braddon's use of implicature extends to her depiction of the act that defines the rest of the narrative: Lady Audley's attempt to murder her husband. Unlike the previous passages discussed, it does not implicate the information which, in retrospect, it is gradually perceived to have represented; instead, it merely indicates that the primary 'secret' denoted in the novel's title has occurred. When interpreted in the context of narrative information later learned, however, the passage implicates Lady Audley's murder of George Talboys. Braddon writes:

> my lady had strolled, book in hand, into the shadowy lime-walk; so [Audley Court] had never worn a more peaceful aspect than on that bright afternoon when George Talboys walked across the lawn to ring a sonorous peal at the sturdy, iron-bound oak door.
>
> The servant who answered his summons told him that Sir Michael was out, and my lady walking in the lime-tree avenue.
>
> He looked a little disappointed at this intelligence, and muttering something about wishing to see my lady, or going to look for my lady... strode away from the door without leaving either card or message for the family.
>
> It was full an hour and a half after this when Lady Audley returned to the house, not coming from the lime-walk, but from exactly the opposite direction. (1998, 80)

After the omitted 'hour and a half' of the narrative, George Talboys disappears from the text, and, as this disappearance is sustained, the implicature asserting George's death gains strength. The above passage provides a quintessential example of implicature in that, by reducing the scene in which Lady Audley pushes George down a well to the undisclosed action of 'an hour and a half', it forces all information the reader has about the pivotal scene to be inferred from the scene's context. While the scene does not immediately implicate George's murder, the scene is physically demarcated (and rendered relevant) by the explicit mention of the passage of time, thereby manifesting its relevance to the interpretation of the overall narrative. The passage is further foregrounded by the detail with which the (unnarrated) encounter is introduced. The scene is set for the long-awaited first interaction between George Talboys and his estranged wife; after this scene is omitted, the reader is told that Lady Audley returns to the house from the opposite direction in which she had been walking—implying that something has interfered with the expected course of her walk and that something (of considerable duration) has happened. What has happened, however, is only communicated by the passage's context and by the accumulation of further speciously irrelevant details in the narrative that follows. Passages such as these are what Brantlinger likely has in mind when he refers to Braddon's use of 'hiatuses' to 'disguise' narrative information; while a hiatus is incapable of 'disguising' information, the one demarcated (by the explicit mention of a lapsed 'hour and a half') in the above passage calls attention to the information which surrounds it, characterizing it as related to the 'secret' and 'criminal case' already introduced into the narrative. Because there are eighty preceding pages on which the reader may draw, the passage reliably communicates that Lady Audley and George have just met; however, it coyly backs away from describing more than how long the meeting took. When reading passages further along in the narrative, the reader is able to recall the omission of this scene; in the context of information that the narrator later adds, it implicates that Lady Audley has killed George Talboys.

The implicatures on which the story builds continue from this point, echoing the deductions Robert makes but teasingly stopping short of the conclusions he reaches. Robert begins to suspect Lady Audley when, shortly after George's disappearance, he notices a bruise on her wrist. When asked how the bruise occurred, Lady Audley responds

> 'I am rather absent in mind, and amused myself a few days ago by tying a piece of ribbon round my arm so tightly, that it left a bruise when I removed it.'
>
> 'Hum!' thought Robert. 'My lady tells little childish white lies; the bruise is of a more recent date than a few days ago; the skin has only just begun to change colour.'
>
> Sir Michael took the slender wrist in his strong hand.
>
> 'Hold the candles, Robert,' he said, 'and let us look at this poor little arm.'
> It was not one bruise, but four slender, purple marks, such as might have been made by the four fingers of a powerful hand that had grasped the delicate wrist a shade too roughly. A narrow ribbon, bound tightly, might have left some such marks, it is true, and my lady protested once more that, to the best of her recollection, that must have been how they were made.
>
> Across one of the faint purple marks there was a darker tinge, as if a ring worn on one of these strong and cruel fingers had been ground into the tender flesh.
>
> 'I am sure my lady must tell white lies,' thought Robert, 'for I can't believe the story of the ribbon.' (1998, 91)

In introducing a discussion of Robert's deductive skills, Jennifer Carnell notes of this passage that the 'reader and Robert Audley think she has George's blood on those hands. Robert shows detective abilities, as he notices clues that no one else does, and Braddon succeeds especially in details like this because the reader follows his thoughts, sharing his investigation' (2000, 253). While Carnell's discussion aptly explains Robert's position as 'detective' in the narrative, her assertions do not address the broader narrative problem of how it is that the information presented in the above passage convinces the reader and Robert that Lady Audley 'has George's blood on those hands'. On an explicit level, Robert only notices that Lady Audley must be lying, a conclusion explicitly linked to the colour of her bruise. According to reader interpretations that are based only on the passage's explicit content, the two paragraphs lying between Robert's assertion and reassertion of this conclusion must be irrelevant; there is no explicit link made between their content and the conclusion that is attributed to Robert. Carnell's assertion that the above details are indicative of Robert's thoughts is untenable, considering that Robert has not yet begun to consider that George might have been physically harmed (two pages later he leaves for London, expecting to find George there). It would also be socially incongruous for an unrelated man to grasp Robert's aunt's hand as the details implicate: in Robert's social context and his current state of awareness, it would be a surprising mental leap for him to form such conclusions.

On a narrative level, the paragraphs are jarringly specific and detailed for an analysis of a bruise: the passage provides a suspiciously detailed speculation as to what 'might have' produced an ambiguous mark. The narrative voice abruptly pulls back from the objectivity it has supposedly practised, and encourages lurid conjectures that far surpass what their context indicates. Moreover, it is only, on an explicit level, a hypothesis that is detailed: the narration leaps from one extreme of minimal commentary to another extreme which details an unlikely hypothesis. This incongruity implicates the truth of what is being posed as conjecture: the specificity of the cause's description clashes with the vagueness expected of discussions concerning hypothetical occurrences, causing the reader to reevaluate his or her view of the description as hypothetical. In relevance theoretic terms, the space devoted to a concept that is explicitly designated as nonfactual is disproportionate. While an interpretation that includes an assumption of literariness would conclude that the passage's implicated factuality is a result of the reader's perception of the description as *deliberately* disproportionate, an interpretation that includes an 'assumption of narratorial omniscience' would be more specific, claiming that the passage is felt to be deliberately disproportionate because the omniscient communicator of the narrative would not devote such space and detail to a description that is irrelevant to the narrative (nonfactual).[10] This fictional-level attribution of narratorial (as opposed to authorial) intention allows the reader to conclude that the information itself is factual and that it is the proposed nonfactiveness of it that is facetious. The reader's assumption of narratorial omniscience, then, is capable of explaining not only why the nonfactual language of the passage seems motivated (which a reader's assumption of literariness explains) but also why it leads the

---

[10] Mary Louise Pratt believes that, in order to experience the literary aspects of a text, the reader must assume that it is literature (1977, 86). For my discussion of Pratt's work, please see the section of the introductory chapter titled 'Pragmatic Stylistics'.

reader to assume that, specifically, Lady Audley 'has George's blood on those hands'.

Like my other readings of novels, the above discussion of *Lady Audley's Secret* attempts not to interpret it in a new light but to clarify and explain existing interpretations and reader reactions to the novel. The reader interpretations assumed by the above pragmatic analysis are corroborated by contemporary reactions to the novel as well as the more recent ones discussed above. An early review in *The Morning Post* lists similar reader reactions and interpretations to the ones examined above: after claiming that the 'identity of Helen Talboys and Lucy, Lady Audley is apparent at once to the reader', the writer goes on to remark upon 'the slow and deliberate revelation of crime' ('Lady Audley's Secret' 1862, 6). This narrative revelation is the result of extended, central uses of implicature. Although the novel is judged as stylish and clever, the reviewer feels the need to point out that the 'story is unredeemed by any touch of the higher sentiments of human nature, and in this lies the grave defect of the author' (1862, 6). The perception of a deliberate humour in the narration of the plot's serious events, enacted by these same implicatures, is responsible for the lack of '[high] sentiments' attributed to Braddon; the real controversy surrounding *Lady Audley's Secret* has to do with its satirical echoing of a dominant narrative mode.

HIDDEN IDENTITIES AND SLY COMMUNICATIONS: NARRATIVE GAMES IN *OUR MUTUAL FRIEND*

Charles Dickens's relationship with sensation fiction is a matter of ongoing discussion and dispute. He was the mentor and close friend of Wilkie Collins, who, more than any other novelist, is given credit for having spurred the sensation movement (Levine *How to Read* 2008, 100; Radford 2009, 3). In fact, it was in the weekly magazine which Dickens edited, *All the Year Round*, that Collins published the seminal novel *The Woman in White*. It is often claimed that Dickens's example provided an important influence on the formation of the genre but that his work is nevertheless to be distinguished from that of the 'true' sensation authors. Although Brantlinger specifies 'the powerful influence of Dickens' as a defining characteristic of the sensation novel (1982, 2) and claims that 'Dickens set the pattern' for the sensation mode (1982, 5), he sets Dickens's work apart from other sensation fictions. For instance, Brantlinger writes that negative 'responses to the sensation novel often echo negative responses to Dickens'—in short, sensation novels are shown to 'echo'

Dickens's work, in that they are consistently characterized as alike yet categorically different (1982, 7). However, other sources indicate that some contemporary readers felt differently. Radford writes

> Was Dickens really a lowbrow sensation author masquerading as a fastidious practitioner of high art, as some declared after reading *Bleak House* (1852–53) and *The Mystery of Edwin Drood* (1870)? *Belgravia* claimed him as the 'founder' of the sensation school, while Margaret Oliphant in *Blackwood's* reviewed *Great Expectations* (1860–61) along with all the other current sensation novels, judging it markedly inferior to Collins's *The Woman in White* as a specimen of the genre. (2009, 5)

Dickens's identification with sensation fiction is demonstrated elsewhere: in *The Morning Post*'s review of *Lady Audley's Secret*, for instance, it is asserted that

> The sensation literature of this day is a variety of the school of fiction inaugurated by Mr. Charles Dickens, and which has departed from the undisciplined imaginativeness and inconsistency of his style, and assumed an elaborate symmetry in the construction of its fancies which invests the most *outré* designs with mathematical precision and realism. ('Lady Audley's Secret' 1862, 6, emphasis in original)

While there are some historical difficulties with the above assertions (as with Radford's claim that 'sensation' might have been used as a derogatory label for fiction as early as 1853), there is a persistent logic in associating Dickens's fiction with a movement he was materially involved in (considering his role as mentor and publisher to Collins). Moreover, it is interesting to note that *The Morning Post*'s characterization of the difference between Dickens's fictions and those of the sensation novelists is one of enhanced 'realism': this claim inherently contradicts conceptualizations of the sensation mode which define it primarily as less realistic than other mainstream fiction, and more particularly contradicts popular conceptions of Dickens's works as having set the stage for sensation fiction but restrained itself, remaining within the arena of the dominant, more 'realistic' mode.

Few discussions of Dickens's relationship with the sensation mode consider how the movement might have affected his own writing. While all of the scholars discussed above note his importance as an influence on sensation fiction, few scholars discuss Dickens's later work within the context of the burgeoning sensation mode. *Our Mutual Friend*, which began serialization in 1864, was written during the peak of sensation's popularity and directly after the mode had been firmly established by the first-noted sensation novels, appearing in 1861 and 1862. In the novel, Dickens makes use of an extended central implicature, which he expects the reader to comprehend during his or her ongoing interpretation of the narrative. Like the extended implicatures discussed in other sections of this chapter, the implicature discussed here is ostensibly unmotivated, largely unrelated to the content which it communicates. In effect, Dickens's non-codified communication of central narrative information imbues the narrative with a slyness reminiscent of that found in *The Dead Secret*, *Lady Audley's Secret*, and other sensation narratives.

The implicature communicates the true identity of the narrative's central character, John Harmon/Julius Handford/John Rokesmith. John Harmon is heir to a large fortune, with the one stipulation that he must marry the girl his now-deceased father chose for him, Bella Wilfer. John has been raised outside England, and upon his return he is poisoned, assumed dead, and thrown into the Thames by a sailor whom he met on his voyage home and whom he has been told he resembles. Within a day the man who poisoned John is found murdered and is declared to be John Harmon. The real John Harmon—now briefly posing as Julius Handford—decides to take advantage of his assumed death by familiarizing himself with his proposed fiancée without the pressure of being known to her as her proposed fiancé. Under the name of John Rokesmith, he establishes himself in the Wilfer family by becoming their lodger and insinuates himself into the home of the elderly couple who have inherited his money upon his (John Harmon's) supposed death. The couple, Mr and Mrs Boffin, are the late Mr Harmon's employees and responsible for what little parental care John experienced as a small child. John, under the assumed last name of Rokesmith, becomes Mr Boffin's secretary and works as his primary financial advisor until Bella proves herself worthy of becoming John's wife. He then marries her, and he eventually reclaims his identity and fortune.[11]

The narration of these events is not as straightforward as this synopsis. Much as Braddon omits the key scene in which Lady Audley pushes George down a well, Dickens begins the novel directly after the murder of the sailor has taken place. As Robyn Warhol-Down has written,

---

[11] The novel has a parallel plot line that occupies as much space as the first; it relates to the daughter of the man who found the sailor's corpse (Lizzie Hexam) and her eventual marriage to a man of much higher social rank (Eugene Wrayburn). Criticism of the novel often concentrates on one plot line or the other. While the second plot line is, functionally, as dominant as the first, one could argue that the storyline described above is intended as the primary narrative of the novel: the phrase 'our mutual friend' is explicitly linked to John Harmon (1997, 115). This discussion is preoccupied with the John Harmon narrative because its use of implicature is more central and extended. Implicature is used, however, to communicate central aspects of the Lizzie Hexam–Eugene Wrayburn narrative as well: Bradley Headstone and Eugene's silent battle over Lizzie's affections, for instance, is initially communicated through implicature (1997, 285, 387).

Our Mutual Friend is essentially a 'novel built on a secret' and in this way functions much as sensation fiction in general is assumed to (2010, 50). Beth F. Herst, in fact, discusses the protagonist's secret as a reason to categorize *Our Mutual Friend* with the sensation fiction of the era:

> Some critics of *Our Mutual Friend*, and of the other novels of Dickens's last decade, both in their own day and since, have viewed them largely in the light of the 'sensation' fiction so popular in the 1860s. And this does suggest one possible means of approaching the problem posed by Harmon and his 'plot'. The 'sensation' form, exemplified by such bestselling titles as *East Lynne* and *Lady Audley's Secret*, relied for its interest on secret guilt and domestic intrigue, bringing violence out of the safely distanced Gothic castle or underworld den and into the 'respectable' English home. With their elaborate machinery of mystery, coincidence and revelation, they placed a premium on plotting in both senses of the term, with an accompanying tendency to subordinate character to situation, larger meaning to local effect. John Harmon, with his secret return from the dead—a favourite 'sensation' device—his assorted disguises and mysteriously murdered double, could certainly qualify as a 'sensation' hero. (1990, 111)

In the above discussion, Herst uses the content of the John Harmon narrative as evidence of the novel's involvement in the sensation mode. In line with George Levine, I have argued that it is the tone rather than the content of the narrative that is decisive in assigning a subgenre to these novels. However, the 'secret guilt' that Herst identifies—which naturally accompanies plots of hidden identities—lends itself to communication through implicature and correspondingly to the type of muted dramatic irony that assumes, rather than overtly draws in, the reader's understanding of an open narrative secret.

The extended implicature concerning Rokesmith's true identity functions partially to fill the gap that is indicated at the beginning of the narrative: it allows the reader to discern John Harmon's actual whereabouts (that he has not, in fact, been mysteriously killed) but simultaneously heightens the mystery surrounding the identity of the corpse that has been found and the mystery concerning how it became a corpse. While Rokesmith's intentions concerning Bella are rendered transparent through implicature, the reader latches on to the mystery surrounding the corpse and links it with his or her perception of Rokesmith's true identity as hidden, a connection which is then complicated by the narrative's omission of any possible motivation for Rokesmith's secrecy. The implicature communicated, then, is strictly related to Rokesmith's true identity and is apparently unconcerned with the motivations underlying that hidden identity; instead, these motivations are abruptly revealed to the reader midway through the novel.[12] In this way, Dickens combines elements of implicature and sudden explication within the same narrative. His alternation between these communicative forms fulfils multiple narratorial characteristics that have been noted of sensation fiction: Brantlinger's sense of the sensation novel's 'structure of abrupt revelation' (1982, 14) and yet its 'gradual discovery—or, better, recovery—of knowledge' (1982, 19), as well as the 'exaggerated concealment of crucial data' noted by Radford (2009, 35). This section argues that Dickens's 'exaggerated concealment of crucial data' correlates with yet another general characteristic of sensation literature: the sense of narrative game playing that creates much of the fiction's non-serious tone. Regardless of *Our Mutual Friend*'s status as a sensation novel or otherwise (a taxonomic decision largely left up to the reader), it rewards discussion within the context of sensation fiction's general use of implicature to create a playful style of narrative.

The implicature communicating Rokesmith's secret identity begins with the characterization of John Harmon's death, which appears in the text before Rokesmith does. Here, Dickens's mode of communication emphasizes the information's defeasibility: the information is initially broken to the reader through a character's speech, when that character is gossiping with other members of a dinner party (1997, 27). The information about Harmon's death is later explicitly declared in a passage notable for its heavy use of ironic free indirect discourse:

> Upon the evidence adduced before them, the Jury found, That [sic] the body of Mr. John Harmon had been discovered floating in the Thames, in an advanced state of decay, and much injured; and that the said Mr. John Harmon had come by his death under highly suspicious circumstances, though by whose act or in what precise manner there was no evidence before this Jury to show. And they appended to their verdict, a recommendation to the Home Office (which Mr. Inspector appeared to think highly sensible) to offer a reward for the solution of the mystery.   (1997, 39–40)

The formal jargon, repetitive clauses, and unconventional capitalization in the passage echo the official language of a jury's verdict, exemplifying the linguistic properties of free indirect discourse. The irony found in the passage results from the discrepancy between the jury's official verdict—what has been decided as 'factual'—and the transparent (even admitted) inconclusiveness of the evidence. The passage as a whole parodies a legal system which aims to distinguish fact from unreliable evidence and which, as the ensuing implicatures communicate, suffers the consequences of its

---

[12] The Boffins' part in Harmon's duplicity is also abruptly revealed, even later in the novel (1997, 751).

ineptitude. Importantly, the jury's (and, correspondingly, the law's) failure allows for an explicit—but markedly defeasible—storyline to be created, and the ensuing implicature details John Harmon's friendly deception while leaving the 'official' storyline undisturbed for hundreds of pages. It is also noteworthy that the episode of Harmon's alleged death is, despite this ruling, still considered a 'mystery'; the passage explicitly problematizes narrative information that would otherwise be assumed.

Harmon's first alias, Julius Handford, appears a few pages before Harmon is officially declared dead. Handford first appears as an 'extremely pale and disturbed' 'stranger' who thinks he might be able to identify the corpse of the drowned man (1997, 32). Upon being questioned, the stranger readily answers that he is not from London and that he is not, contrary to his appearance at the morgue, seeking John Harmon (1997, 33). Further questioning, however, proves almost fruitless: it serves only to expose the unwillingness with which the stranger speaks of himself and of the connection he holds to the corpse he has come to see (1997, 34–5). Upon a police inspector's pressing request, he provides the name 'Mr. Julius Handford', a name whose initials match those of John Harmon's. This unsubtle hint towards the man's true identity understandably escapes the characters, who are operating in their own 'actual world' rather than in a fictional 'alternative possible world' in which every detail is interpreted as significant.[13] The matching initials of Julius Handford and John Harmon, then, provide the first instance of the dramatic irony that pervades the communication of Harmon's true identity in the narrative.

As Julius Handford's name disappears from the text, John Rokesmith's appears. Rokesmith is first presented as a newly instated lodger of the Wilfers (1997, 47). Pages afterwards, a concrete association between Julius Handford and John Rokesmith is explicitly stated, when Dickens writes that 'if Mr. Julius Handford had a twin brother upon earth, Mr. John Rokesmith was the man' (1997, 51). The sentence is the last of the chapter and is clearly intended to end the chapter portentously (the preceding sentence shows Bella thinking of Rokesmith as a 'suspicious lodge[r]'). Taken in any but the most literal sense, the final sentence of the chapter indicates the likelihood of Handford and Rokesmith being the same person. It is the conditional quality of the sentence that indicates the questionable veracity of the explicit assertion. The narrative voice is, noticeably, practising omniscience by simply claiming the possibility of a fraternal connection between the two characters; the rest of the paragraph is focalized through Bella, and there is no possibility of her knowing enough of Rokesmith's (or

---

[13] See the section of the introductory chapter titled 'Pragmatic Stylistics' for a discussion of actual worlds and alternative possible worlds.

Handford's) life to form such a conjecture. The sentence functions as a narratorial intrusion, reminding the reader of the omniscience of the narrative voice. Interestingly, then, it holds back, as the narrative voice only exercises its powers of omniscience to a seemingly moveable limit, refusing to comment as a certainty on the information it has postulated. The very arbitrariness of this limitation is what calls it into question: there is no readily apparent reasoning behind it. In this way the sentence makes manifest its more-than-explicit meaning, entailing the identical (or at least very similar) appearances of Handford and Rokesmith but implicating that they are one and the same person.

Rokesmith's character is soon rendered still more suspicious. After securing his lodgings with the Wilfers, Rokesmith continues his odd activities by approaching Mr Boffin on the street and, as a stranger, asking to become the man's secretary. A series of intentionally vague answers to Mr Boffin's reasonable questions characterizes Rokesmith as secretive, and his behaviour as incongruous in a man earnestly seeking employment:

> 'Where do you come from?' asked Mr. Boffin.
> 'I come,' returned the other, meeting his eye, 'from many countries.'
> Mr. Boffin's acquaintance with the names and situations of foreign lands being limited in extent and somewhat confused in quality, he shaped his next question on an elastic model.
> 'From—any particular place?'
> 'I have been in many places.'
> 'What have you been?'
> Here again he made no great advance, for the reply was, 'I have been a student and a traveller.'
> 'But if it ain't a liberty to plump it out,' said Mr. Boffin, 'what do you do for your living?'
> 'I have mentioned,' returned the other, with another look at him, and a smile, 'what I aspire to do. I have been superseded as to some slight intentions I had, and I may say that I have now to begin life.' (1997, 101)

Rokesmith's uninformative answers to a potential employer are coupled with his odd willingness to work for two years without pay (1997, 101). Together, they make Rokesmith's advances wholly incongruous with the expected scenario of a man seeking employment, and they indicate a hidden motivation which Mr Boffin is characterized, here, as too naive to perceive. Rokesmith's vagueness in response to questions about his identity and his past has an added effect on the reader's interpretation of the passage. Besides assigning Rokesmith hidden motivations, the vagueness of Rokesmith's answers highlights the mystery of his background, a mystery that is not indefeasibly solved until Rokesmith is explicitly revealed to be

John Harmon 258 pages later. In the context of Rokesmith's probable identification with Julius Handford (and, further, Handford's questionable relationship to and markedly possible identification with John Harmon), Rokesmith's evasiveness casts doubt upon the identity he is operating under and makes his identification or non-identification with Handford and Harmon more relevant to the overall interpretation of the developing narrative.

Rokesmith's flimsy identity is further associated with Harmon's when, in another bout of incongruous behaviour, he shows an extreme reaction to an unexpected use of John Harmon's name. Bella Wilfer is sitting with the Boffins when Rokesmith is first introduced to Mrs Boffin. Dickens writes that, upon Rokesmith's arrival, Mrs Boffin

> gave him a good day, and he bestirred himself and helped her to her seat, and the like, with a ready hand.
>
> 'Good-bye for the present, Miss Bella,' said Mrs. Boffin, calling out a hearty parting. 'We shall meet again soon! And then I hope I shall have my little John Harmon to show you.'
>
> Mr. Rokesmith, who was at the wheel adjusting the skirts of her dress, suddenly looked behind him, and around him, and then looked up at her, with a face so pale that Mrs. Boffin cried:
>
> 'Gracious!' and after a moment, 'What's the matter, sir?'
>
> 'How can you show her the Dead?' returned Mr. Rokesmith.
>
> 'It's only an adopted child. One I have told her of. One I'm going to give the name to!'   (1997, 116)

It should be noted that Harmon's supposed death is well known by this point in the narrative (it has been, as the opening chapters of the book indicate, the talk of the town), and there is no narrative incongruity in Rokesmith's knowledge of Harmon's death. But the extremity of Rokesmith's reaction is sufficient enough to be registered by another character. His unusual reaction to Mrs Boffin's use of 'John Harmon' strengthens an implicature that has formed over one hundred pages; the flimsiness and incongruity of characterization manifested by John Rokesmith and Julius Handford are explained by the hidden identity they have in common: John Harmon. A relevance theoretical account of this extended implicature is straightforward: salient incongruities in the text communicate ostensively to the reader that the primary meaning of certain passages is not explicit. These incongruities then motivate the reader to reconsider these passages' relevance in light of their narrative context. The collapsed identity of John Harmon, Julius Handford, and John Rokesmith provides the most relevant 'solution' to these narrative incongruities by simultaneously being the most comprehensive and the least difficult solution to reach. The cementation of the implicature in the reader's mind, then, brings with it a solution to the narrative puzzle, accompanied by the enjoyment inherent in puzzle solving and the effects of dramatic irony. In consequence, the central implicature in *Our Mutual Friend* must be understood for substantial aspects of the narrative experience to be felt.

In its contemporary review of *Our Mutual Friend*, the *London Review* complained that the revelation of Rokesmith/Harmon's history was awkward. 'Young Rokesmith, or Harmon', writes the reviewer, '*tells himself* his own previous history, in a sort of mental soliloquy (in which a long series of events is minutely narrated), evidently for no other purpose than to inform the reader' (Collins 1971, 456, emphasis in original). This abrupt revelation of narrative events (which dispels the mystery of 'how' Harmon became Handford and Rokesmith) is introduced by a few last instances of the extended implicature (1997, 359, 360), and the first explicit linking of all three names does not generate any additional contextual effects (1997, 366). While Dickens's working notes indicate that he still meant to 'work on to possessing the reader with the fact that he [Rokesmith] is John Harmon' (indicating that Dickens was aware his implicatures might not have been detected by all readers), his most explicit discussion of the Harmon plot suggests otherwise (Cotsell 1986, 175).[14] This discussion forms the opening of Dickens's postscript to the novel:

> When I devised this story, I foresaw the likelihood that a class of readers and commentators would suppose that I was at great pains to conceal exactly what I was at great pains to suggest: namely, that Mr. John Harmon was not slain, and that Mr. John Rokesmith was he. Pleasing myself with the idea that the supposition might in part arise out of some ingenuity in the story, and thinking it worth while, in the interests of art, to hint to an audience that an artist (of whatever denomination) may perhaps be trusted to know what he is about in his vocation, if they will concede him a little patience, I was not alarmed by the anticipation. (1997, 798)

Dickens's explanation of what he was 'at great pains to suggest' offers rare evidence of a Victorian author consciously privileging implicature over more explicit communication. The authorial intentionality that Brantlinger withholds from Braddon is impossible to withhold from Dickens, who explicitly discusses his intentional use of implicature in the postscript.[15]

---

[14] Dickens's working notes were necessarily truncated, and the least favourable interpretation for my argument is provided in the parentheses above. The note concerns a chapter in which Harmon is yet again disguised as another person; Dickens could be referring to the need to indicate that particular disguise, and not the two others which Harmon has previously adopted.

[15] Brantlinger claims that Braddon 'pushes third-person omniscient narration to its logical limits' 'without any consciously experimental intention' (1982, 14).

Interestingly enough, Michael Cotsell notes that it 'has been remarked... that Dickens had before him Wilkie Collins's defence of such a method of plotting in the preface to the 1861 edition of *The Dead Secret*' (1986, 283). Cotsell goes on to mention that 'Collins made a similar defence in the preface to *No Name* (1862)' (1986, 283). Dickens would certainly have been familiar with both of these novels: in 1861 *The Dead Secret* was published in Dickens's journal *Household Words* (Collins *Dead Secret* 2008, xxvi), and in 1862 *No Name*, like *The Woman in White* before it, was published in his journal *All the Year Round* (Collins *No Name* 2008, xxii). Dickens's dismissive reference to the 'denomination[s]' of art, then, may be interpreted as a show of solidarity with his mentee Collins and other sensation authors (as well as a possible excuse for participating in a commercially successful subgenre). Regardless of the official 'denomination' of *Our Mutual Friend*, its tone was demonstrably influenced by the sensation fiction that formed its historical context.

REPRESENTING FATE IN FICTION: ARTIFICIAL PLOTTING IN *ARMADALE*

By 1863, Wilkie Collins had established himself as a leading writer of the era and, arguably, the leading writer of the sensation movement. According to both contemporary and modern scholars, his 1860 publication of *The Woman in White* 'launched the fashion for "sensation fiction"', and Collins's new-found fame guaranteed him years of work (Law 2006, 97). The publication of *Armadale* was one result. The publishing firm of Smith & Elder had offered £500 for the rights to *The Woman in White*—a sum rejected by Collins and subsequently proven to be laughably low by the novel's watershed success. Recognizing their earlier mistake, in 1861 Smith & Elder eagerly offered Collins £5,000 for the rights to an as yet unwritten novel. Due to other writing engagements and illnesses, Collins took two years longer on the novel than Smith & Elder had foreseen; in November 1864, however, he turned in the first instalment of *Armadale*.

The novel's complicated plot was another factor in the delay of its publication. In November of 1863, Collins was 'getting ideas—as thick as blackberries—for another book' (Collins 1999, 238), but by January he had realized that constructing the plot would take him longer than he had expected, and he wrote to his mother that it was 'a very difficult job this time' (Collins 1999, 244). Unlike many other authors, Collins fully laid out the plots of his novels before beginning serialization; in 1865, he explained to a fan that

> the great stages of the story, and the main features of the characters, invariably lie before me on my desk before I begin my book. In the story

I am now writing ('Armadale'), the last number is to be published several months hence—and the whole close of the story is still unwritten. But I know at this moment who is to live and who is to die—and I see the main events which lead to the end as plainly as I see the pen now in my hand—as plainly as I see the ground laid, months since, in the published part of the story, for what (if I am spared to finish it) you will read months hence.

(Collins 1999, 259)

Collins's description of his writing practices emphasizes the careful construction of his plots and explains the year-long interval between his initial structuring of the novel and the appearance of its first instalment in the *Cornhill*.

Armadale contains a plot that justifies the extended time Collins spent constructing it. Winifred Hughes famously labelled it 'one of the most over-plotted novels in English literature'; its plot is certainly one of the most complicated and tortuous in Victorian fiction (1980, 155). The greater part of the novel involves the consequences of an embedded story, one that the critic Peter Thoms refers to as the 'inherited story' (1992, 116). The inherited story is first communicated to the reader as it is narrated by Allan Armadale on his deathbed, to a witness charged with penning the story for Armadale's son (also named Allan Armadale), so that he may read it when he turns twenty-one. The narrating Allan Armadale was born Allan Wrentmore, christened after a wealthy relative of his father named Allan Armadale. When Wrentmore is twenty-one, he receives a letter from this same relative, explaining that he has disinherited his own son (another Allan Armadale) and that if Wrentmore adopts the last name of Armadale, he will make him heir to his West Indian property. Wrentmore agrees, and throughout the rest of the text is also referred to as Allan Armadale. When this Armadale agrees to his mother's suggestion that he marry the beautiful daughter of a wealthy English family, the original Armadale's son impersonates the new Armadale and, with the help of the daughter's devious maid, marries the daughter first in revenge. The new Armadale, enraged by the loss of his expected wife, joins the crew of a boat on which the other Armadale is voyaging and locks him in an inner cabin when the boat sinks during shipwreck, effectively murdering him. The widow returns to England to give birth to a son (another Allan Armadale), while the surviving Allan Armadale (the one narrating the 'inherited' story) marries a woman of Afro-Caribbean descent and fathers a last Allan Armadale. The narrator Armadale dies within a few years of his son's (and the other Allan Armadale's) birth, but leaves the letter communicating the inherited story along with a warning to 'avoid the widow of the man I killed—if the widow still lives. Avoid the maid whose wicked hand smoothed the way to the marriage—if the maid is still in her service.

And more than all, avoid the man who bears the same name as your own' (1989, 56). The rest of the plot involves the unwitting realizations of the actions warned against and their apparently fated consequences. The son of the once-narrator Armadale is maltreated and leaves home at an early age, assuming the name Ozias Midwinter. He is harshly treated throughout his early life as a vagrant and develops a nervous, if worldly, disposition. Having not yet received the letter his father wrote him, he happens to fall ill in a town where the other Allan Armadale and his mother live. Midwinter is nursed back to health by this new Allan, who is open and friendly but naive to the point of stupidity. The two become close friends. When Midwinter turns twenty-one, he receives his father's letter and becomes terrified of bringing fated harm upon Allan by remaining near him. He enlists only the confidence of the Armadales' close family friend, Mr Brock, who insists that Midwinter's warm feelings for Allan can do nothing but good for him and that Midwinter's fears are empty superstitions.

When Allan's mother dies, Midwinter and Allan take a sailing voyage, and in their travels they end up spending a night aboard the shipwreck that Allan's father died in. While asleep on the wreck, Allan has a dream that Midwinter subsequently interprets as an omen. After seeing a figure that Midwinter (and the reader) interpret as Allan's drowned father, Allan is shown shadowy scenes involving a man and a woman. Midwinter interprets these images as warnings of pivotal scenes in Allan's future life.

Midwinter is eventually shown to be the man in Allan's dream, and 'the maid whose wicked hand smoothed the way to the marriage' is shown to be the woman. Only twelve years old when she helped Allan's mother wed the wrong Armadale, Lydia Gwilt is still a relatively young woman (and looks younger) when Allan and Midwinter are both twenty-one. Having previously extorted money from Allan's mother while she was alive, Gwilt decides to con Allan (who has never heard of her) into marrying her when he unexpectedly succeeds to a large property. Gwilt, hired by a neighbouring family as their governess, ultimately fails in seducing Allan after his attempts to learn more of her history take him to a notorious house in London. Midwinter, however, falls in love with Gwilt, and the two marry after she uncharacteristically reciprocates his love. After Midwinter tells Gwilt his real name (and signs the marriage registrar as 'Allan Armadale'), she plots to acquire the other Allan's wealth by posing as his widow after killing him. After a few failed and detected attempts to kill Allan, she poisons herself, and Midwinter's fears concerning Allan are finally laid to rest as he reinterprets the dream's omens as warnings for him to stay near and protect Allan.

While the above paragraphs outline (a much reduced synopsis of) the novel's plot, they do not communicate narrative information in the same style as it is communicated in the novel.[16] Essentially, *Armadale*'s entire plot is derivative of the 'inherited' story's warnings: for Midwinter to avoid Allan, Allan's mother, and Allan's mother's maid. For much of the novel, narrative information is continuously (if at times implicitly) related back to this original warning, and is represented as pertaining to the overall narrative only if it is represented as pertaining to the narrator-Armadale's letter. Although the novel is coloured with hidden identities, shipwrecks, seduction, murders, attempted murders, bigamy, and spying, it is essentially Allan's, Midwinter's, and Gwilt's proximities to each other that propel the plot and create the possibility that Midwinter's superstitious fears will come true. Consequently it is dramatic irony that drives the reader's interest: for most of the novel, none of the three characters is fully aware of each other's true identity and the foretold disastrousness of their proximity. The 'fated' quality of these consequences is teasingly played out in Collins's sustained use of implicatures to introduce Midwinter and Gwilt into the text. Their introductions are the basis of the ensuing plot as well as of the realization of the narrator-Armadale's warnings. In this way, primary aspects of *Armadale*'s plot are communicated through sustained implicature, and Collins relies on the defeasibility of implicatures to create suspense regarding whether the narrator-Armadale's fears will be realized. Although the reader must read Midwinter's and Gwilt's implicated appearances as certain in order to make sense of the emphasis placed on (and space devoted to) discussion of their identities, the defeasibility of implicatures allows Collins to keep plot twists in reserve, a technique which he uses in communicating more peripheral aspects of the plot. In *Armadale*, the possibility of the implicatures' defeasibility is highlighted by character dialogue, and Collins's continual strengthening (and eventual confirmation) of his most central implicatures lends a teasingly deterministic tenor to the narration of events.

While contemporary reviews of the novel were generally mixed, Collins's execution of *Armadale*'s complex plot was generally admired. The *Spectator* wrote that Collins had 'raised "plot interest" to the rank of a science' (Page 1974, 150) while the *London Quarterly Review* noted of Collins that

> He is a pure story-teller, spending comparatively little care on anything but his plot; but in his own department he is unrivalled. There is no one who, with more consummate skill, can weave an exciting tale out of the most slight and unpromising materials, leading his reader on from point to point with ever-growing interest, concealing the mystery on which the whole

---

[16] This synopsis may appear lengthy, but the convoluted nature of the plot is such that it cannot be shortened further.

depends till the proper time for disclosure comes, and, meanwhile, ever dangling it before the eye with an art that tantalizes even while it stimulates the curiosity. (Page 1974, 156)

One of my aims is to clarify seemingly oppositional statements such as the one given in the last sentence of this quotation—this section will argue that the mystery of *Armadale* is at no point truly 'conceal[ed]' and that it is implicature which allows Collins to create the 'dangling' effect which 'tantalizes' the reader. However, this quotation is also an example of reviewers' generally mixed feelings about Collins's plots: while they admired the skill with which he could 'weave an exciting tale', they often derided his tendency to spend 'comparatively little care on anything but his plot', and more often than not did not appreciate its content. The *Saturday Review*, for instance, wrote of *Armadale*'s plot that 'it is subtle and well-sustained, and the unity of purpose and aim which pervades it is very perceptible' but objected that without 'the incidents of the plot, the characters in *Armadale* would be very wearisome' and that there 'is such a thing as economy in the free use of improbabilities, . . . the story of *Armadale* hinges almost entirely on miraculous combinations, the arithmetical chances against which are simply infinite' (Page 1974, 153).

The *Athenaeum* was less generous, writing that those 'who make plot their first consideration and humanity the second,—those, again, who represent the decencies of life as too often so many hypocrisies,—have placed themselves in a groove which goes, and must go, in a downward direction, whether as regards fiction or morals' (Page 1974, 146). The *Athenaeum*'s moral objections are generalized to the sensation mode: the writer initially characterizes *Armadale* as a '"sensation novel" with a vengeance' (Page 1974, 146) and accuses Collins of belonging 'to the class of professing satirists who are eager to lay bare the "blotches and blains" which fester beneath the skin and taint the blood of humanity', 'without any such genuine motive as led formerly Hogarth and latterly Mr. Dickens not to show a horror without a suggestion towards its cure' (Page 1974, 147). The author of the review appears to link Collins's emphasis on plot construction (as well as the sensation mode as a whole) with satiric tendencies that are devoid of moral purpose. In short, the plot of *Armadale* is portrayed as unnecessarily 'ugly', to use the term of the *Saturday Review* (Page 1974, 155).

Reviewers' portrayals of Collins's plotting as the sole asset of *Armadale* may have fed contemporary and ongoing perceptions of the novel as unusually constructed and artificial. Sue Lonoff, for instance, notes more generally that the '"good things" in Collins's fiction are his taut, suspenseful plotting, his skill at construction, and his effective blend of realism and sensationalism' (1982, 50). According to Lonoff, however,

Collins's 'skill at construction' becomes overbearing in *Armadale*; she writes that

> *Armadale* suffers from an excess of contrivance. The mechanics of the plot are obtrusive, and while Collins is ingenious, he is also overzealous; he strains for effect, heaps ploy on ploy, supplies too many cues and warnings. Still, the games within his novels can be highly effective, especially when he combines them with strategies that engage the reader as an active participant. (1982, 120–1)

It is telling that, where Lonoff characterizes the narrative voice as supplying 'too many cues and warnings', Brantlinger notes 'the unobtrusiveness of the narrator' in *Armadale* and his occasional 'abdication of omniscience' (1982, 18). These oppositional claims are both warranted: as will be shown in close readings of *Armadale*, implicatures and character dialogue repeatedly communicate narrative information concerning Midwinter's and Gwilt's identities and pasts (as well as other, more peripheral narrative detail)—information that the narrative voice conspicuously does not comment on. It is the narrative voice's marked break from omniscience that communicates the presence of an implicature to the reader. Collins's 'cues and warnings', however, are part of why many scholars feel that '*Armadale* suffers from an excess of contrivance'. Shortly after discussing Anthony Trollope's claim that he could 'never lose the taste of the construction' when reading a Collins novel (qtd. in Hughes 1980, 138),[17] Hughes claims that Collins believed in two fundamental structures for novels: 'the novel in which everything is hinted at beforehand and that in which everything is found out afterward. In the first half of *The Woman in White*, as in *Armadale*, the future impends ominously and is partially foreshadowed' (1980, 138–9). The narrative voice's evident omniscience and its superficially unwarranted breaks from it, then, are a large part of the artificial effect of *Armadale*: the breaks from omniscience render the narrator's ability to foreshadow the future problematic, emphasizing the fictionality of the omniscience displayed.

Peter Thoms believes that the artificiality other scholars have attributed to *Armadale* is intended rather than a failure of the author's skill. Thoms writes that in '*Armadale* Collins emphasizes the artificiality of the narrative

---

[17] The rest of Hughes's quote from Trollope explores the general feeling that many scholars have about the perceived artificiality of Collins's work: 'the construction is most minute and most wonderful. But I can never lose the taste of the construction. The author seems always to be warning me to remember that something happened at exactly half-past two o'clock on Tuesday morning; or that a woman disappeared from the road just fifteen yards beyond the fourth milestone. One is constrained by mysteries and hemmed in by difficulties' (qtd. in Hughes 1980, 138).

sequence (with its coincidences and allusions to fate) to suggest Midwinter's status as a mere character trapped within an impersonal story' (1992, 128). The end of the novel sees Midwinter empowered by the narrated events: he both recognizes the existence of fate (which the novel seems to endorse) and realizes that it does not equate to a complete inability to control the consequences of his actions. The artificiality of the narrative, then, mimics Midwinter's feelings about the pre-scripted nature of his life, evoking a deterministic narrative world in which characters cannot truly act as free agents, even within their narrative plane. Brantlinger also links the artificial quality of the narrative with the explicit discourse on fate within the book, writing that because 'of the dream and the heavy doses of coincidence, everything in *Armadale* seems to be laden with a preternatural—if not quite supernatural—significance' (1982, 17–18).

The following close readings are meant to bolster Thoms's and Brantlinger's assertions, and show that the sustained implicatures which Collins employs help to create the 'artificial' quality of his narration. Collins's implicatures rely heavily on the dominant use of narratorial omniscience in the novel, in that he uses breaks in omniscience to make the implicatures salient to the reader. His inconsistent use of omniscience breaks the realist convention of (relatively) unobtrusive narration, highlighting the fictionality of the narrative and, in association, its 'plotedness'. As a piece of fiction, the evolution of the plot is necessarily pre-scripted, and Collins brings the reader's attention to the story's fictional status in order to parallel Midwinter's concerns about his fate. Because this fate has been communicated through warnings and sinister omens, the defeasible qualities of the implicatures propel the narrative, engaging the reader's interest in whether or not Midwinter's and Allan's fates will be overturned and the implicatures voided.

Ozias Midwinter's identity is rendered questionable, and his association with the narrator-Armadale's son implicated, with his first appearance in the text. After the 'inherited story' has been presented in a fifty-eight-page prologue, the first book of the novel opens with a chapter titled 'The Mystery of Ozias Midwinter' (1989, 59). Just as the 'secret' mentioned in the title of *Lady Audley's Secret* characterizes Lady Audley as secretive and spurs the reader to detect her secret, the 'mystery' attributed to Midwinter (ambiguously indicating either a mystery surrounding his identity or a mystery in his keeping) characterizes Midwinter as mysterious and spurs the reader to detect a mystery concerning him. After this introduction, however, the narrative is unexpectedly focalized through Mr Brock and concerns only Allan and his mother; Midwinter is first mentioned under his alias (and the name he continues to be referred to as) ten pages later

(1989, 69). In the interim, an account is given of a newspaper advertisement that appeared five years prior, publicizing the disappearance of an Allan Armadale who is roughly the same age as the Allan Mr Brock knows and who Mrs Armadale insists is of 'Another family, and other friends'—although she mysteriously refuses to explain her knowledge of him (1989, 64). The narration then omits five years, and Midwinter's appearance in the village is recounted.

The initial description of Midwinter notes that he is 'young' and that his 'tawny complexion, his large bright brown eyes, and his black beard, gave him something of a foreign look' (1989, 67). It is soon established that Midwinter is roughly the same age as Allan (1989, 74), and Midwinter's 'brown fingers', 'bright brown eyes', 'yellow face', and 'rough black beard' (1989, 73) are recounted repeatedly along with, again, his 'tawny' complexion (1989, 73, 98) and 'brown hands' (1989, 98). This emphasis on Midwinter's 'tawny' complexion recalls the extensive description given of his beautiful Afro-Caribbean mother in the prologue, the one other character whose physical description involves primarily discussion of skin tone (1989, 12, 23, 24, 27, 34, 35). The possibility of Midwinter's racial difference (and, specifically, a difference that identifies him with the Allan Armadale who has an Afro-Caribbean mother) is reemphasized when a second advertisement appears, noting that 'Twenty Pounds Reward will be paid to any person who can produce evidence of the death of ALLAN ARMADALE, only son of the late Allan Armadale, of Barbadoes [sic], and born in Trinidad in the year 1830' (1989, 88). It is noteworthy that the only descriptors of the missing Armadale concern his lineage and the place where he was born (implicating, non-intrusively, his potential racial difference). Descriptors that would not indicate Midwinter's identification with the missing Armadale in real life implicate just that when presented within a fictional context: while it would be ludicrous to assume, outside fiction, that one person of a darker complexion may secretly be another person who is likely to have a darker complexion, the presumed relevance of all presented narrative information in fictional, omnisciently narrated texts dictates that the reader assume exactly that.

The reader's interpretive process is mimicked and ridiculed by Mrs Armadale's reaction to the advertisements and Midwinter's appearance in the village. Mrs Armadale is consistently portrayed as 'obstinately and fretfully uneasy on the subject of her son'; until Midwinter's appearance, the reader's interpretations of events do not correspond with Mrs Armadale's, whose views are often overly fearful and pessimistic (1989, 66). The defeasibility of the implicature concerning Midwinter's hidden identity is then highlighted when Mrs Armadale is noted to have 'passionately declared that the vagabond Armadale of that advertisement, and the vagabond Midwinter at the village inn, might, for all she knew to the contrary, be one and the same' (1989, 77). This statement creates one of the many narrative 'games' Lonoff identifies in *Armadale*: although Collins has emphasized the defeasibility of the implicature by explicitly attributing the resultant inference to a character whose perspective is consistently unreliable, he continues to strengthen the implicature. Midwinter is shown abruptly leaving the village in a 'violent hurry' directly after reading the newspaper with the advertisement concerning his death (1989, 89), and, upon turning twenty-one, is shown with the letter the narrator-Armadale wrote in the prologue (1989, 102). One page later, Midwinter is referred to as 'the inheritor of the fatal Armadale name'. The ensuing chapter explicitly clarifies his hidden identity and past life. After drawing attention to the defeasibility of the implicature, then, Collins explicitly confirms it, teasingly leading the reader back to the determinism that has been debated in character dialogue.

Lydia Gwilt's introduction into the narrative is, in many ways, a prolonged version of the revelation that Midwinter is the missing Armadale. In her introduction to the novel, Catherine Peters notes that 'the deliberately delayed and carefully prepared first appearance of Miss Gwilt [takes place] more than a third of the way through the book' (1989, ix); while this is technically false,[18] the first appearance of Miss Gwilt that does not communicate her identity through implicature is indeed as delayed as Peters indicates. Lonoff notes that Miss Gwilt's youthful appearance 'prolongs the riddle of her true identity for hundreds of pages' (1982, 120), explaining that

> The riddle is highly complex. Her first appearance in Book One, as a heavily veiled woman who attempts to extract money from Allan's mother, and her second, as an attempted suicide, are conundrums in themselves. Her identity becomes clear to the reader at the time she first exchanges letters with her confidante, Mother Oldershaw, but her mysterious past is not revealed until the fifteenth chapter of Book Three. Meanwhile, the characters are variously aware of her scheme and her identity, and some, like the two Allans, never perceive the solution that Collins gives the reader.
> (1982, 255)

Lonoff's description illustrates the fragmented nature of what constitutes a 'true identity': while Miss Gwilt's identity as 'the maid' is clarified on page 83, she is first named in Mother Oldershaw's correspondence with her (1989, 189) and, as Lonoff indicates, her past life is not narrated until

---

[18] Miss Gwilt appears within the first tenth of the novel, and of course is referred to in the prologue as 'the maid whose wicked hand smoothed the way to the marriage' (1989, 56).

late in the novel (1989, 632). For the purposes of Collins's discourse on fate, however, it is Miss Gwilt's identity as Mrs Armadale's maid that is important.

The implicature that communicates the maid's presence is sustained, rather than confirmed, because it is not immediately made explicit that the same woman who extorts money from Mrs Armadale (explicitly identified as the maid) appears again in the novel. The first description of Miss Gwilt is focalized through Mr Brock, when he is

> accosted in the village by a neatly-dressed woman, wearing a gown and bonnet of black silk and a red Paisley shawl, who was a total stranger to him, and who inquired the way to Mrs. Armadale's house. She put the question without raising the thick black veil that hung over her face. Mr. Brock, in giving her the necessary directions, observed that she was a remarkably elegant and graceful woman. (1989, 81)

This woman is almost immediately identified as Mrs Armadale's previous maid (1989, 83) and as antagonistic in her extortion of money from Mrs Armadale. However, her name is teasingly withheld from the reader; when pressed to divulge it by Mr Brock, Mrs Armadale answers:

> 'The name I knew her by,' she said, 'would be of no use to you. She has been married since then—she told me so herself.'
>
> 'And without telling you her married name?'
>
> 'She refused to tell it.' (1989, 83)

This namelessness is carried forward into the woman's next appearance, in which she jumps ship in a suicide attempt, only to be saved by a man (Arthur Blanchard) who then falls ill, dies, and instigates the chain reaction that ends in Allan's improbable inheritance. In popular reports of the incident, she is described as 'neatly dressed in black silk, with a red Paisley shawl over her shoulders, and she kept her face hidden behind a thick veil. Arthur Blanchard was struck by the rare grace and elegance of her figure' (1989, 92). The woman's description is rendered pointedly identical to that of Mrs Armadale's former maid, but the lack of an explicit identification with the other woman renders the ensuing implicature defeasible. This lack of explicit identification is emphasized by the narrative voice: 'Who was the woman? The man who saved her life never knew. The magistrate who remanded her, the chaplain who exhorted her, the reporter who exhibited her in print—never knew' (1989, 94). The defeasibility implied by the woman's namelessness is made explicit in a discussion in which Mr Brock and Midwinter realize that the woman who extorted money from Mrs Armadale and the woman who caused Blanchard's death have identical descriptions:

'Can it be the same?' [Midwinter] said to himself, in a whisper. '*Is* there a fatality that follows men in the dark? And is it following *us* in that woman's footsteps?'...

'My young friend,' [Mr. Brock] said kindly, 'have you cleared your mind of all superstition as completely as you think?... Let your own better sense help you; and you will agree with me, that there is really no evidence to justify the suspicion that the woman whom I met in Somersetshire, and the woman who attempted suicide in London, are one and the same. Need an old man, like me, remind a young man, like you, that there are thousands of women in England, with beautiful figures—thousands of women who are quietly dressed in black silk gowns with red Paisley shawls?' (1989, 125–6)[19]

The defeasibility emphasized here illustrates the dependence of the implicature upon its fictional context: as with the implicature indicating Midwinter's hidden identity, the implicature concerning the maid's description would prove ludicrous if attempted in a nonfictional context (there would have been, truly, 'thousands' of women who matched the description of Lydia Gwilt). It is only within fiction, and specifically within omnisciently narrated fiction, that the length of the discussion devoted to this possibility may be interpreted as evidence of its factuality, because its factuality would prove most relevant to the narrative. But, despite Brock's logical objections to the implicated information (which function like Mrs. Armadale's perverse endorsement of an implicature, highlighting the defeasibility of it), the implicature is still recognized and continues to strengthen as the text progresses. Mrs Oldershaw's letter identifies the name 'Lydia Gwilt' with the maid who aided Mrs Armadale's marriage (1989, 189–90), and Mr Brock's coincidental sighting of 'the woman with the red Paisley shawl' as she is discussing Allan Armadale with a woman who matches Mother Oldershaw's description strongly links the various facets of Gwilt's identity together (1989, 250–1). In the case of Lydia Gwilt, Collins does not rely on omniscient third-person narration to confirm the implicature's verifiability; instead, Brock's observation of Gwilt and Mother Oldershaw begins a novel-length trend in which pivotal information is communicated through character dialogue and first-person narration, allowing for a continuance of the dramatic irony that was effected by the early use of implicature.

In *Armadale*, then, Collins's sustained use of implicatures institutes playful narrative games, teasing the reader and highlighting the dramatic

---

[19] Interestingly, this point is one of the red herrings of the novel, in which Collins does employ a plot twist. While Gwilt's participation in both passages is later confirmed explicitly, the second-order implicature concerning her identity here is that she purposefully caused Blanchard's death. This is later denied in the first person by Miss Gwilt, which voids the implicature.

irony that engages the reader's interest. The implicatures Collins uses evoke the artificial, constructed feeling common to sensation novels, emphasizing the narrative art of the text. In *Armadale*, however, the over-constructed feeling of the narrative also echoes the novel's themes, and specifically Midwinter's preoccupation with his questionable agency. The salient artifice of the narrative highlights instead the author's agency, exposing the necessary personality behind all texts (including those which are posed as objective). The dramatic irony which propels the narrative necessarily undercuts the realist endeavour: as Hughes notes, more 'than any other sensation novel, *Armadale* depicts an entire populace down on its knees before its neighbours' keyholes, prying into their unsavory secrets.... but in spite of the unbridled curiosity, no single character ever finds out the entire story' (1980, 158). Both the content and narration of *Armadale* illustrate that the realist endeavour towards a serious, 'truthful' fiction is necessarily flawed; because omniscience is impossible, its representation is inherently fictional. Any fiction exhibiting omniscient narration and aspiring to nonfictional truths is, one could argue, essentially fraudulent: unlike the newspaper articles that sensation plots imitate, novels communicate stories that are created rather than reported. The narrative games endemic to the sensation mode, and *Armadale* in particular, incessantly remind their readers of the text's fictional status, primarily entertaining where many of their predecessors have attempted primarily to inform.

Conclusion

The analyses presented here were prompted by my initial encounter with scholarship on *Lady Audley's Secret*. While there is a wealth of insightful criticism on the novel, there is little that attempts to account for the playfully indirect tone of much of its narration. Patrick Brantlinger's scholarship is the primary exception to this generalization, and my admiration for his ground-breaking discussion is acknowledged in Chapter Three. However, I was not completely convinced by the analyses that I read in Brantlinger, Carnell, and others: while I found that my general impressions of the novel's tone were often reflected in this scholarship, little was said about how those impressions had been achieved. Moreover, significant details of those impressions sometimes failed to resonate with my own: unlike Brantlinger, for instance, I did not feel that the 'reduct[ion]' of the information explicitly presented was due to the focalization of the narrative through Robert Audley, and, unlike Carnell, I did not make an unproblematic connection between the premature suspicions of the narrative voice and Robert's blossoming 'detective abilities' (Brantlinger 1982, 18; Carnell 2000, 253). (Side by side, it is clear that these two claims contradict each other: they both entail that the narrative is focalized through Robert, but Brantlinger aligns this focalization with less narrative information being made explicit, while Carnell aligns this focalization with more being made explicit.) At the time I did not know the term 'implicature', but felt that the effect produced by the novel's narration could be explained more satisfactorily by an acknowledgement of its pronounced reliance on a gradual accumulation of contextual details rather than on explicit narration—in other words, by an acknowledgement of the centrality of the text's implicatures.

In attempting to explicate reader reactions that are described elsewhere, I have followed the established aim of pragmatic stylistics. The originality of my contribution to the field lies primarily in my focus on strong and central implicatures, as opposed to weak implicatures and those that communicate background information. My approach is, moreover, somewhat unusual for pragmatic stylistics in that it concentrates more on the authorial techniques employed to generate certain narrative effects than on the reading processes involved in interpreting those effects. A further contribution to the field arises out of the stances I have adopted from narrative theory: in contradiction to the prevailing pragmatic stylistic assumption that there is little difference in reader interpretations of fiction and nonfiction, I have argued that fictionality should be recognized as a context which may affect the interpretation of utterances. Specifically, I have discussed the potential for narratorial omniscience that fiction allows, and how the reader's assumption of this potential affects what narrative information (or lack of narrative information) the reader regards as most relevant to his or her interpretation of the text. This last contribution has implications for future studies within pragmatic stylistics: more needs to be written about the potential differences that are involved in interpreting fictional and nonfictional texts, and current formulations that attempt to encompass all 'literature' need to be reevaluated. Similarly, I hope that recognizing narratorial omniscience as a potential reader assumption, rather than solely a potential characteristic of a text, will allow theorists to articulate various ways in which this assumption can be exploited to generate narrative effects.

My contributions to Victorian studies are necessarily more diffuse, reflecting both the pervasive applicability of the concept of implicature and my distinct engagements with various aspects of Victorian culture. At a local level, the relationships between the narrative effects uncovered here and their Victorian contexts need to be further explored. Acknowledging Robyn Warhol's basis of organization in her discussion of narrative gaps, each chapter concentrated on a specific authorial motivation that could have prompted the central implicatures discussed. This organizational principle allowed me to comment on the use of implicature to represent specific issues within a chosen Victorian context. It was found that, while the politeness-driven implicatures discussed in Chapter One (in relation to illegitimate pregnancy) could be related to Warhol's concept of the antinarratable, those discussed in Chapter Two and Chapter Three could not be assigned 'unnarratable' status. Instead, the implicatures in Chapter Two mimicked characters' semiconsciousnesses of their romantic feelings for other characters, and those in Chapter Three posed transparent narrative puzzles, satirizing the conventional constraints on narratorial omniscience within realism and effecting a playful tone. More can be done with these findings: as each case study shows, even authors with similar motivations fashioned implicatures suited especially for their texts and tailored according to their specific intentions. Consequently, the analysis of other central implicatures in any of these subcategories would build on my discussion.

Conclusion 171

Further research is also possible within the broad categories into which my case studies were grouped. Implicatures are obviously capable of communicating antinarratable topics other than illegitimate pregnancy, semiconscious states other than those relating to romantic desire, and narrative games not found in sensation fiction. But it is not only antinarratable content, character semiconsciousness, and narrative games that are sometimes communicated through implicature. To begin with, unnarratable content other than the antinarratable is also capable of being narrated through implicature. However, it is important to look beyond the bounds of the 'unnarratable' when discussing narrative gaps within fiction: although the concept has been of considerable use to narrative theory, its recent prevalence has led to neglect of other effects of and motivations for narrative silence. The subject matter discussed in my second and third chapters cannot be categorized as 'unnarratable', but there are still other potential authorial motivations behind the central use of implicature that cannot be categorized under any of the topics I have noted here. Even within the fictional context I have discussed, there is a wide range of meanings implicatures could generate, regardless of their centrality. Through my chosen subject matter, I have attempted to elucidate some of the more common discussions I have encountered in Victorian literary criticism and narrative theory, but the method of interpretation discussed here could be applied far more widely.

In several sections, for instance, I have provided brief analyses of how the representation of blushes functions within fictional narratives. I have often related these analyses to discussions of semiconscious character states, but the character states implicated by blushes are not always semiconscious. Blushes are often discussed as a gendered form of character expression, seen as indubitably sincere because beyond the character's control: they are considered more a betrayal of the character's thoughts than a willing expression of them (Homans 1993, 168; Levine 2003, 115–16). However, a close examination of the narrative blushes encountered in Victorian novels suggests conclusions that do not align with their commonplace representation in criticism: both male and female characters blush for a wealth of reasons that are not often textually inscribed, and characters are sometimes (if rarely) depicted as conscious of, and enjoying, their blushes (Caroline Levine rightly notes that Hetty blushes 'with perfect complacency' (2003, 115)). These representations are further complicated by the presence of rouged women in Victorian literature; the connotations of rouge within the Victorian era present a further context in which (unadulterated) narrative blushes are sometimes explicitly entangled (if only because of the necessary dichotomy between real and fake blushes). An examination of how represented blushes function within narratives must take into account that they almost always function by way of implicature and that these implicatures carry information of a more certain cast when the narrative voice is sure of the cause of the blush (that is, when it is omniscient). A detailed analysis of the implicatures associated with narrative blushes would inform prominent strands of criticism within Victorian studies, feminist theory, and narrative theory.

This work has examined only the conspicuous use of implicature within third-person omnisciently narrated Victorian novels; while there is more to write about this use of implicature in particular, there is also much to explore about how especially salient implicatures might function in second- or first-person narration as well as in other types of literature (both fictional and nonfictional). In the introductory chapter, for instance, I discussed Mary Louise Pratt's analyses of certain passages in *Tristram Shandy*. Her larger point is that the passages' effects are partly derived from the reader's assumption that the text is 'composed, edited, selected, published, and distributed' (1977, 170), but she also mentions that they are partly derived from the perceived duality of the sources that communicate the content—that is, from the reader's assumption that there is both an author and a narrator of the story (1977, 174). Although Pratt does not discuss the point further, this perceived duality is only possible when a narrative is assumed to be fiction. The effects she isolates differ from those discussed here, and, if analysed further, could inform current conceptions of how dramatic irony is effected within first-person fictional narratives. Although, as in many first-person narratives, *Tristram Shandy* sometimes slides into the third person (in that, although the narrative is largely about him and his birth, Tristram digresses into stories about other characters), it is still categorically a first-person narrative. Tristram is decidedly not omniscient but rather humorously fallible. Whereas I have examined implicatures that are generated by a narrative voice's assumed omniscience, Pratt discusses those which are generated by a narrator's perceived ignorance. The narratives I have discussed are often interpreted as having narrators who know more than they explicitly communicate to the reader; in *Tristram Shandy*, the narrator knows decidedly less, unwittingly communicating more information than he is aware of. While dramatic irony may be created by both narrative situations, it is inherent in the situation that Pratt describes. Pratt's focus, however, is on illustrating the relevance of the Cooperative Principle to literary analysis and characterizing narration as an imitation speech act, not on the dramatic irony that necessarily results from the implicatures which she describes (1977, 173). An analysis that concentrates on the dramatic irony generated from such implicatures, and that fully acknowledges the fictional context in which they must operate, would be a worthwhile addition to both pragmatic stylistics and narrative theory.

I have attempted to explicate a method of authorial communication that has been, both within primary texts and within the realm of much literary theory, too often invisible even as its effects have been recorded at length (if at times misattributed to other authorial techniques). My conclusion has centred primarily on the potential benefits to be derived from making implicature more visible within literary theory—that is, it has explored the use of discussing the narrative effects implicature is capable of generating within fiction. By articulating these processes, it will be possible to clarify not only readily described reader experiences such as 'reading between the lines' but also relatively elusive ones, such as reactions to narratorial 'tones'. These tones often result from the author's skilful exploitation of general pragmatic principles; it is only by acknowledging the author's conscious use of implicatures that we can fully understand this aspect of his or her craft.

Reference List

Abbott, H. Porter. 2008. *The Cambridge Introduction to Narrative*, 2nd ed. Cambridge: CUP.
'Advertisements & Notices'. 1842. *Caledonian Mercury*, 19 December. n. pag. *19th Century British Library Newspapers*. Web. 17 June 2010.
Ayres, Brenda. 2002. 'Introduction'. In *Frances Trollope and the Novel of Social Change*, edited by Brenda Ayres, 1–10. London: Greenwood.
Bal, Mieke. 1997. *Narratology: Introduction to the Theory of Narrative*, 2nd ed. London: U of Toronto Press.
Black, Elizabeth. 2006. *Pragmatic Stylistics*. Edinburgh: Edinburgh UP.
'Blasphemous Publications'. 1842. *Caledonian Mercury*, 19 December. n. pag. *19th Century British Library Newspapers*. Web. 17 June 2010.
Boring, Edwin G. 1957. *A History of Experimental Psychology*, 2nd ed. London: Prentice-Hall.
Boyle, Thomas F. 1984. '"Morbid Depression Alternating with Excitement": Sex in Victorian Newspapers'. In *Sexuality and Victorian Literature*, edited by Don Richard Cox, 212–33. Knoxville: U of Tennessee Press.
Braddon, Mary Elizabeth. 1998. *Lady Audley's Secret*. London: Penguin.
Brandser, Kristin J. 2000. 'In Defence of "Murderous Mothers": Feminist Jurisprudence in Frances Trollope's *Jessie Phillips*'. *Journal of Victorian Culture* 5 (2): 179–209.
Brantlinger, Patrick. 1982. 'What Is "Sensational" about the "Sensation Novel"?'. *Nineteenth-Century Fiction* 37 (1): 1–28.
Brown, Gillian and George Yule. 1983. *Discourse Analysis*. Cambridge: CUP.
Brown, Penelope and Stephen Levinson. 1999. *Politeness: Some Universals in Language Usage*. Cambridge: CUP.
Brownlow, John. 1864. *Thoughts and Suggestions Having Reference to Infanticide*. London: Charles Jaques.
Bruner, Jerome and Carol Fleisher Feldman. 1994. 'Metaphors of Consciousness and Cognition in the History of Psychology'. In *Metaphors in the History of Psychology*, edited by David E. Leary, 230–8. Cambridge: CUP.
Butte, George. 2004. *I Know That You Know That I Know: Narrating Subjects from Moll Flanders to Marnie*. Columbus: Ohio State UP.
Carnell, Jennifer. 2000. *The Literary Lives of Mary Elizabeth Braddon: A Study of Her Life and Work*. Hastings: Sensation Press.
Carpenter, William Benjamin. 1998. 'The Power of the Will over Mental Action'. In *Embodied Selves: An Anthology of Psychological Texts 1830–1890*, edited by Sally Shuttleworth and Jenny Bourne Taylor, 95–101. Oxford: OUP.
Christie, Christine. 2007. 'Relevance Theory and Politeness'. *Journal of Politeness Research* 3: 269–94.
'The Church of England Female Penitentiary'. 1854. *The Times*, 30 January.

Clark, Billy. 2009. 'Salient Inferences: Pragmatics and *The Inheritors*'. *Language and Literature* 18 (2): 173–212.
Clark, Billy. 2011. Personal interview, 7 December.
Cobbe, Frances Power. 1998. 'On Unconscious Cerebration'. In *Embodied Selves: An Anthology of Psychological Texts 1830–1890*, edited by Sally Shuttleworth and Jenny Bourne Taylor, 93–5. Oxford: OUP.
Cohn, Dorrit. 1978. *Transparent Minds: Narrative Modes for Presenting Consciousness in Fiction*. Princeton: Princeton UP.
Cohn, Dorrit. 1999. *The Distinction of Fiction*. London: John Hopkins UP.
Collins, Philip, ed. 1971. *Dickens: The Critical Heritage*. London: Routledge and Kegan Paul.
Collins, Wilkie. 1989. *Armadale*. Oxford: OUP.
Collins, Wilkie. 1999. *The Letters of Wilkie Collins: Volume 1, 1838–1865*, edited by William Baker and William M. Clarke. London: Macmillan.
Collins, Wilkie. 2008. *The Dead Secret*. Oxford: OUP.
Collins, Wilkie. 2008. *No Name*. Oxford: OUP.
Conley, Carolyn A. 1991. *The Unwritten Law: Criminal Justice in Victorian Kent*. Oxford: OUP.
Cotsell, Michael, ed. 1986. *The Companion to* Our Mutual Friend. London: Allen & Unwin.
Cox, Jessica. 2004. 'Representations of Illegitimacy in Wilkie Collins's Early Novels'. *Philological Quarterly* 83 (2): 147–69.
Culpeper, Jonathan. 2001. *Language and Characterisation: People in Plays and Other Texts*. London: Pearson Education.
Davis, Michael. 2006. *George Eliot and Nineteenth-Century Psychology: Exploring the Unmapped Country*. Aldershot: Ashgate.
'The Dead Secret'. 1857. *The Saturday Review*, 22 August.
Dickens, Charles. 1997. *Our Mutual Friend*. London: Penguin.
'Died'. 1843. *Jackson's Oxford Journal*, 20 May.
Downing, Laura Hidalgo. 2000. *Negation, Text Worlds, and Discourse: The Pragmatics of Fiction*. Stamford: Ablex.
Easson, Angus, ed. 1991. *Elizabeth Gaskell: The Critical Heritage*. London: Routledge.
Eliot, George. 1994. 'George Eliot to John Blackwood, July 9, 1860'. In *The Mill on the Floss*, edited by Carol T. Christ, 430–1. London: Norton.
Eliot, George. 1994. *The Mill on the Floss*, edited by Carol T. Christ. London: Norton.
Eliot, George. 1998. *The Journals of George Eliot*, edited by Margaret Harris and Judith Johnston. Cambridge: CUP.
Eliot, George. 2005. *Adam Bede*, edited by Mary Waldron. Plymouth: Broadview.
Ellenberger, Henri F. 1970. *The Discovery of the Unconscious: The History and Evolution of Dynamic Psychiatry*. London: Penguin.
Emmott, Catherine. 1997. *Narrative Comprehension: A Discourse Perspective*. Oxford: Clarendon Press.
Finkelstein, David. 2002. *The House of Blackwood: Author–Publisher Relations in the Victorian Era*. University Park: Pennsylvania State UP.

Fludernik, Monika. 2001. *The Fictions of Language and the Languages of Fiction: The Linguistic Representation of Speech and Consciousness*. London: Routledge.
Fludernik, Monika. 2009. *An Introduction to Narratology*. London: Routledge.
Fowler, Roger. 1996. *Linguistic Criticism*, 2nd ed. Oxford: OUP.
Freud, Sigmund. 1995. *The Freud Reader*, edited by Peter Gay. London: Vintage Books.
'From *Saturday Review*, April 14, 1860: The Mill on the Floss'. 1994. In *The Mill on the Floss*, edited by Carol T. Christ, 444–8. London: Norton.
Furlong, Anne. 2007. 'A Modest Proposal: Linguistics and Literary Studies'. *Canadian Journal of Applied Linguistics* 10 (3): 325–47.
Furlong, Anne. 2011. 'The Soul of Wit: A Relevance Theoretic Discussion'. *Language and Literature* 20 (2): 136–50.
Ganz, Margaret. 1969. *Elizabeth Gaskell: The Artist in Conflict*. New York: Twayne.
Gaskell, Elizabeth. 2008. *Ruth*. Oxford: OUP.
Gérin, Winifred. 1976. *Elizabeth Gaskell: A Biography*. Oxford: OUP.
Ginsburg, Michal Peled. 1980. 'Pseudonym, Epigraphs, and Narrative Voice: *Middlemarch* and the Problem of Authorship'. *ELH* 47: 542–58.
Graff, Ann-Barbara. 2002. '"Fair, Fat, and Forty": Social Redress and Fanny Trollope's Literary Activism'. In *Frances Trollope and the Novel of Social Change*, edited by Brenda Ayres, 53–70. London: Greenwood.
Graff, Ann-Barbara. 2008. 'Introduction'. In *Jessie Phillips: A Tale of the Present Day*, edited by Brenda Ayres, ix–xix. London: Pickering & Chatto.
Grice, H. Paul. 1975. 'Logic and Conversation'. In *Syntax and Semantics: Volume 3, Speech Acts*, edited by Peter Cole and Jerry L. Morgan, 41–58. London: Academic Press.
Grundy, Peter. 2000. *Doing Pragmatics*, 2nd ed. London: Arnold.
Guy, Josephine M. 1996. *The Victorian Social-Problem Novel: The Market, the Individual and Communal Life*. New York: St. Martin's Press.
Hamer, Mary. 1987. *Writing by Numbers: Trollope's Serial Fiction*. Cambridge: CUP.
Hamilton, Andy. 1998. 'Mill, Phenomenalism, and the Self'. In *The Cambridge Companion to Mill*, edited by John Skorupski, 139–75. Cambridge: CUP.
Hamilton, William. 1998. 'Three Degrees of Mental Latency'. In *Embodied Selves: An Anthology of Psychological Texts 1830–1890*, edited by Sally Shuttleworth and Jenny Bourne Taylor, 80–3. Oxford: OUP.
Harris, Mason. 1983. 'Infanticide and Respectability: Hetty Sorrel as Abandoned Child in *Adam Bede*'. *English Studies in Canada* 9 (2): 177–96.
Heineman, Helen. 1984. *Frances Trollope*. Boston: Twayne.
Herman, David. 2007. 'Introduction'. In *The Cambridge Companion to Narrative*, edited by David Herman, 3–21. Cambridge: CUP.
Herst, Beth F. 1990. *The Dickens Hero: Selfhood and Alienation in the Dickens World*. London: Weidenfeld and Nicolson.
Higginbotham, Ann R. 1992. '"Sin of the Age": Infanticide and Illegitimacy in Victorian London'. In *Victorian Scandals: Representations of Gender and Class*, edited by Kristine Ottesen Garrigan, 257–88. Athens: Ohio UP.
'Hints on the Amendment of the New Poor Law'. 1841. *Times*, 25 May.

Homans, Margaret. 1993. 'Dinah's Blush, Maggie's Arm: Class, Gender, and Sexuality in George Eliot's Early Novels'. *Victorian Studies* 36 (2): 155–78.

Horn, Laurence R. and Gregory Ward. 2006. *The Handbook of Pragmatics*. Oxford: Blackwell.

Hughes, Linda K. and Michael Lund. 1999. *Victorian Publishing and Mrs. Gaskell's Work*. London: UP of Virginia.

Hughes, Winifred. 1980. *The Maniac in the Cellar: Sensation Novels of the 1860s*. Princeton: Princeton UP.

'The Increase of Infanticide'. 1867. *Times*, 29 January.

Infanticide and Its Cause. 1862. London: George Phipps.

'Infanticide in the Metropolis'. 1862. *Times*, 9 September.

Iser, Wolfgang. 1975. 'The Reality of Fiction: A Functionalist Approach to Literature'. *New Literary History* 7 (1): 7–38.

Jary, Mark. 1998. 'Relevance Theory and the Communication of Politeness'. *Journal of Pragmatics* 30: 1–19.

'Jessie Phillips'. 1843. *New Monthly Magazine and Humorist*, February.

'Jessie Phillips'. 1843. *New Monthly Magazine and Humorist*, November.

'Jessie Phillips: A Tale of the Present Day'. 1843. *The Athenaeum*, 28 October.

Jones, Miriam. 2004. '"The Usual Sad Catastrophe": From the Street to the Parlor in *Adam Bede*'. *Victorian Literature and Culture* 32 (2): 305–26.

Khayati, Abdellatif. 1999. 'Representation, Race, and the "Language" of the Ineffable in Toni Morrison's Narrative'. *African American Review* 33 (2): 313–24.

Knight, Stephen. 2010. *Crime Fiction since 1800: Detection, Death, Diversity*, 2nd ed. Basingstoke: Palgrave Macmillan.

Knoepflmacher, U. C. 1994. 'Tragedy and the Flux: *The Mill on the Floss*'. In *The Mill on the Floss*, edited by Carol T. Christ, 502–20. London: Norton.

Krueger, Christine L. 1997. 'Literary Defenses and Medical Prosecutions: Representing Infanticide in Nineteenth-Century Britain'. *Victorian Studies* 40 (2): 271–94.

'Lady Audley's Secret'. 1862. *The Morning Post*, 17 October.

Law, Graham. 2006. 'The Professional Writer and the Literary Marketplace'. In *The Cambridge Companion to Wilkie Collins*, edited by Jenny Bourne Taylor, 97–111. Cambridge: CUP.

Law, Graham and Robert L. Patten. 2009. 'The Serial Revolution'. In *The Cambridge History of the Book in Britain: Volume 6, 1830–1914*, edited by David McKitterick, 144–71. Cambridge: CUP.

Leech, Geoffrey. 1990. *Principles of Pragmatics*. London: Longman.

Levine, Caroline. 2003. *The Serious Pleasures of Suspense: Victorian Realism and Narrative Doubt*. London: U of Virginia Press.

Levine, George. 1994. 'Intelligence as Deception: *The Mill on the Floss*'. In *The Mill on the Floss*, edited by Carol T. Christ, 489–502. London: Norton.

Levine, George. 2008. *How to Read the Victorian Novel*. Oxford: Blackwell.

Levine, George. 2008. *Realism, Ethics and Secularism: Essays on Victorian Literature and Science*. Cambridge: CUP.

Lewes, George Henry. 1998. 'Feeling and Thinking'. In *Embodied Selves: An Anthology of Psychological Texts 1830–1890*, edited by Sally Shuttleworth and Jenny Bourne Taylor, 87–8. Oxford: OUP.
Li, Hao. 2000. *Memory and History in George Eliot: Transfiguring the Past*. London: Macmillan.
'The Literary Examiner'. 1843. *The Examiner*, 28 October.
'Literature'. 1843. *Bell's Life in London and Sporting Chronicle*, 8 January.
'Literature'. 1843. *Caledonian Mercury*, 13 March.
'Literature'. 1843. *John Bull*, 20 November.
Lodge, David. 2002. *Consciousness & the Novel: Connected Essays*. London: Secker & Warburg.
Lonoff, Sue. 1982. *Wilkie Collins and His Victorian Readers: A Study in the Rhetoric of Authorship*. New York: AMS Press.
Macherey, Pierre. 1986. *A Theory of Literary Production*, translated by Geoffrey Wall. London: Routledge & Kegan Paul.
MacPike, Loralee. 1984. 'The Fallen Woman's Sexuality'. In *Sexuality and Victorian Literature*, edited by Don Richard Cox, 54–71. Knoxville: U of Tennessee Press.
Marck, Nancy Anne. 2003. 'Narrative Transference and Female Narcissism: The Social Message of *Adam Bede*'. *Studies in the Novel* 35 (4): 447–70.
Margolin, Uri. 2007. 'Character'. In *The Cambridge Companion to Narrative*, edited by David Herman, 66–79. Cambridge: CUP.
Mason, Michael. 1994. *The Making of Victorian Sexuality*. Oxford: OUP.
Matus, Jill L. 1993. 'Disclosure as "Cover-Up": The Discourse of Madness in *Lady Audley's Secret*'. *University of Toronto Quarterly* 62 (3): 334–55.
Matus, Jill L. 2009. *Shock, Memory, and the Unconscious in Victorian Fiction*. Cambridge: CUP.
McDonagh, Josephine. 2003. *Child Murder and British Culture: 1720–1900*. Cambridge: CUP.
Mey, Jacob L. 1999. *When Voices Clash: A Study in Literary Pragmatics*. Berlin: Mouton de Gruyter.
Mey, Jacob L. 2001. *Pragmatics: An Introduction*, 2nd ed. Oxford: Blackwell.
Mey, Jacob L. 2006. 'Literary Pragmatics'. In *Encyclopedia of Language & Linguistics*, 2nd ed., edited by Keith Brown, 255–61. Elsevier.
Miller, John Hawkins. 1978. '"Temple and Sewer": Childbirth, Prudery and Victoria Regina'. In *The Victorian Family: Structure and Stresses*, edited by Anthony S. Wohl, 23–43. London: Croom Helm.
'Monthly Publications'. 1843. *John Bull*, 7 January.
Nemesvari, Richard. 1995. 'Robert Audley's Secret: Male Homosocial Desire in *Lady Audley's Secret*'. *Studies in the Novel* 27 (4): 515–28.
'The New Fictions by Boz and Mrs. Trollope'. 1843. *The Spectator*, 7 January.
'New Novels'. 1857. *The Athenaeum*, 20 June.
Osborne, Sidney Godolphin. 1835. *A Familiar Explanation of that Part of the New Poor Law which Relates to the Maintenance of Illegitimate Children*. London: T. and W. Boone.

OUP. 2009. 'Omniscience'. In *The Oxford English Dictionary*. Oxford: OUP. 24 Nov. 2010.
OUP. 2011. 'Intersubjective'. In *The Oxford English Dictionary*. Oxford: OUP. 1 May 2011.
Page, Norman, ed. 1974. *Wilkie Collins: The Critical Heritage*. London: Routledge & Kegan Paul.
Palmer, Alan. 2004. *Fictional Minds*. London: U of Nebraska Press.
Pascal, Roy. 1977. *The Dual Voice: Free Indirect Speech and Its Functioning in the Nineteenth-Century European Novel*. Manchester: Manchester UP.
Paxton, Nancy L. 1991. *George Eliot and Herbert Spencer: Feminism, Evolutionism, and the Reconstruction of Gender*. Princeton: Princeton UP.
Peters, Catherine. 1989. 'Introduction'. In *Armadale*, by Wilkie Collins, vii–xxiii. Oxford: OUP.
Pilkington, Adrian, Barbara MacMahon, and Billy Clark. 1997. 'Looking for an Argument: A Response to Green'. *Language and Literature* 6 (2): 139–48.
'The Poor Law'. 1843. *The Times*, 30 December.
Pratt, Mary Louise. 1977. *Toward a Speech Act Theory of Literary Discourse*. London: Indiana UP.
Prince, Gerald. 1988. 'The Disnarrated'. *Style* 22 (1): 1–8.
Pykett, Lyn. 2006. 'Collins and the Sensation Novel'. In *The Cambridge Companion to Wilkie Collins*, edited by Jenny Bourne Taylor, 50–64. Cambridge: CUP.
Radford, Andrew. 2009. *Victorian Sensation Fiction*. Basingstoke: Palgrave Macmillan.
Richards, Graham. 1996. *Putting Psychology in Its Place: An Introduction from a Critical Historical Perspective*. London: Routledge.
Rimmon-Kenan, Shlomith. 2006. *Narrative Fiction: Contemporary Poetics*, 2nd ed. London: Routledge.
Rose, Lionel. 1986. *The Massacre of the Innocents: Infanticide in Britain 1800–1939*. London: Routledge & Kegan Paul.
Rubery, Matthew. 2009. *The Novelty of Newspapers: Victorian Fiction after the Invention of the News*. Oxford: OUP.
Ryan, A. 2004. 'Hamilton, Sir William Stirling, Baronet (1788–1856)'. In *Oxford Dictionary of National Biography*. Oxford: OUP.
Ryan, Marie-Laure. 1991. *Possible Worlds, Artificial Intelligence, and Narrative Theory*. Bloomington: Indiana UP.
Rylance, Rick. 2000. *Victorian Psychology and British Culture: 1850–1880*. Oxford: OUP.
Schor, Hilary. 1990. 'The Plot of the Beautiful Ignoramus: *Ruth* and the Tradition of the Fallen Woman'. In *Sex and Death in Victorian Literature*, edited by Regina Barreca, 158–77. London: Macmillan.
Sell, Roger D. 1991. 'The Politeness of Literary Texts'. In *Literary Pragmatics*, edited by Roger D. Sell, 208–24. London: Routledge.
Sell, Roger D. 1994. 'Literary Gossip, Literary Theory, Literary Pragmatics'. In *Literature and the New Interdisciplinarity: Poetics, Linguistics, History*, edited by Roger D. Sell and Peter Verdonk, 221–42. Amsterdam: Rodopi.

Sell, Roger D. 2001. 'A Historical but Non-determinist Pragmatics of Literary Communication'. *Journal of Historical Pragmatics* 2 (1): 1–32.

Shuttleworth, Sally. 1986. *George Eliot and Nineteenth-Century Science: The Make-Believe of a Beginning*. Cambridge: CUP.

Small, Helen. 2012. 'Subjectivity, Psychology, and the Imagination'. In *The Cambridge History of Victorian Literature*, edited by Kate Flint, 487–509. Cambridge: CUP.

Spencer, Herbert. 1998. 'On Consciousness and the Will'. In *Embodied Selves: An Anthology of Psychological Texts 1830–1890*, edited by Sally Shuttleworth and Jenny Bourne Taylor, 83–7. Oxford: OUP.

Sperber, Dan and Deirdre Wilson. 1999. *Relevance: Communication and Cognition*, 2nd ed. Oxford: Blackwell.

St Clair, William. 2009. 'Following up *The Reading Nation*'. In *The Cambridge History of the Book in Britain: Volume 6, 1830–1914*, edited by David McKitterick, 704–35. Cambridge: CUP.

Summers, Leigh. 2001. *Bound to Please: A History of the Victorian Corset*. Oxford: Berg.

Taylor, Jenny Bourne. 1988. *In the Secret Theatre of Home: Wilkie Collins, Sensation Narrative, and Nineteenth-Century Psychology*. London: Routledge.

Taylor, Jenny Bourne and Russell Crofts. 1998. 'Introduction'. In *Lady Audley's Secret*, by Mary Elizabeth Braddon, vii–xli. London: Penguin.

Taylor, Jenny Bourne and Sally Shuttleworth, eds. 1998. *Embodied Selves: An Anthology of Psychological Texts 1830–1890*. Oxford: OUP.

Thackeray, William. 1968. *Vanity Fair*. London: Penguin.

Thoms, Peter. 1992. *The Windings of the Labyrinth: Quest and Structure in the Major Novels of Wilkie Collins*, Athens: Ohio UP.

Thorn, Jennifer. 2003. 'Introduction'. In *Writing British Infanticide: Child-Murder, Gender, and Print, 1722–1859*, edited by Jennifer Thorn, 13–44. Newark: U of Delaware Press.

Trollope, Anthony. 2008. *Orley Farm*. Oxford: OUP.

Trollope, Frances. 2006. *Jessie Phillips: A Tale of the Present Day*. Stroud: Nonsuch.

Trudgill, Eric. 1976. *Madonnas and Magdalens: The Origins and Development of Victorian Sexual Attitudes*. New York: Holmes & Meier.

'Unsigned Notice, *National Magazine*'. 1969. In *Trollope: The Critical Heritage*, edited by Donald Smalley, 164. London: Routledge & Kegan Paul.

Waldron, Mary, ed. 2005. 'Appendix A: Realism, Morality, and Fiction'. In *Adam Bede*, by George Eliot, 575–86. Plymouth: Broadview Editions.

Waldron, Mary, ed. 2005. 'Appendix D: The Reception of *Adam Bede*'. In *Adam Bede*, by George Eliot, 610–18. Plymouth: Broadview Editions.

Waldron, Mary. 2005. 'Introduction'. In *Adam Bede*, by George Eliot, 9–52. Plymouth: Broadview Editions.

Wall, Geoffrey. 1986. 'Preface'. In *A Theory of Literary Production*, by Pierre Macherey, translated by Wall, vii–ix. London: Routledge & Kegan Paul.

Walsh, Richard. 2007. *The Rhetoric of Fictionality: Narrative Theory and the Idea of Fiction*. Columbus: Ohio State UP.

Warhol, Robyn R. 2007. 'Narrative Refusals and Generic Transformation in Austen and James: What Doesn't Happen in *Northanger Abbey* and *The Spoils of Poynton*'. *The Henry James Review* 28: 259–68.

Warhol, Robyn R. 2006. 'Neonarrative; or, How to Render the Unnarratable in Realist Fiction and Contemporary Film'. In *A Companion to Narrative Theory*, edited by James Phelan and Peter J. Rabinowitz, 220–31. Oxford: Blackwell.

Warhol-Down, Robyn. 2010. '"What Might Have Been Is Not What Is": Dickens's Narrative Refusals'. *Dickens Studies Annual: Essays on Victorian Fiction* 41: 45–60.

Watt, Ian. 2000. *The Rise of the Novel: Studies in Defoe, Richardson and Fielding*. London: Pimlico.

Index

Abbott, H. Porter 9
Adam Bede 6, 9, 37, 53, 74–85, 133
action tendencies 97, 98
antinarratable 7, 8, 43–4, 48–50, 58–60, 64, 69, 71–2, 124
assumption of coherence 21, 81, 82
assumption of literariness 12–13, 147, 172
assumption of narratorial omniscience 27, 30, 99, 105, 147, 170
Austen, Jane 9, 12–13, 95–6
 Pride and Prejudice 12

Black, Elizabeth 44, 47
Braddon, Mary Elizabeth 33, 128, 135, 150, 156
 Lady Audley's Secret 33, 130, 131, 135, 138–48, 149, 151, 169
Brantlinger, Patrick 127, 128–9, 130–1, 133, 134–6, 138, 142–3, 144, 152, 163, 169
Brown, Penelope 44–5

Carpenter, William 89, 90, 93–4, 102, 112, 121
Cobbe, Frances Power 92–3, 121
Cohn, Dorrit 25n11, 26–7, 67, 96, 97, 98
Collins, Wilkie 33, 136, 148, 149
 Armadale 33–4, 128, 130, 131, 157–68
 The Dead Secret 123–6, 127, 129, 131–2, 141, 157
 No Name 157
 The Woman in White 126, 129, 148, 149, 157, 162

Dickens, Charles 33, 44, 52, 124n, 128, 148–57, 161
 Our Mutual Friend 33, 128, 148–57
disnarration 9, 63–4, 109–10

echoic, *see* irony
Eliot, George 44, 124
 Adam Bede 6, 9n, 32, 36, 37, 53, 74–85, 124, 133, 134
 The Mill on the Floss 33, 87, 100–12, 117n, 133
Emmott, Catherine 23n
explicitness, definition 19–20

face 44–5, 47–8, 132, 134
 face-threatening act 45, 47–8, 50, 73, 80, 83
fictional worlds theory 12, 14–16, 23, 24
 actual world 14–16, 153
 alternative possible world 14–16, 153
 recentering 15, 16n
free indirect discourse 20, 21, 33, 66–7, 95, 96, 99, 107–8, 115, 116, 117n, 119–20, 152

Gaskell, Elizabeth 37, 124
 Ruth 32, 36, 37, 60–74, 124, 133, 134
Grice, H. P. 11, 17–18, 20, 50, 127
 Cooperative Principle 17, 18, 46–7, 49–50
Grundy, Peter 44, 45–6

Hamilton, Sir William 91–2, 93n
Herbart, Johann Friedrich 88–9, 90, 96

imitation speech acts 14, 172
implicature, definition 2–3, 78, 169
 defeasibility 17n, 104–5, 152–3, 160, 163, 164–5, 166–7
 evolution of concept 17–19
indicative description 97, 105, 106, 108, 110, 113, 115, 117
infanticide 32, 40, 42, 72, 74, 76, 84
 and the New Poor Laws 32, 40, 53, 56, 60, 76
irony 10, 16, 44, 67, 77, 98, 107, 110, 117, 118, 127, 136, 137, 138, 152
 definitions of 20–1, 67
 dramatic 13–14, 33–4, 68, 106, 130, 144, 151, 153, 156, 160, 167–8, 172
 as echoic 20–1, 67, 107, 126, 127, 134, 142

Levine, Caroline 75–6
Levine, George 127–8, 132–3, 136–8, 151
Levinson, Stephen 44–5
Lewes, George Henry 89–90, 101, 102

Mey, Jacob L. 11, 22–3, 43
Libraries 35–6, 73

narrative refusal 9, 10, 63n
New Poor Laws of 1834 32, 40, 42, 52–4, 57, 59, 60, 76
  Bastardy Clause 40, 42, 58, 59, 60, 64
New Poor Laws of 1844 60

omniscient narration 3–4, 25–9, 30, 33, 63, 65, 77, 98, 99, 105, 110, 114, 120, 124, 126, 127, 132, 135–8, 142, 147, 153–4, 162, 163, 164, 167, 168, 170, 172
ostensive-inferential communication 18–19, 49, 50, 65, 77–8, 97, 141, 155

Palmer, Alan 27, 95, 97, 98, 99
  action tendencies 97, 98
  indicative description 97, 105, 106, 108, 110, 115, 117
paranarratable 6, 7–8, 10, 43, 59
politeness 32, 36–7, 43–50, 64, 70, 73, 84, 85, 124, 126, 132, 141, 170
  presentational 46–7, 48–50, 58, 62, 64, 72, 78, 79, 80, 124n, 132
  selectional 46, 48–50, 59, 64n
Pratt, Mary Louise 12–14, 15–16, 26, 27, 28, 147n, 172
pregnancy 39, 41–2, 51, 55, 59, 70–2, 80–5
  abortion 41–2
  concealment 39, 40, 42, 82, 83
  illegitimate 32, 36, 38–43, 53, 55–6, 59, 61, 70–2, 73, 76, 77, 80–5, 124n
  quickening 41, 42n

realism 74, 75–6, 84, 127–8, 129, 132–3, 136–8
relevance theory 18–21, 43, 44n, 50, 78, 86, 97, 100, 138
Ryan, Marie-Laure 14–16, 26, 27, 28

Searle, John 11, 12n, 16
Sell, Roger D. 11, 23, 44, 46–7, 49, 64
social problem novel 37, 51, 76, 133
speech act theory 11, 12, 15, 23, 24
Spencer, Herbert 90–1, 92, 101–2, 103n, 112, 121
Sperber, Dan 18–21, 49, 50, 67, 97, 107
Sterne, Laurence 12–13, 13–14, 48
  Tristram Shandy 12–13, 13–14, 172
subnarratable 6, 8, 10, 77, 87, 100, 109, 110
supranarratable 6, 8, 10, 69

Trollope, Anthony 87, 112–22, 133, 162
  Orley Farm 33, 87, 112–22
Trollope, Frances 37, 51–2, 64
  Jessie Phillips: A Tale of the Present Day 32, 36, 37, 50–60, 64, 72, 124, 134

unnarratable 5–6, 7–8, 9, 10, 170, 171
unnarration 9

Vanity Fair 1–4, 10, 23, 49, 98, 137–8

Walsh, Richard 24–5, 27–8
Warhol, Robyn 5–10, 63n, 110n, 150–1, 170
  Robyn Warhol-Down, *see* Warhol, Robyn
Wilson, Deirdre 18–21, 49, 50, 67, 97, 107